Appropriate Methodology
and Social Context

CAMBRIDGE LANGUAGE TEACHING LIBRARY
A series of authoritative books on the subjects of central importance
for all language teachers.

In this series:

Appropriate Methodology and Social Context

Adrian Holliday

CAMBRIDGE
UNIVERSITY PRESS

Published by the Press Syndicate of the University of Cambridge
The Pitt Building, Trumpington Street, Cambridge CB2 1RP
40 West 20th Street, New York, NY 10011-4211, USA
10 Stamford Road, Oakleigh, Melbourne 3166, Australia

© Cambridge University Press 1994

First published 1994

Printed in Great Britain by Bell and Bain Ltd, Glasgow

A catalogue record for this book is available from the British Library

Library of Congress Cataloging-in-Publication Data
Appropriate methodology and social context / Adrian Holliday.
    p.   cm.   (Cambridge Language Teaching Library)
Includes bibliographical references and index.
ISBN 0 521 43156 5. ISBN 0 521 43745 8 (pbk.)
1. English language – Study and teaching.
2. English language – Study and teaching – Social aspects.
3. Comparative education.
4. Educational anthropology.
I. Title
II. Series.
LB1576.H626 1994
428.4'07 dc20   93-34915
                                              CIP

ISBN 0 521 43156 6 hardback
ISBN 0 521 43745 8 paperback

Contents

Contents

Chapter 9 Teachers' and students' lessons

Part C Appropriate methodology design

Chapter 10 A culture-sensitive approach

Chapter 11 Solving classroom problems

Chapter 12 Curriculum and project design

Thanks

By way of acknowledgement, I am indebted to the Syrian, Egyptian, American and British colleagues with whom I worked on aid projects between 1980 and 1990 – especially, but not only, at Damascus University, Warka Barmada, Nafez Shamas and Terence Cooke; at Helwan University, Mona Zikri, Lucy Hakim and Salwa Farag; at Ain Shams University, Amal Kary, Shaker Rizk, Sanaa Tamman, Mohammad Shawkat and Layla Rizk; at Tanta University, with their classes of 400, Hany Azer, whom I quote extensively, Tim Riney, Darab Barjesteh, Hasan Gaballa and Mohammad Negm; Hasan Tamam at Alexandria University, Sirvart Sahakian at Mansoura University, Saber Galal at Assiut University, David Bell and Stephen Boeshaar in el Arish, William Martin at Damietta and Qena, Carol Geren and Peter Herworth in the Fayyoum, Margaret Connely at Shibin el Kom, and the late Abd el Messih Daoud. It is through trying to understand their points of view, and sometimes 'observing' them more than they were aware, that I was both inspired and made able to write this book. I would also like to thank Tony Wright and Hywel Coleman, who read various drafts and made critical, yet very supportive comment, and Katharine Mendelsohn who made sense of the text in final editing. At CUP, Annemarie Young, Elizabeth Serocold and Colin Hayes provided support and advice at different stages. Mike Breen and Dick Allwright provided unfailing and inspiring supervision for those parts of the argument which come from my doctoral research. My 1992 and 1993 MA students at Canterbury Christ Church College acted as a participant sounding board for most of the ideas, as well as providing me with continual motivation. Brian Martin continued to provide very precise comment on Chapter 10 long after graduation.

Acknowledgements

The author and publishers are grateful to the authors, publishers and others who have given permission for the use of copyright material. It has not been possible to trace the sources of all the material used, and in such cases the publishers would welcome information from copyright holders.

The British Council for the extract from R. Phillipson (1991) 'Linguistic imperialism' in *The Dunford Seminar Report of 1991* on p. 99; The Centre for Developing English Language Teaching, Ain Shams University for the extract from D. Barjesteh and A. R. Holliday (1990) 'How to introduce inductive learning in the teaching of grammar' in M. Abousenna (Ed.) *Proceedings of the National Symposium on Teaching English in Egypt: Linguistics, Literature and Culture, 1989* on p. 187, and the extracts from H. Azer (1990) 'Can a communicative approach to university grammar cope with large classes?' in *Occasional Papers in the Development of English Language Education* 12 on pp. 184–6, 188; Hywel Coleman for the extracts from *Society and the Classroom: Social Explanations for Behaviour in the Language Class* on pp. 101–2 and 106–7; the extracts from *The Social System* by Talcott Parsons. Copyright © 1951, 1979 by Talcott Parsons. Reprinted with the permission of The Free Press, a Division of Macmillan, Inc., and Routledge & Kegan Paul on pp. 24, 25; Martin Hyde for extracts from *The Moroccan Association of Teachers of English XIIth Conference* (1992) on pp. 100, 103; The Institute for English Language Education, Lancaster University and Prentice Hall International for the extract from A. R. Holliday and T. M. Cooke (1982) 'An ecological approach to ESP' in A. Waters (Ed.) *Issues in ESP, Lancaster Practical Papers in English Language Education* 5 reprinted as Figure 15 on p. 200; the extracts from A. Schultz (1964) 'The stranger' reprinted by permission of Kluwer Academic Publishers on pp. 23, 24, 26; Leicester University Press for the extracts from D. Tomley (1980) 'The selection of curriculum content: Issues and problems' on pp. 70, 75, and for the extract from T. Eggleston (1980) 'Action and reaction in science teaching' on p. 88, both in M. J. Galton (Ed.) *Curriculum Change: The Lessons of a Decade*; The Macmillan Press Ltd for the extracts from D. Holly (1990) 'The unspoken

Acknowledgements

curriculum – or how language teaching carries cultural and ideological messages' in B. Harrison (Ed.) *ELT Documents 132: Culture and the Language Classroom* on p. 98; Methuen & Co for the extracts from M. D. Shipman, D. Bolam and D. R. Jenkins (1974) *Inside a Curriculum Project* on pp. 111, 114–16, 136; The Open University Press for the extracts from I. Goodson (1988) 'Beyond the subject monolith: Subject traditions and sub cultures' in A. Westoby (Ed.) *Culture and Power in Educational Organisations* on pp. 70, 76; Oxford University Press for the extracts from A. R. Howatt (1984) *A History of English Language Teaching* on p. 168, and from T. Hutchinson and A. Waters (1984) 'How communicative is ESP?' in *English Language Teaching Journal* 38 (2) on pp. 173, 175; Figure 6 on p. 121 reprinted from *System* 18, A. R. Holliday, 'A role for soft systems methodology in ELT projects' pp. 77–84, Copyright 1990, with permission from Pergamon Press Ltd, Headington Hill Hall, Oxford OX3 0BW, UK; Sherill Pociecha for the extract from Open Letter to the Peace Corps, the US Embassy Teaching Office, NJKO Directors, and whom it may concern, in *IATEFL Newsletter* No 117, 1992 on p. 124; Prentice Hall for the extracts from R. E. Murphy (1986) *Culture and Social Anthropology: An Overture* on p. 26; Tavistock Publications for the extracts from M. Hammersley and P. Atkinson (1983) *Ethnography* on pp. 204, 208; the extract on p. 137 reprinted from Fullan, Michael, *The New Meaning of Educational Change*: 2nd Edition. (New York: Teachers College Press, © by Teachers College, Columbia University. All rights reserved.) Excerpt from p. 4 – under 500 words; The University of Alaska Fairbanks for the extracts from M. Collier *A Film Study in Classrooms in Western Alaska* © M. Collier 1979 on pp. 35, 147, 155; Weidenfeld and Nicholson for the extracts from E. Gellner (1964) *Thought and Change* on pp. 25, 27.

Preface

In this book, I present an argument for making English language education more appropriate to the social requirements of students and educators in different environments throughout the world. The argument is that any methodology in English language education should be appropriate to the social context within which it is to be used. The scope is broad. Although finally I am concerned with appropriate methodology for classroom teaching, I deal with three basic types of methodology, all of which sooner or later affect what happens in the classroom.

The first is the methodology for carrying out the work of teaching English, which includes what the teacher does in the classroom – what we normally think of as 'methods and approaches'. This can be extended to the work of training or educating teachers; and the focus is not only on the nature of classroom or seminar room activities, but also on the nature of the curriculum as a whole. This area might be defined as the methodology for *doing* English language education.

The second is the methodology for carrying out the work of *designing* and *managing* English language education. This includes many activities from writing textbooks or examinations, which might involve a small number of people, to designing, setting up and managing large projects for developing anything from textbooks to teacher training curricula. I put this under the general heading of curriculum development. Four out of the twelve chapters focus on this area.

The third methodology is that of *collecting* the *information* about the particular social context in question, which teachers or curriculum developers need to make the other two methodologies appropriate. This methodology also has to be appropriate to the social context. I therefore argue for an ethnographic action research, which enables social investigation in a gradual, non-prescriptive way, as work proceeds.

To achieve appropriacy, we must investigate, try to understand, and then address, whichever social context we are working within. To illustrate both the need for, and the nature of this task, the first two parts of the book constitute an exploration of how different social contexts affect what happens in the classroom and in curriculum development, and show what

1

can go wrong when the social context is neither acknowledged nor addressed. The third part looks at the nature of the practice required to make methodology appropriate.

What are my motivations for writing this book? Where is the need for this type of work? English language education by its nature extends over a world-wide canvas through an immense variety of social contexts. Largely through aid projects, but also through a variety of other international activity, a relatively united approach to classroom instruction has been proclaimed across the globe. The outcome has nevertheless in more than a few cases been littered with failures and anxieties. In ministry of education offices, colleges and universities, shelves of teaching materials remain unused. Teachers return from training programmes unable to implement what they have learnt, because it does not fit the conditions, needs and philosophies of their classrooms, students, institutions and communities. Expensive projects have often failed to have significant sustainable effect. Several years after their conclusion there is sometimes little trace that anything has happened.

The approach to English language education has been largely prescriptive. The knowledge of linguistics is considerable, as is our understanding of the psychology of language learning; and the methodology of classroom teaching has been developed to a fine science. However, these pillars of our profession have been based upon experience of a narrow set of conditions within a limited social context. The problem has not been neglected; but attempts at solutions have often involved a further refinement of existing classroom methodologies, and training methodologies which will enable teachers to use them, rather than getting at the root of the problem. In the late 1970s we had a revolution in syllabus design. It was stated that prescribing syllabuses before considering the linguistic needs of students was putting the cart before the horse. To rectify this state of affairs, the needs analysis was developed first into a precise and then into a more sensitive instrument – to enable student language needs to drive syllabuses. I suggest that in the design of methodologies, the cart is still before the horse. We are still paying insufficient attention to the social needs of all the people we expect to use them. Methodologies for teaching, for educating teachers, for designing curricula, and for designing and carrying out curriculum projects, continue to be refined, but without sufficient attention to, or knowledge of the people who will be involved.

But what about 'the teacher as researcher', and the 'reflective' approach to teacher education – well-developed methodologies to enable teachers and trainees to adapt and re-create classroom practice to suit their own situations through action research? Developments such as these have shown relative success in British schools. What about all the techniques which management has brought to English language education – such as the science of innovation and change? What about base-line studies and formative and summative evaluation – to enable us to plan, monitor and adjust the impact of what we do in classrooms, courses and projects? All of this might be fine if the designers of methodologies and the people they intended to use them were compatriots. In such a case there would be an intuitive knowledge of shared social backgrounds to guide the design. As it is, the designers often come from very different backgrounds from the users, who are other people, from other societies and other cultures, who have different ways of doing things, thinking, deciding what is important in education, and of solving problems; and unless these ways are understood and acknowledged, methodologies are not going to work beyond the familiar domains in which they are created. Even when the designers and the users are from the same country and the same institution there are problems, as I shall show in a report of the Keele curriculum project in Britain. On the world scale of English language education the propensity for breakdown in communication is enormous. Indeed, the literature is full of models and checklists about *how* to do and *what* to do; but hardly anywhere is there advice on what we need to know about people, and how we can find this out.

It is not my intention to offer definitive solutions to the problem of making methodologies appropriate, nor to offer models or checklists. First of all, it is paramount that I acknowledge that *I* do not have sufficient knowledge of what happens between people in diverse social contexts to enable me to do this. Instead, I explore the *types* of information we need to collect, and *how* we might collect this information. The purpose of this exploration is to demonstrate the complex nature of the diverse social contexts surrounding English language education, to demonstrate the immensity of the area we need to address. Through case studies – from solving classroom problems through enabling professionals from different cultural backgrounds to work with each other to avoiding conflicts in English language projects – I consider where and how we might begin to look for solutions.

There is currently an outcry against linguistic or cultural imperialism which says that English language education is creating a world hegemony to keep the less advantaged dependent on the technology and commerce of the West. That this outcry exists is not surprising, considering the unilateral professionalism which has carried English language education across the world. I argue that this professionalism is ethnocentric, failing to appreciate the social backgrounds of others, using international English language education to feed its own expansionism. I hypothesise about how this imperialism works, not at the government or agency level, but in the more piecemeal relations between 'native-speaker' teachers and students, and between 'native-speaker' curriculum developers, project managers and

3

trainers and their colleagues from the rest of the world. However, my aim is not to pass judgement on the rights and wrongs of this 'imperialism'; and I do not believe it to be an inevitable outcome of an uneven world order.

There are various aspects of the imperialist paradigm which I do not agree with. First, the paradigm is patronising – assuming that the 'recipient' of English language education is passive, without agency. The power of English is a current fact of life; but it is a commodity which everyone has the right to use in ways which are socially appropriate. By showing how diverse social contexts can be understood and acknowledged, I hope also to show how English language education can be used for the mutual benefit of all concerned parties.

Secondly, the imperialist paradigm seems to work on a West-against-the-developing-world principle. The conflicts I speak about are not between the advantaged and the disadvantaged, but between professional groups with different ways of looking at education, within the developed world as well as the less developed world. My premiss is not that the recipient of English language education is vulnerable to a superior technology, but that there are different, but equally 'sophisticated' types of educational technology in different, but equally 'sophisticated' types of social context. My aim is not to describe an inevitable imperialism, but to show how lack of knowledge of how other types of people think and do things, from *both* sides, can create the conditions for imperialism. This lack of knowledge is rife, but avoidable.

The conflict I try to analyse is between two halves of the English language teaching profession – that which is oriented towards the private sector in Britain, North America and Australasia on the one hand, and state education in the rest of the world. The dominant professional literature has emanated from the former and paid very little constructive attention to the wider educational needs of the latter. Where attention *has* been paid it has tended to be stereotypical and has often seen the state sector as deficient. I take the 'communicative approach' to language teaching as a core element in private sector English language education and, on the one hand, explain why, in its narrow form, it fails to meet the needs of state education, but, on the other hand, how it can, in a wider, more truly communicative form, be made more sensitive and adaptable to state education in its diverse social contexts.

Because little has been written which addresses individual social contexts, there has been little documentary evidence at my disposal. Much of the substance is based upon a professional experience gained while working in different parts of the world. A large proportion of the data I collected myself while working on a curriculum development project in Egypt. This is supported by papers written by colleagues working in similar situations in other countries, such as Poland, Indonesia and Pakistan, and by a richer literature from general education. Nevertheless, I write with conviction that this small amount of evidence has a universal relevance. If the reader says, 'This makes sense to me, but where is the evidence?', I will feel that I have succeeded, especially if the reader then goes off to collect evidence in her or his own world of operation. The reader will then be relating to her or his own professional experience of the world just as I am; and a dialogue will have been set up. I begin my argument with a quote from Dick Allwright that there is very little real evidence about much of what we have been led to believe in English language education. We are all dealing with the perceptions, feelings and expectations of people, whether they be teachers or students. Whatever can be scientific about our work must be very *soft* science. We have built up structures and statistics on controlled experiments in clinical conditions. These can tell us a great deal; but out in the real world these findings only scratch the surface.

In the final part of the book I suggest that the curriculum developer, trying to find out necessary information about the cultures of the classroom and the institution, must embark upon *thick description*. This means that, within a complex world of human interaction, the investigator will make sense of fragments. A picture – never the whole picture – will gradually be built up; and each fragment will only make sense when compared with other fragments. The examples I present throughout the book make up a thick description. I possess only some of the fragments. However, each reader will also possess fragments from experience of her or his own world, and from this point of view will be able to judge what makes sense or does not make sense. Whichever way round, the problem of appropriate methodology will have been engaged, which is the most important thing of all. I advocate the application of ethnography as a means for looking at the social context. The thick description upon which I myself embark is part of this ethnography, and fully within its spirit.

The discussion questions at the end of each chapter are designed to invite the reader to participate in this ethnography – to help the reader to think deeply about how some of the principles discussed in the book may relate to her or his own professional experience.

I do not intend to provide clear answers to the problems which different social contexts present. Indeed, it would be naive to suggest that there are clear answers. Social scientists have long sought to clarify the realities of the sort of human interaction with which I am concerned, and find layer upon layer of perplexing complexity. Looking out from the viewpoint of one particular professional community, and familiar with a small number of social contexts, this writer cannot even presume to know sufficient about the larger picture, which includes many other professional communities and social contexts, to present any clear answers. Instead, I present a starting discussion which might precipitate thought in others, who may be in a better position than I to find answers relating to their own social contexts.

I am aware of my own bias. I argue against a professional ethnocentricity originating in Britain, North America and Australasia; and yet I myself have been brought up in this tradition and therefore will automatically be influenced by this same ethnocentricity. This is unavoidable; but at the same time I feel that there can be no such thing as an impartial view from any side. The ethnography which I advocate acknowledges the bias of the investigator as natural, as long as this bias is realised and accounted for. This I believe I do. Ethnographers see the cultures they study more acutely as they respond to the observer. As an outsider in the cases I discuss, I might see more clearly that which insiders hold tacit and never appreciate.

Conflict of interests is a recurring theme in my argument – between different professional groups, between curriculum developers and teachers, and between teacher and students, especially where there are cultural differences. It is not my intention to be divisive: I fully support current efforts to bind our profession internationally. Nevertheless, that there are conflicting interests is a fact of life which must be addressed if we are to come anywhere near solving important professional problems. Also, conflict does not have to be destructive. When a curriculum developer or a teacher is confronted by teachers, students or an institution which seem to go against the new, 'modern' methodology, it is *not* time for each side to close ranks and become more extreme in their defence against the other. This is what is worrying about the term 'culture' when it is used as a rallying point against change – either as something to be preserved against the imperialism of new ideas, or something which acts as a constraint against innovation. Instead, constructive dialogue and mutual learning can be healthy and productive. English language educators are in a rare and remarkable position to experience a rich variety of viewpoints and experiences from across the world.

I try to get away from stereotypical national cultural definitions, which are often the basis of destructive ethnocentricity, and to look at culture in a smaller, more precise way. It is more useful to talk about the cultures of individual classrooms and of individual teacher and student groups. These are entities which are close to us, in which we participate and about which we know a great deal. They are more tangible and definable than an 'Arab culture' or a 'Western culture'. Also, because these smaller cultures are less connected with partisan national feelings, more neutral in their connotations, it is easier to talk of, for example, cultures changing and being influenced by each other. In this micro-cultural landscape of teachers, students and classes, one can begin to see, too, dynamics of change and interaction in what amounts to a cultural market place, where new ideas or practices are traded between different groups according to their needs.

Rather than the destructive notion of a cultural imperialism, I prefer the market place analogy, where all parties are equal and there is tremendous potential for industry. Also, this analogy helps reduce the 'us' and 'them' problem. Market places are essentially cosmopolitan societies, where people come from afar to buy and sell; and 'afar' might be anything from a village down the valley to a distant land. Yet within the intimacy of dealing, outsiders and insiders of all sorts of different types might begin to lose their foreignness and become just people with different types of personalities. My presentation of a professional community from Britain, North America and Australasia, sweeping like a Mongol horde over educational institutions in the rest of the world – essentially a cultural imperialist metaphor – becomes redundant if the market-place analogy becomes real. Outsiders cease to become expatriate teachers and curriculum developers set against local teachers and students. In the smaller market place, all teachers are outsiders to the cultures of their students, and vice versa, and all curriculum developers are outsiders to the cultures of teachers, and vice versa. Similarly, trade of English language teaching technology may be between a group of teachers from the same community, as well as between local teachers and experts from foreign lands.

On a technical point, throughout I use the terms 'local' and 'expatriate' to refer to personnel who belong to the country in question, and who come from Britain, North America or Australasia respectively. I do not intend that 'local' should imply less worldly. These are simply convenient technical terms. 'Native' might be a more accurate term; but this has other connotations which I also wish to avoid.

What appear throughout the text as 'observation notes' are descriptions of classroom events in Egypt. In my references to teachers or lecturers in these observation notes, the gender bears no relationship to true identity. I sometimes use male and sometimes female gender quite arbitrarily. I also use fictitious names. Wherever anyone may feel they recognise themselves in any of these descriptions, I wish to stress that no offence is meant. If any inaccuracies exist my apologies are forthcoming; and it just goes to show that my perceptions of colleagues, no matter how much I search and research, are still liable to be incomplete. Hence the whole reason for this book – to demonstrate that everyone needs to think a great deal *more* about other people's intentions and expectations if anything appropriate is to result.

Part A The cultures of the classroom

1   The social context

Put very briefly, my aim in writing this book is to search for what we need to know about the social context of English language education in order to achieve appropriate classroom methodologies. This involves three areas of concern: a) what we know and what we need to know about the social context; b) how far this provides, or should provide a basis for more appropriate classroom methodologies, and c) the research techniques which are necessary for finding out what we need to know about the social context.

In this chapter I am going to set the scene by looking at why the social context of language teaching and learning is important – at the value of looking beyond the immediate classroom to the wider society – and at some of the implications this has for research and development in English language teaching.

1.1   In search of what happens between people

A great deal of research has been done in all aspects of English language education, and yet there are still significant gaps in our knowledge which prevent us from achieving classroom methodologies appropriate for different situations.

Much has been learnt about how people learn or acquire second languages. Second language acquisition research tells us how learning can or might take place at the individual level, but we do not know enough about how learning might be affected by the attitudes and expectations that people bring to the learning situation, which are influenced by social forces within both the institution and the wider community outside the classroom, and which in turn influence the ways

9

in which people deal with each other in the classroom. According to Breen, the experimental laboratory metaphor for the classroom, which second language acquisition research presents, although seeing the classroom as providing an optimal input or re-enforcer of good strategy, reduces language learning to linguistic or behavioural conditioning independent of learners' social reality. This metaphor is therefore asocial and psychologically naive (1986:137–9).

In the 'post-Munby era', syllabus and curriculum designers try hard to consider the socio-political, logistical, administrative, psycho-pedagogic and methodological constraints on their work. (In the epilogue to his book on communicative syllabus design, Munby 1978:217 describes these features as constraints on syllabus design, but sees them as factors which should be dealt with *after* rather than in conjunction with the design stage.) However, they have not succeeded in finding out what they need to know about the social forces deep in local settings which affect language learning. The issue of how to practise English language teaching in other countries and other social settings compounds these problems.

Now attention is moving on to the management of English language education (Hutchinson 1989:29–31; Robinson 1989:146; White 1988:21, 1987, 1989b); but there is a danger of emptiness in this movement. Management is a device for organising people and their activities in time and space; it cannot provide answers for *what* to manage. The research and development process can be managed, but management cannot provide the *data* necessary for the appropriate design of a product. The management itself has not only to be appropriate to the task in question, it also needs to be informed by this data. The key area is still lacking: we still do not have enough data about what really happens in the classroom between people.

The 'communicative approach' with its new awarenesses is now over a decade old, and yet it is still not conclusive that this or any other classroom methodology is the best. Allwright maintains:

> that method probably doesn't really matter very much ... but that what happens in the classroom still must matter. All the research so far described has involved the implicit assumption that what is really happening in the classroom is simply that some particular method or technique is being used, and that more or less efficient learning might be taking place accordingly. It is however clear that much more than this is happening. People are interacting in a multiplicity of complex ways. ... We need studies of what actually happens, not of what recognisable teaching methods, strategies or techniques are employed by the teacher, but of what really happens between teacher and class.
>
> (1988:51)

It is this area, of what 'really' happens between teacher and class, that I shall be concerned with throughout this book. The social context with which I shall be concerned is the social interaction within and around classroom language teaching and learning which affects and therefore helps explain what really goes on. The classroom is the place where the multiplicity and complexity of interaction referred to by Allwright takes place. However, I shall argue that it is not sufficient to look only within the classroom to understand this interaction. I emphasise within and *around* the classroom because I wish to maintain that much of what goes on within the classroom is influenced by factors within the wider educational institution, the wider educational environment and the wider society.

1.2 A division in the profession

There are two basic problems to which this lack of information about what really happens between teacher and class relates, and to which we seem to find no solutions.

1.2.1 *Foreign students and foreign methodologies*

On the one hand there are curriculum developers or teachers trying to effect appropriate English language teaching with students who are foreign to them, either at home or abroad, and trying to understand their attitudes and ways of doing things, which, to the outsider, are often obscure and opaque. On the other hand, there are teachers and curriculum developers who are native to the countries where they work, and the same nationality as the students they teach, but who are trying to make sense of methodologies developed in Britain, North America or Australasia for 'ideal' teaching-learning situations which are very different from their own. In this latter scenario, the question of what *is* the optimum classroom situation, or how far received classroom methodologies *are* the most appropriate, becomes very important. Not only do we have insufficient data about what really happens between people in the classroom, we lack this data for the wide range of social settings in which English language education is carried out around the world.

The two problem scenarios represent a basic division in the English language education profession. Current literature on the subject of appropriate methodologies often distinguishes between Western and non-Western or between the developed and the developing world, arguing that the transfer of methodologies from the first to the second, in each case, is problematic because of different attitudes towards education or lack of resources. However, I wish to argue that these distinctions are misleading. There is indeed a problem of technology transfer which I see not only in terms of teaching methodology, but in terms of the whole *technology* of English language education. However, it is not simply a Western-non-Western problem, because it is sometimes difficult to implement the methodology in continental Western Europe. Neither is it simply a developed-developing problem, because there are difficulties in implementing the methodology in developed countries such as Japan. It is rather a problem of English language teaching methodologies developed specifically in Britain, North America and Australasia being implemented almost everywhere else. Almost all the internationally established literature on English language education is published in these countries, which, at present, seem to have a virtual monopoly on received methodology.

1.2.2   Instrumental versus state

A probable reason for the difficulty of transporting these received English language teaching methodologies is that they are designed very much with a particularly instrumental approach in mind. By 'instrumental' I mean that there is a relatively clear contract between institutes and mainly adult groups who come specifically to learn English, or a special type of English. This can be found in institutes which tend to be either private language schools or annexes to university departments in Britain, Australasia and North America. Abroad, they are either these countries' cultural centres, or are private language schools in some way managed or spawned from the British, Australasia and North American model. I shall refer to this entity throughout as 'BANA' – derived from the initial letters of the countries in question.

It is not surprising that methodologies designed for this type of situation may not adapt easily to the other part of the English language education profession, which is found in state education, either in primary and secondary schools or in universities and colleges. These institutions are non-commercial in orientation and have a clientèle for whom English may not have such a clearly instrumental purpose. The influence of wider educational policies and, especially, but not only, in developing countries, of fewer resources, makes state English language education a very different type of activity from that in BANA language institutes. I shall refer to this entity throughout as 'TESEP' – derived from '*te*rtiary, *se*condary, *p*rimary'.

Because of the hegemony of the received BANA English language teaching methodology, and because there are few examples of high-status methodologies grown from the TESEP sector, the latter sector automatically becomes second class in that it is forced to make difficult adaptations of methodologies which do not really suit. Kharma and Hajjaj (1985) is only one example of published articles which complain of the unsatisfactoriness of the so-called 'communicative' approach, one form of which, I shall argue in Chapter 10, is too narrowly BANA in its orientation.

My thesis has two parts. First, the problem of technology transfer between instrumentally-oriented BANA and state-oriented TESEP English language education is largely created by the lack of concerted concern that research has shown for the different social contexts which bear upon these different scenarios. This is accompanied by a failure to see the state scenario as anything but sub-standard, and its features more as constraints than factors for design. Indeed, Phillipson (1992:57) argues that the recipients of the technology are seen as 'periphery' to a technology-producing 'centre'. Second, the two scenarios constitute two *cultures* in English language education, which contain different parameters for what happens between people in the classroom, and which must be considered, in all their variety, if appropriate methodologies are to be found.

These arguments will be pursued throughout the coming chapters. I do not wish to discuss the issue of culture in detail in this chapter, but to talk more generally of the aspects of social context with which investigation must begin. Also, in Chapter 10, I shall address the issue of how the so-called 'communicative' approach fits into all this. The reader might get the impression, from my early comments on failure in technology transfer, that I see this as a failure in the communicative approach. This is not the case. I shall argue that in its widest, strongest form, this approach has the potential to bridge the BANA-TESEP divide, provided that it pays heed to the differing social contexts that are involved.

1.3 Which social context?

Interest in the social context of English language education has been considerable and varied. As with other literature on the subject, I wish to deal only with certain aspects of the social context. The main focus of this book is on what I wish to call the *macro* aspects of the social context of language education.

I distinguish the macro from the micro aspects of social context in the following way. The macro context includes the wider societal and institutional influences on what happens in the classroom. Van Lier

13

describes the macro view as involving the wider community – 'home-school relations, L1-L2 relative status, learners' attitudes and reference groups and so on' (1988:7–8). In contrast, the micro social context consists of the socio-psychological aspect of group dynamics within the classroom. Van Lier describes the micro view as involving a discoursal or interactive context (ibid.).

I choose to focus on the macro social context because it concerns the influences from outside the classroom, which, I shall argue, are key in helping us understand what happens between people. Although the final focus, on what happens between people, is micro, these relationships can only be fully understood in terms of the wider, macro picture. A major part of my argument will be that it is the attitudes derived from relationships of status, role and authority brought by students and teachers from outside the classroom that influence those aspects of classroom interaction about which we know least. Furthermore, we need to understand how these factors are different in different countries in order to determine what can be appropriate in terms of classroom methodology. Therefore, a sociology and anthropology of the classroom is necessary.

A *sociology* is important because it can determine principles of influence across societies – generalisable principles about social action which can be applied to all classroom situations. An *anthropology* is important because it can determine how these influences are different within specific societies – social features of specific classroom situations. These two will be interwoven in the arguments and descriptions throughout the book. An anthropology is particularly important because it transcends the macro-micro continuum, connecting an understanding of the wider social picture with a deep exploration of what happens between people. Central to seeing the actors in the classroom as people with lives that originate outside, I feel it necessary to refer to the majority member of the classroom as 'student' rather than, as has become more common recently, 'learner'. This is because 'learner' carries the implication that the only purpose for being in the classroom is to learn. It will become apparent during the course of the book that there are often other purposes for being in the classroom, amongst which learning may be minor. 'Student', on the other hand, implies roles and identities outside the classroom.

The macro view of the social context is less frequently dealt with elsewhere, probably because it is the view least connected with applied linguistics. Indeed, there is a growing realisation within our profession that applied linguistics, as we have known it, is not sufficient to enable us to understand all that we need to know about language teaching andlearning, that it is necessary to look at the wider picture (Bowers 1986:1; White 1989b; Swales 1980:70; Savignon 1991; Phillipson 1992:175–6).

14

1.4   The classroom and its environment

A macro view of the social context of teaching and learning requires that we look at how the classroom relates to the world outside. Indeed, there are many ways in which what happens within the classroom reflects this world outside. As Bowers (1987:8–9) suggests, 'the classroom is a microcosm which, for all its universal magisterial conventions, reflects in fundamental social terms the world that lies outside the window'. This realisation from within English language education is supported by discussions already taking place elsewhere, which place the classroom, as a culture, within a wider complex of cultures, between which there are many complex channels of influence. The way in which the classroom mirrors the world outside can also be seen in the interest taken in it by 'a variety of disciplines: sociology, anthropology, social psychology, communicative ethnography' (Allwright 1988:x, citing Candlin). Van Lier (1988:9–10) suggests that the classroom possesses special features which crystallise the social world, such as routines and scripts, which occur in a controlled context, and which make it particularly attractive to researchers.

I shall deal with the question of the classroom as a culture in Chapters 2 and 3, and with its relationship with cultures outside the classroom in Part B. Here, by way of introduction, I shall describe briefly how the complex interconnection between the classroom and the world outside looks on the surface. (This is illustrated in Figure 1 on page 17.)

First of all, the classroom is situated in a host institution, which could be anything from a state school, to a private language institute, to a university or college. The host institution is in turn situated within a host educational environment. In state education, the host educational environment provides strong influences, from parents, employers and so on in the local community, which bear on the classroom. In some cases in English language education, local community influences might be less important. I therefore define the host educational environment as any type of environment which influences the host institution and in turn, the classroom. In private language institutes, this might consist of the market – client companies who send students, potential clients, the whole population of customers and potential customers, and other institutes in competition. This host educational environment would often not be local, but world-wide. In an English language aid project, the host educational environment would consist of the host country's ministry of education, aid agencies and other involved government institutions from both the host and donor countries, which also might be considered as contributing to market forces. Besides these different types of influence, in all cases the host educational environment also includes influences on students and teachers from their respective peer and reference groups. A reference group is the group of people which an individual looks to for self-evaluation, who provide the individual with values, standards and goals (Shipman *et al.* 1974:103, citing Merton; Stenhouse 1975, citing Johnson). For students, these would include other students and other parties such as family members who provide role models. There would also be expectations brought to the classroom from other classroom experiences, perhaps in other host institutions. For teachers, the major peer and reference groups would be colleagues, both in and out of the host institution; these would in turn be influenced by professional associations, as well as by training and other sources of attitude towards expertise, such as universities. What van Lier (1988:8) refers to as attitudes and expectations, prior schooling, socio-economic status, preferred learning styles, teacher and 'learner' roles, would all be involved here.

A third important participant in the classroom, after students and teachers, is the materials and the content and methodologies which they carry. These are of course created by teachers, to greater or lesser degrees through interaction with students. However, publishers, libraries and production facilities within the host institution are important contributory elements within the host educational environment. All of these are also influenced by teacher and student groups. There is thus a complex network of influences and interests within the host educational environment; and it is important not to forget the role of the economy, and other political and bureaucratic institutions within the wider society, influencing a wide range of resources, from salaries to furniture.

I began this section by stating that the classroom was a microcosm. It is a microcosm in the sense that what happens within the classroom reflects, affects and is affected by the complex of influences and interests within the host educational environment. In many ways, classroom interaction is an acting out of these influences and interests. Figure 1 illustrates this.

1.5 Finding out what we need to know

I have already referred to Allwright's (1988:51) point that there is a need for research which looks at what happens between people in the classroom [1.1]. I shall not be so much concerned with research in the formal sense as with the sort of on-the-job research which can be carried out by teachers and curriculum developers – and in the latter I

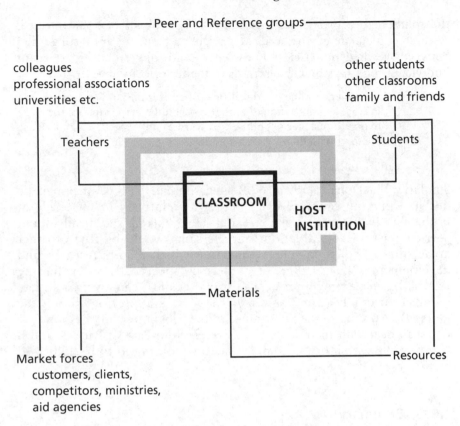

Figure 1 The classroom and the host educational environment

include those working in English language projects. In order to arrive at appropriate methodologies, practitioners need to take time to investigate what happens in the classroom. They need to incorporate into their approach to the classroom the capacity to look in depth at the wider social forces which influence behaviour between teachers and students, and to take a broad view of how these are in turn influenced by social forces from outside the classroom. This concept of 'teacher-researcher' is not new in education (Stenhouse 1975; Ruddock and Hopkins 1985).

My concern will be with action research, that is, research needed to create something which works – an appropriate classroom methodology – research as in 'research and development'. I shall not necessarily be looking for a research method that does more than provide sufficient guidelines to enable the next stage in the development of a product, or the solution to a problem. Hoyle (1970:18) explains how 'unfinished' research is adequate for the needs of curriculum planning. He distinguishes between 'verified but useless knowledge' and 'unverified but relevant knowledge' and says that the latter is of higher priority where:

> Our understanding of educational organizations and of curriculum development is so limited ... that it would be inappropriate for anyone to put [her or] himself forward as an 'expert', least of all as an expert who guarantees a solution.
>
> (Ibid.:16)

Similarly, MacDonald (1971:167n) suggests that the type of pragmatic decision making required can operate at relatively lower levels of probability than conventional research. He is talking specifically about curriculum project evaluation; but the same would be true of other areas within English language education which require research and development. Elley (1989:271), referring specifically to evaluating English language programmes, also warns against 'employing a sledge-hammer to crack a nut' and says that 'time and effort should be tailored' according to the importance of the programme in question.

I shall deal with the nature of this research in Part C. Parts A and B will be a discussion of the complex factors which need to be addressed by this research.

1.6 Summary

The following points have been made in this chapter:
a) After major advances in SLA research, more than ten years of the communicative approach and a realisation of the importance of the social context of the classroom in syllabus and curriculum design, we still do not know enough about what happens in the classroom between people. There are problems with the movement towards management because the data needed to inform management decisions is not sufficient.
b) This state of affairs is particularly problematic where i) practitioners need to understand the 'foreign' behaviour of students from other countries, and ii) practitioners are native to the countries where they work, and the same nationality as the students they teach, and who are trying to make sense of 'foreign' methodologies.

c)   There are two basic contexts – that of instrumentally oriented English language education based in Britain, Australasia and North America (BANA), and that of state English language education in the rest of the world (TESEP). Lack of knowledge of what is happening between people in these contexts makes it difficult to be certain about what the optimum methodology or classroom situation might consist of.

d)   The aim of the book will therefore be concerned with what happens between teacher and students within these different contexts, which form two cultures within English language education.

e)   The means for investigating the micro concern of what happens between teacher and students will be through looking at the macro context: the wider social relationships between classroom participants and influences from outside the classroom.

f)   This macro view of the social context involves the classroom being seen as a microcosm of wider society. Relationships with the host institution and the host educational environment will be investigated, as will influences upon classroom interaction from students' and teachers' peer and reference groups.

g)   One aim of the book is to look for a means whereby teachers and curriculum developers can carry out on-the-job research to investigate the macro view of the social context.

1.7.   Questions for discussion

The following questions are to provoke thought. They raise issues which will be addressed again in later chapters.

1   What sort of things would you list under the heading *What happens between people in the classroom*?
    Do you think it is true that we know very little about these things? Would it be truer to say that they are not dealt with in the literature?

2   What aspects of your job put you either in the BANA or the TESEP branch of English language education?
    What sort of people might fall into both groups?

3   The term 'instrumental' is used to describe the relationship within the educational environment between BANA institutions and their clientèle. How far is this a commercial or a business relationship?

4   Does 'appropriate methodology' refer to things like the structural approach or audio-lingualism?

5   List some important features of the educational environment in
    which you work.
    In what ways do these features affect the attitudes and practices of
    your colleagues, and the expectations of your students?
    To what extent is your educational environment different from
    that of teachers you know about in other regions, countries, or
    other types of institutions?

2 'Coral gardens'

The next two chapters demonstrate the value of looking at the classroom as a culture.

2.1 Metaphors for the classroom

Breen (1986) suggests that two common metaphors for the classroom have directed our attention away from crucial aspects of classroom interaction. I have already referred to the *experimental laboratory metaphor*, which involves second language acquisition research (SLA). Breen finds this asocial and psychologically naive [1.1]. He finds the *discourse metaphor* similarly inadequate. It reduces the classroom to what is observable in teacher-student talk. It takes into consideration the social aspects of the classroom, but it is psychologically naive because it does not sufficiently take into account the feelings and intentions of actors behind the words (ibid.:139–42). Breen sees *classroom as culture* as a more meaningful metaphor, addressing the interactive, social and often opaque features of the classroom which are instrumental in language learning. Where Allwright (1988:51) suggests that it is difficult to know exactly what is going on between people [1.1], Breen claims that it is only through looking at the classroom as culture that we can begin to understand.

Culture is a concept which needs to be handled carefully. Nowadays it is much used, often far too loosely. One of the problems is that the most common use of the word – as national culture – is very broad and conjures up vague notions about nations, races and sometimes whole continents, which are too generalised to be useful, and which often become mixed up with stereotypes and prejudices. It is easy to talk about, for example, the learning problems of a particular group of students as being influenced by 'Arab culture', or 'Confucian culture'; but such cultures, if indeed they are identifiable, are so complex and vast that they are no longer useful devices for investigating what is happening in the classroom between people. It is necessary to be far more precise than this. Bowers makes the cogent point that so-called cultural differences in the educational context can be much more in terms of class and educational differences between or within societies than between societies *per se* (1980a:105), and that it is thus 'both impracticable and unprofitable' to attempt to define these differences in terms of national cultures (ibid.:113).

In the following discussion I shall attempt to find a notion of culture which is more precise. One of the difficulties is that 'culture' is a pre-scientific concept. It already exists in common parlance, and carries with it many connotations which are not scientific. This is in contrast to, for example, 'social structure', which is a scientific concept developed to express aspects of sociological theory (Murphy 1986:40). However, I wish to use the notion because it is already in use, and because it contains many scientific connotations which are, I shall claim, extremely useful. As Mills states, despite 'the sponge-like quality and limitations of the word "culture"' in describing 'the social in man's depths' – indeed, he suggests it is one of the 'spongiest words in social science' – it is, 'perhaps for that reason, in the hands of an expert, enormously useful' (1970:177n).

Rather than attempt a concise definition of such a complex notion as culture, I shall build up a picture of the various features of culture, and show how each of these features can relate to the classroom. Indeed, the discipline of going through these features in relation to the classroom draws attention to aspects of classroom interaction which might otherwise escape the analysis. I shall refer to several writers in the social sciences. In doing this my intention is not to attempt an exhaustive survey of the literature, but to represent a wide range of views on the subject of culture, all of which can be absorbed into a workable notion.

2.2 Cultures of specific activities

In common parlance, as I have already suggested, the term culture can refer to whole societies. In sociological and anthropological terms, 'culture' can also refer to sections of societies. Stonequist (1937:4) refers to religious, class, urban, rural and sexual cultures. Whatever their size, these cultures have histories and traditions, implying a sense of permanence. How, therefore, can the term 'culture' be used for classroom groups, which are essentially temporary by comparison, forming only when the classroom group meets at appointed times?

Social science also refers to the cultures of specific activities, such as scientific cultures (ibid.:4). In management studies there are organisational cultures (Handy 1985:186). In education, similarly, references are made to school and teacher cultures (Hargreaves 1986:170; Swales 1985:212). Closer to home, Smith (1989:2–3), using Handy's concept, refers to the organisational cultures of the English language curriculum project, the donor agency and the recipient educational system, which will be the subjects of later chapters. These cultures do not have permanent membership or long histories and traditions when compared with the cultures of whole societies. They are temporary in the sense that they form when the groups in question meet to carry out specific activities. Individuals can be members of several of these cultures, switching as they move from one activity to another, rather as they would switch roles. The classroom culture is of this type, only existing when the class is in session.

As well as individual class groups, both learning and teaching can be said to have cultures of their own, as can different approaches and methodologies. The communicative approach, the audio-lingual method and so on all evolve their own cultures which influence the culture of the classroom. English language teaching produces a culture within the classroom which is different from that of teaching other subjects. I shall discuss this further in Chapter 5.

2.3 Patterns for group life

Given that classroom cultures, involving specific activities, are different from the permanent cultures of, say, family and religion, the value of seeing the classroom as a culture is in its similarities to these permanent cultures. Knowledge of how culture works generally can reveal much about the workings of classroom interaction. There are key features which relate to all types of cultures, whether classroom or national.

As a pre-scientific concept, in everyday usage culture becomes 'a loose reference to social milieux plus "tradition"' (Mills 1970:177n). The term can thus embrace a huge range of social labels:

> In customary terminology ... we use the term 'cultural pattern of group life' for designating all peculiar valuations, institutions and systems of orientation and guidance (such as folkways, mores, laws, habits, customs, etiquette, fashions) which, in the common opinion of sociologists of our time, characterise – if not constitute – any social group at a given moment in history.
>
> (Schutz 1964:92)

Nevertheless, all these labels are concerned with different types of patterns for behaviour. These patterns are taken for granted and unquestioned in normal circumstances, and are passed on by authoritative institutions within the society. They involve recipes for interpreting the social world:

> Any member born or reared within the group accepts the ready-made standardised scheme of the cultural pattern handed down to him by ancestors, teachers, and authorities as an unquestioned and unquestionable guide in all the situations which normally occur within the social world. The knowledge correlated to the cultural pattern carries its evidence in itself – or, rather, it is taken for granted in the absence of evidence to the contrary. It is knowledge of trustworthy *recipes* for interpreting the social world and handling things and men in order to obtain the best results in every situation with a minimum of effort by avoiding undesirable consequences.
>
> (Ibid.:95)

They involve tacit 'master patterns' which behave rather like deep structures:

> Culture is a common set of previously assimilated master patterns from which an infinite number of individual patterns directly applicable to specific situations are generated.
>
> (Bourdieu 1971:192)

They regulate interaction:

> Cultural elements are elements of patterned order which mediate and regulate communication and other aspects of the mutuality of orientations in interaction processes.
>
> (Parsons 1951:327)

Culture can similarly be seen as a system 'of interrelated symbols that provide coherent and meaningful ways of life for their bearers' (Murphy 1986:327). Also emerging from this interpretation is the notion of culture as a regulator of and a medium for communication (Gellner 1964:155, Stenhouse 1975:8), as a subset of behavioural recipes.

The culture of the classroom also provides tradition and recipe for both teachers and students in the sense that there are tacit understandings about what sort of behaviour is acceptable. These understandings are strengthened by common acceptance by peers. This provides the bonding which has the capacity to bear the conflicts of interest between teacher and students – the asymmetric relationships to which Breen (1986) refers. Asymmetric relationships are created when students give the teacher the right to allocate rights and duties to the students (ibid.:146). Culture also provides the conservatism which is seen particularly at times of innovation (ibid.:147). It may well be that these elements of culture transcend the pedagogic functions of classroom interaction. I shall discuss this in more detail in Chapter 3.

Through using the culture metaphor, Breen argues that the interactive aspect of the classroom is brought into focus:

> This interaction exists on a continuum from ritualistic, predictable, phatic ... to dynamic, unpredictable, diversely interpreted communication ... motivated by the assumption that people can learn together in a group.
>
> (Ibid.:143)

There is a juxtaposition of interaction *through* and *about* languages, and a frequent conflict between the established interaction of the classroom and the innovation created by new language (ibid.:143).

2.4   Transmission and learning

Culture transmits tradition, which is shared and learned, to produce systems which are sometimes created as well as being sometimes taken for granted – socialisation, and knowledge as a social construction of reality from the past yet unquestioned in the present:

> Culture is *transmitted*, it constitutes a heritage or a social tradition; ... it is *learned*, it is not a manifestation, in particular content, of man's genetic constitution; ... it is *shared*. Culture, that is, is on the one hand the product of, on the other hand a determinant of, systems of human social interaction.
>
> (Parsons 1951:15)

The cultures of individual classrooms are transmitted to new members. Both teachers and students have to learn and share them if they are to be fully accepted into the group.

2.5   Personality and ethics

There is an expressive aspect of culture in that it provides outward signs of the personality of a social group:

> Membership of a group is signified by wearing a certain kind of cloth, and that marital status is reflected in the manner of taking part in collective dances, is part of the culture of the society in question.
>
> (Gellner 1964:153–4)

In the classroom culture, every teacher has experienced the different personalities and ethics which different classroom groups evolve. They mediate in the agendas which individual members wish to pursue in classroom activities. They assert a social force which prevents teachers from replicating their lesson agendas with different classroom groups.

2.6   Change and stress

Another aspect of culture is that it can be changed:

> Cultures are not rooted in absolutes. They are the products of human activity and thinking and, as such, are people-made. The elements of culture are artificial, contrived and changeable.

(Murphy 1986:25)

Looking back to the point which Schutz makes about knowledge and culture, 'it is taken for granted [only] in the absence of evidence to the contrary' (1964:95). Schutz argues that the cultural system maintains a status quo, successfully eliminating questioning ideas from outside which might upset the:

> ...'of course' assumptions of its members, until a 'crisis' [arises to] ... overthrow precipitously the actual system of relevances. The cultural pattern no longer functions as a system of tested recipes at hand; it reveals that its applicability is restricted to a specific historical situation.

(Ibid.:96)

The crisis 'interrupts the flow of habit and gives rise to changed conditions of consciousness and practice' (ibid.:96, citing Thomas). This means that cultures are not something static: they can change as they come into contact with each other, as the influences of culture are 'diffused from group to group' (Stonequist 1937:18).

The power of change can create different dependencies on cultural identity. In more static situations, people's roles in organisations or society are relatively fixed and secure. Individuals base their identity on where they are placed within a hierarchy or social structure; and the culture surrounding their role supports this identity. Indeed, membership of a specific position or class in society is largely prescribed and determined by membership of cultural groups and vice versa (Gellner 1964:154–7). For example, in a more static educational situation, the job of senior teacher might be secured by being a grade A graduate of College X. The culture of the College X grade A group would be tied to and support the job and position of senior teacher. The role of senior teacher is thus prescribed, as is its connection with the cultural group.

However, in more dynamic situations, the job of senior teacher might not be secured by being a member of the College X grade A group, but according to competition, supply and demand and performance. Permanent identity can no longer be attached to 'senior teacher', but remains attached to the more portable culture of the College X grade A group. Thus, for the purpose of identity:

> Culture does not so much underline structure: rather it replaces it
> ... Man does not possess citizenship in virtue of prior membership
> of some organic sub-part of it. He possesses citizenship – if he
> possesses it at all – *directly*.

(Gellner 1964:155)

There is 'an erosion of the *given*' which can cause tremendous strain and interpersonal friction (ibid.:157). Without the support of a prescribed membership within a hierarchy or social structure, culture thus becomes central to identity and a sense of security:

> If a man is not firmly set in a social niche, whose relationship as it
> were endows him with his identity, he is obliged to carry his
> identity with him, in his whole style of conduct and expression: in
> other words, his 'culture' becomes his identity.

(Ibid.:157)

Culture is, therefore, particularly at issue in the lives of people in dynamic, complex situations, especially when their identity is at stake.

A word of warning is necessary when talking about dynamic or static contexts. I do not support the way in which Gellner attaches static to 'primitive' societies and dynamic to 'modern' societies. It is very likely that the former *appear* static to outsider, Western anthropologists who do not understand the nature of their dynamism. There has been a tendency for the West to see countries of the developing world as static and therefore in need of change – to overcome the strictures of prescription (Phillipson 1992:39, 42). To avoid this kind of excuse for imperialism (ibid.), I wish to emphasise that I see dynamism and static situations as existing alongside each other within the same society, whether that society is 'Western' or 'developing'.

Although the classroom culture is largely conservative [2.3], it is also open to large degrees of change. This is especially the case in English language education, which has given birth to a proliferation of new methodologies. Where the change is too harsh, crisis leads to the closing of ranks among both teachers and students. If the structure they are used to seems at risk, they hang on to their cultural values and resist. As I shall argue in Chapter 11, change can only be effective if crisis is avoided, through deep understanding of the classroom culture. Teacher agendas easily fail, and classrooms fall into irreconcilable conflict when classroom cultural forces are not understood and worked with. I shall discuss this in more detail in Chapter 9. In some cases, where classroom conditions are harsh, crisis becomes a regular state of affairs, and creates a vigorous co-operation within student groups. This co-operation can be capitalised on in the introduction of new methodologies, as I shall show in Chapter 12.

Classroom interaction represents an 'amalgam and permutation' of different and often conflicting social contexts for the different types of people involved. There is a tension between the 'internal world of the individual and the social world of the group' (Breen 1986:144).

The changeability of classroom cultures provides them with the capacity to bear the mobility of members from classroom group to group. Teachers move frequently from classroom to classroom and have to become expert at learning and being accepted by new classroom cultures; to a lesser degree students also have to become expert at moving between courses, and meeting their peers in a range of combinations in different groups.

2.7   Diversity and interconnection

I have already referred to the possibility that cultures can be any size, from very large to very small, from a national or tribal culture to a family culture [2.2]. In the concept, 'European culture', one sees even a continental culture. There can also be a system of cultures which are not mutually exclusive, with cultures overlapping, containing and being contained by other cultures. Relations between cultures can be both vertical, through hierarchies of cultures and subcultures, or horizontal, between cultures in different systems.

It is important to look at the classroom culture in terms of wider cultures. The classroom is part of a complex of interrelated and overlapping cultures of different dimensions within the host educational environment [1.4].

Figure 2 shows schematically how this culture complex may interrelate. It consists of the classroom, host institution, student, professional-academic, wider international education-related and national cultures. I have already said something about the host institution [1.4], and indeed the representation of interrelated cultures here is a deeper interpretation of the set of relationships shown in Figure 1. *Student cultures* will be dealt with in Chapter 4. The figure shows that although these are a major contributor to the classroom, they also partly derive from outside the classroom. Their influence comes partly from the wider society, and is also carried between classrooms within the corridors of the host institution.

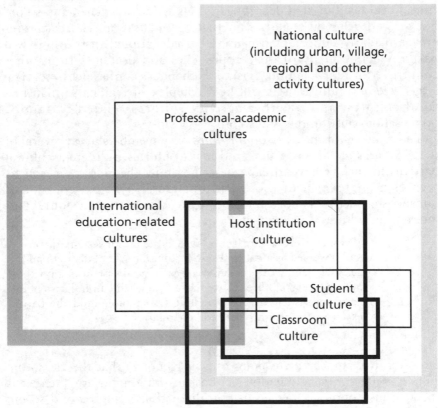

Figure 2 *Host culture complex*

Professional-academic cultures will be dealt with in detail in Chapter 5. It is sufficient to say here that they are the cultures connected with professional peer and reference groups, schools of academic thought and practice, professional approach etc., generated by professional associations, unions, university departments, publishers etc. It is significant that these extend beyond the boundaries of the national culture: in particular, English language teachers, in countries where English is not the mother tongue, where the subject matter, the language, is considered to be foreign, have *inter*national links which they depend on for much of their sense of professional-academic belongingness.

Apart from these links within the English language teaching community, there is also a wider *international education-related* culture. This involves the wider ethos of what constitutes education, an educational institution, a department, a discipline, a teacher, and so on. For many developing countries international education-related cultures are particularly important because local educational institutions will partially derive many of their approaches and practices from other countries, through training, visits, exchanges, conferences etc. The larger *national* culture itself will be a complex of regional, urban and rural cultures, and of other activity cultures related to family, organisations, institutions and so on.

The members of the *classroom culture* have membership in several of these cultures at the same time and may conform to different cultural patterns in each. I have already described how the classroom can be seen as a microcosm of the world outside [1.4]. This concept of microcosm becomes more meaningful if it is seen in a context of interrelated cultures. Lutz explains:

> ... that a classroom may be observed as a cultural system, the school observed as a cultural system, and the school district and the larger society may each be observed as cultural systems – all within a single national culture. As we move from each cultural system to the broader system, the actors in each system often hold alternative roles across the arbitrary cultural boundaries.

(1981:60)

However, it is important to point out, in Figure 2, that the classroom culture is not *completely* within the host institution culture. Neither is the host institution completely within the national culture, and so on. This is because they are influenced by elements within other, outside cultures, including international education cultures. Both the classroom and host institution cultures will be part of a larger educational system which will also have a culture which will itself be complex. Teachers bring tradition to the classroom, derived from professional-academic cultures. Professional-academic cultures derive influence from both within and outside the host institution, as well as partly from international education-related cultures. Innovations, the cultures of methodologies and approaches also derive from outside the classroom through professional-academic cultures and other educational and scientific cultures. Students, too, bring tradition to the classroom, passed from generation to generation of students and formed partly in the corridors of the host institution, partly through reference groups which may extend to other institutions, through the media and the family. The students' role and influences on the classroom culture will be discussed in detail in Chapter 3.

It becomes clear, therefore, that many aspects of what happens within the classroom can be understood fully only by looking at the influences of all the cultures outside the classroom.

2.8   'Coral gardens'

The many aspects of culture and of the classroom culture which I have so far mentioned reflect the complex multiplicity of classroom interaction referred to by Allwright [1.1]. In similar vein, Breen compares the complexity of the classroom culture with the interrelated myriad life forms found in a coral reef (1986:142). Little of this life can be seen on the surface of the reef; but beneath the surface, the complexity of life forms is immense. Similarly, what can be seen of classroom interaction constitutes *'epiphenomena'* – mere surface manifestations of far more complex things going on under the surface. All that we can so far understand of classroom reality is the 'rim of a socio-cognitive coral reef' (ibid.:149).

An important implication of seeing the classroom as a culture is that more is going on between people than the transfer of knowledge and skills between the members of the classroom group. Researchers and teachers – if not teacher-researchers [1.5] – must submit themselves to the knowledge that there are mysteries which they cannot fathom. Breen makes the point that 'anthropological humility' must be applied when looking at the classroom (ibid.:142). Just as anthropologists must humble themselves to the mysteries of the communities they are studying, so must teacher-researchers humble themselves to the class-rooms with which they are involved.

Where the classroom has a culture as complex as the coral reef, the teacher cannot afford to be anything but a researcher. All techniques and methodologies must be continuously in question, and *interpretive ethnography* becomes the essential research approach. I shall deal with this in Chapter 10.

2.9   A note on terminology

One problem connected with the type of culture analysis begun in this chapter is that of terminology. Where almost every sphere of human behaviour is looked at in terms of culture, the word 'culture' is in danger of appearing so frequently that, stylistic questions apart, the concept becomes weakened. Having made the point in this chapter, therefore, that it is necessary to look at the different types of culture surrounding teacher and student behaviour, in the rest of the book I shall sometimes use other terms. I shall sometimes refer to national culture as society, and to permanent cultures within society by their names – the family, religion and so on. Professional-academic cultures and student cultures will be referred to as teacher and student groups or communities, the latter implying something larger, and the former implying something smaller. It is not my intention to present these as scientific terms. On the one hand, their boundaries are vague, and on the other hand, as has already been mentioned [1.5.1], relevance is more important than exhaustive precision.

2.10   Summary

The following points have been made in this chapter:
a)   A culture metaphor for the classroom draws attention to the complexity of classroom interaction. It is less asocial and psychologically naive than the SLA metaphor, and looks deeper than the discourse metaphor at what is observable in teacher-learner talk.
b)   Tradition and recipe, expressiveness and complexity, and the capacity for change and stress in culture, can all be seen in classroom culture. That cultures can be of different sizes and types, related hierarchically or in other ways, sometimes overlapping, underlines the importance of seeing classroom culture as related to a complex of other cultures in the host educational environment.

2.11   Questions for discussion

1   List important aspects of a) your culture, b) the culture of a class which you teach, and c) the culture of your institution.
   Is a) a different type of thing from b) and c), or just bigger than b) and c)?
   Do you have different class groups which have different cultures? How are they different?
2   Is the culture of your classroom completely governed by the culture of your country or region?

How far is the culture of your classroom influenced by the cultures of schools, universities or professional groups in other countries or regions?

3   Do you agree that cultures are constantly changing and being affected by other cultures?

Is culture change a good or a bad thing?

Have you ever experienced changes in the culture of one of your own class groups?

3   The variety of classroom cultures

In this chapter I wish to describe some cases which illustrate the variety of classroom cultures, and some of the typologies which have been employed to describe them. These cases are interesting in that they illustrate how various classroom cultures can be influenced by different combinations or weightings of influences from the various other cultures seen in Figure 2 on page 29.

Also, as these cases are described, some beginning attempts at appropriate English language teaching methodology design will be observed. At the same time, these cases will illustrate how essentially problematic such ventures are. Perhaps because these attempts at methodological change intend to be sensitive to the cultures of the classroom and respective educational environments, without sufficient knowledge, they are in danger of creating far-reaching unforeseen consequences. The cases referred to here will thus serve to raise weaknesses and possibilities upon which later discussion will be based.

Existing literature on classroom culture is very slight. It is therefore not possible to attempt anything approaching a representative account of classroom cultures across the world. Rather, I present a preliminary exploration on the basis of some of the little data which exists. Much of this data I have collected myself in Egyptian university classrooms. It is my intention, therefore, not to describe cultures *per se*, but to illustrate, by looking at *some* cultures, their general complexity and variety, and therefore the implications for designing appropriate methodologies.

3.1   Pace and flow

In his study of the non-verbal classroom behaviour of Alaskan school children, Collier (1979) notices a marked type of movement in classrooms, which he calls 'pace' and 'flow'. Pace is 'the rate of movement, actions and events', which 'affects the meaning and course of communication'. Flow is 'the interrelatedness of the movements of people who are interacting or attempting to interact'; it is high when movements are interrelated, and low when they are not related (ibid.:1–2). He distinguishes two patterns in the classes he observes. The first is when the teacher's pace is different from that of her or his pupils, resulting in low flow. The second pattern is when the teacher's pace is in harmony with that of the pupils, resulting in high flow (ibid.:42).

Collier sees these distinctions, within the classroom culture, as influenced by the wider community. He sees pace as something which 'varies from culture to culture' (ibid.:1), and observes that although:

> There was some variation in pace with changes in activity ... it was essentially the same in all circumstances: in school, around the villages, at home and in church. ... The consistency of this pace style and the fact that it was shared by both adults and children suggests that it is the characteristic pace of Eskimos in this section of Alaska.
>
> (Ibid.:42)

At the same time, the varying pace amongst teachers was observed as largely to do with whether they were outsider American 'Anglo' teachers – different pace from their pupils, producing low flow – or local Eskimo teachers – same pace as their pupils, producing high flow (ibid.:42–3).

Although Collier does not refer to differing professional-academic cultures, it could be argued that they are an instrumental factor in the differences of pace between the teachers in the study. In contrast to the local teachers, the 'Anglo' teachers tended to belong to a culture which promoted a more rationalised, technical teaching approach, which was less sensitive to local pace amongst pupils (ibid.:44).

Collier is more an anthropologist than an educationalist and does not concern himself with action to be taken as a result of what he observes. However, his pace-flow distinctions can be seen as typologies – as means for describing classroom cultures, which might be applied to other situations. The implication of what Collier says for the search for appropriate English language teaching methodologies is considerable, for it reveals an aspect of deep, tacit classroom behaviour which is difficult for the outsider curriculum developer or teacher to understand, and a potential for conflict between the outsider teacher who does not conform to this behaviour, which could seriously inhibit learning. I shall say more about this in Chapter 9, when I discuss sources of conflict between teachers and students.

3.2 Teaching spectacles and learning festivals

Coleman uses Handelman's anthropological distinction between spectacle and festival in cultural events when he distinguishes between 'teaching spectacles', in which students are largely passive and behave like an audience watching the spectacle of the teacher's teacher-centred performance, and 'learning festivals', where students participate in the activity of learning as they would participate in a festival (1987:97–8). Although Coleman draws relationships with the Indonesian national culture – the Hasanuddin University lectures in Indonesia, which he categorises as teaching spectacles, are similar to Indonesian puppet shows, where the audience watches and does not participate (ibid.:97) – this typology can be applied to any classroom situation.

Coleman demonstrates the value of this type of classroom culture analysis in curriculum development. He uses his distinction between teaching spectacle and learning festival as a 'model on which we can base an attempt to introduce new forms of classroom behaviour'. His agenda as a curriculum designer is to improve the effectiveness of lessons at Hasanuddin University by increasing student participation. Hence, the teaching spectacle-type lesson is seen as ineffective because students do not participate. 'The implication is that if the "teaching spectacle" is to be abandoned, then a "learning festival" must be instituted' (ibid.:98). Thus, by looking at the cultural nature of the classroom in question, Coleman is able to define what he considers the nature of the problem, and to see the solution in alternative cultural terms.

However, the situation is not that simple. Coleman observes that the 'teaching spectacles' at Hasanuddin have value as *ritual* – much as the puppet shows with which they are compared. Hence, the main function of classes is not necessarily for students to learn a content but to take part in the ritual of the 'lesson' for other than educational reasons. Learning English takes place elsewhere in private language schools (Coleman in process).

This understanding of the cultural *function* of the classroom enables Coleman to see that, given the deep cultural nature of the classroom in this particular situation, it is not possible to *change* the form of the lesson, because to these particular students and teachers the 'lesson' is essentially a teaching spectacle.

> In other words, it becomes necessary to put the participants – both
> teachers and students – into situations which will no longer be
> perceived as 'lessons', so that all who are involved can avoid falling
> back into roles which are inextricably associated with the lesson
> format.
>
> (Coleman 1987:98)

It is only this understanding of the culture which enables Coleman to
see that change requires a shift to a whole different ball game – to
something which is not considered a 'lesson' – to a *festival* situation in
which what he considers the preferable type of learning can take place.

Coleman reports significant success in the change which he subse-
quently engineers through this knowledge of the classroom culture. His
Risking Fun material, which was designed to help produce a 'learning
festival', was adopted by junior lecturers (1992a:229), although of
course, as Coleman admits, it is difficult to get reliable, quantitative
feedback from teachers and students, because there are other
motivations for saying things are better than they really are (ibid.:233).
(See also my discussion in Chapter 7 of hidden curricula.) More
recently, during a 1989 workshop to evaluate the new methodology, the
lecturers who had been involved stated that they did not wish to go
back to the old methods (Coleman 1991, personal communication).

Although Coleman's concern seems to be largely with the influence of
national culture on the classroom, changes from teaching spectacle to
learning festival in the classroom would involve changes in the
professional-academic culture of the teachers and the local institution
culture. I shall come back to this at the end of the chapter.

3.3   Large- and small-class cultures

I myself made the following observations of undergraduate classroom
culture in Egyptian faculties of education, for the purpose of informing
the design of a new English language teaching methodology. (I shall
describe in Chapter 12 how this information helped curriculum design.)
A significant typological distinction was between *small-class* cultures, in
classes with fewer than 50 students, and *large-class* cultures, in classes
with up to 450 students (Holliday 1991a:279–90, in process).The small-
class culture seemed to be based on tacit, implicit relationships. I
compare this type of culture with the sociological concept of *Gemeinschaft*, in which small-scale community relationships are characterised
by 'traditional' forms of behaviour which have 'thorough adherence to

customary ways of behaving' (Murphy 1986:149–50). This type corresponds with the Eskimo-taught Eskimo classes described in Collier [3.1]. The relationship between teacher and students seemed not so much a product of an explicit methodology; it was rather derived more naturally from existing unspoken role expectations perhaps originating outside the classroom.

On the other hand, the large-class culture was a relatively new development brought about in the long term by urbanisation and population increase. It thus precipitated the need for a new, more consciously organised, explicit, classroom management. This type of culture can be compared to a *Gesellschaft* or 'large' society in which relationships involve greater distance and special behaviour has to be developed to cope with the situation. It is thus characterised by 'rational' forms of behaviour 'in which the validity of social usage is found in the logicality of its fit with other usages' after the event, rather than the adherence to prescribed recipes for action (Murphy 1986:149–50). (Murphy takes the concepts of 'rational' and 'traditional' behaviour from Max Weber. It is not my intention to suggest that small groups of the *Gemeinschaft* type never rationalise their behaviour, but that there are *more* ready-made recipes for action at hand, based on traditional ways of doing things, which reduce the need to develop special methodologies.)

The large-small-class typology relates to professional-academic culture. In the small-class culture, the local lecturers followed traditional classroom processes, which belonged to attitudes about human interaction which were beyond and prior to professional, pedagogic issues of the classroom. In Egyptian faculties of education such classes were characterised by tacit communication rules which I, as an outsider expatriate observer, found difficult to perceive. For example, in a local lecturer's translation class:

> Anyone walking in would have thought there was chaos because a lot of students were talking at once and the lecturer did not always seem to be in control. ... The lecturer asked some students to be quiet, but not some others who appeared to be talking out of turn. ... One particular student in a group which always seemed to be talking out of turn was clearly in contact with the lesson because they often initiated very cogent comments. ... The end of the lesson was left apparently without a concrete conclusion (the Arabic version of the final sentence dealt with, with changes by the lecturer as a result of student suggestions, was not finished with).

> (Observation notes)

Despite apparent lack of order in the classroom, in discussion with the local lecturer:

> She said that ... she knew exactly what was going on and that, yes, it was culturally normal to be talking and listening at the same time ... and that although some students were talking a lot, perhaps only 60% about the lesson, they were very much in touch. The ones she told to be quiet were [the ones who were] really off the point.

(Observation notes)

However, the large-class culture seemed to force an entirely different situation. With the breakdown in the proxemics necessary for the natural, community approach, the local lecturers' traditional approach appeared no longer to produce the same type of rapport. Such classes in Egyptian faculties of education were characterised by teacher-centred lectures in which there was very little contact between lecturer and students. I therefore hypothesised that the professional-academic culture of local lecturers was failing to cope with the changing classroom situation brought about by increasing class sizes at tertiary level.

Of course, my hypothesis might well have been coloured by the notions of what an 'effective' classroom should be like, produced by my own BANA professional-academic culture which I shall describe in Chapter 5. However, it is supported by literature on population growth and urbanisation in the wider society. Abou-Lughod, in her study of the effects of urbanisation in Egypt, cited in Safty *et al.* (1985:235), reports the difficulty which society has in coping with the 'anonymity and secondary contacts' of urban life, by which it is not normally characterised. Thus, in the large-class situation, the relations between teacher and student, which had traditionally been close, had been reduced to more anonymous secondary contacts. It was certainly common for lecturers to know only a small proportion of their students.

Two more relationships between the Egyptian faculty of education classroom culture and the wider society supported the notion of a development of a new classroom culture found in the large-class situation. They show that *Gesellschaft* was also becoming a feature of the national culture. Anawati, in her study of men-women student relationships, cited in Safty *et al.*, claims that the 'colleagueship and friendship' common between undergraduate students of both genders is a reflection of urbanisation, and would have been unknown at the beginning of the twentieth century (ibid.:215). Rugh takes this connection further and argues that the classroom's provision of 'non-kin' collaboration is a substitute for small-community relations lost in the advent of urbanisation. These types of relations are essential to enable young adults to meet each other in the relative respectability of the classroom, where the credentials of peers are known (1985.:283, 256–60). Thus, work places, clubs and classrooms provide a valuable social function external to the purely educational function of passing on knowledge, and are an example of classroom cultural forces transcending the pedagogic function.

3.4   Deep and surface action

A further typological distinction which proved useful in my investigation of Egyptian classrooms, which is applicable to any classroom culture, is that between deep and surface action. Whereas surface action is plain to see, deep action phenomena are those which are opaque to outsiders and perhaps only tacitly understood by insiders to the culture. Deep action phenomena are within the realm of tacit recipes for action [2.3] deep within the fabric of the culture. (I shall look at deep and surface action again in Chapter 8, within the context of English language project management.) The pace and flow of classroom movement which Collier describes [3.1], and the ritual aspect of classroom behaviour described by Coleman (in process) [3.1, 3.2], can be seen as examples of deep action phenomena.

3.4.1   Hidden communication

I have already referred [3.3] to one example of deep action in the tacit rules for communication evident in the more traditional, small-class culture, which were difficult to fathom by the outsider observer. They seemed to represent an ability for the students to talk and listen at the same time. In an examination situation this ability to handle several channels of communication at once was evident when I was told:

> that I should attend my students' examination for a short while near the beginning to answer any questions about the paper that may be causing problems. This seemed to be a routine thing: I had done something similar with my postgraduate students.

> (Observation notes)

The students appeared to have no difficulty doing the exam while question answering was going on. Similarly, at a local preparatory school, while watching students on teaching practice, it was very difficult to see *how* communication was taking place, although there were clear signs that communication *was* taking place:

> During the first five minutes of each lesson it was difficult to know whether the teacher was speaking English or Arabic – both equally unintelligible. There was little overt reference to the textbook or to separate parts of the lesson. There clearly was organisation; but if the pupils were aware of it it was because the communication was

deep set or because there was a communication going on which I was not aware of. I feel that the former was the case. The pupils were very enthusiastic regardless, apparently, of what was happening, and took part in a ritual snapping of fingers against the thumb caused by a sudden flick downward of the wrist as they lunged their hands forward, rather than up, to show that they knew the answers to the questions. Most pupil responses were in the form of uttering a word in Arabic to show that they understood a new word in English.

(Observation notes)

These incidents may seem unmysterious after description. They are examples of deep action in the sense that within a curriculum development context they had not been formally acknowledged by either insiders or outsiders to the situation.

3.4.2 Classroom instructions

Another example of deep action was in the rules for giving classroom instructions (Holliday 1991a:247–50). Classes observed with local lecturers contained lower percentages of explicit instruction regarding classroom procedure than classes observed with expatriate lecturers. Whereas local lecturers generally gave instructions about overall classroom procedure and appropriate behaviour once at the beginning of the course, the expatriate lecturers tended to spend a large amount of time on instructions about individual activities within each lesson. For example, on one local lecturer's class: – 'No time was spent on explaining procedure – everyone seemed to know what to do and got on with it from the moment of start' (Observation notes). Indeed, this routine was often set up at the beginning of the course; and it was often felt that there was no need to reinforce it during the process of lessons. In the discussion at the end of her class, a local lecturer said that in her lesson:

> She was in a better position than [expatriate lecturers] ... who constantly reconfirmed procedures, to know *when* the students had got the message and therefore when she could stop reconfirming. She added, unelicited, that she and her compatriots were always annoyed in the United States when they went to airports, train stations etc., and they were constantly being retold what the procedures were. She said that this constantly insulted their intelligence.

(Observation notes)

The issue here seems to be with the timing of classroom instructions. In giving instructions too frequently expatriate lecturers interfered with the *protocol* of the classroom culture in the sense that the students were treated as less than competent (see Holliday 1992a). Again, this protocol was too deep to be seen by outsiders and had not been stated formally by insiders to the situation.

3.4.3 Sanctity and hospitality

Further deep aspects of the protocol of the classroom culture were revealed in the interaction with myself and others entering the classroom as observers (Holliday 1991a:254–66). A particularly opaque deep action was evident in the apparently paradoxical relation between lesson sanctity and the overall hospitality offered by the classroom culture.

The fairly common phenomenon of classroom sanctity being preserved by being closed to colleagues, and of observation being seen as evaluative 'inspection', was in evidence when local lecturers did not appear eager to have me watch them teaching. However, they generally seemed keen to allow me into their classes to do the teaching myself. This was surprising, as one would have thought local lecturers, in fear of inspection, would rather not risk letting an 'expert' show up their inadequacies in front of their students by teaching in an innovatory way better than they would be able to do. It may have been the case that these local lecturers hoped I would discredit the new methodology by 'failing' in my demonstration, thus letting them off the hook. In fact it might have rather shown that the methodologies already in use were deep, traditional methodologies [3.3], which could not be easily compromised by outsider interference.

Whatever the local lecturers' hidden agenda might have been, I did not get the impression that there was a relationship between lecturer and students which was sufficiently sacrosanct as to require protection from the eyes of the outsider observer. On the contrary, I sensed an unexpected *hospitality* towards the outsider. An example of this was seen in one class where a local lecturer finished half an hour early because, she said, 'she was worried about *me* getting tired' (Observation notes). Whether or not this was really concern for the well-being of a guest in the classroom, or – if one is cynical – an excuse for finishing early, the *statement* of hospitality is significant.

The notion of outsider observer in the classroom as honoured guest, despite the inconvenience which intrusion might create, was supported by the way in which outsiders are received into homes in the wider community. It was also seen in the way in which, when observing classes, despite wishing to sit out of the way at the back as observers 'should', I was asked to sit in the front, facing the students, with the lecturer – a more honoured position. This action was all the more significant because lecturers sat at a desk on a platform that raised them two to three feet above the students. This brings home the fact that when one enters a classroom as an observer, one is invited into a new society with its own deep culture whose norms may go against standardised instructions on how to observe and how to have minimal observer effect. Again, I use the term 'deep' because it is never clear exactly what *is* going on. My outsider interpretation on being seated at the front rather than being allowed to be unobtrusive may have been wrong. The point is that there is something going on which is strange, and only by going along with and addressing this can one begin to understand what is happening between people in any given classroom. At the beginning of this section I also use the term 'revealed'. Understanding what is happening in the classroom is accompanied by a process of *revelation* of deep action – of the never-ending mysteries of the 'coral garden' [2.8]. I take this notion of revelation partly from Sussex's (1975) discussion of a revelatory tradition, which allows events to speak for themselves within their own rhythm, as opposed to an illustrative tradition, which develops a prescribed theme, in documentary film making.

3.4.4 Resilience in the face of outsider interference

This notion of classroom hospitality suggested a classroom culture sufficiently resilient to cope with the intrusion of outsiders. Evidence of this was the apparent indifference on the part of the students when outsiders entered, despite their being seated at the front of the class. A very *revealing* event was when I found it impossible to avoid taking two other observers into a classroom. The lecturer was an expatriate:

> I had just been to pay a courtesy call on the dean with the head of department and had met a lecturer from the curriculum department. They both escorted me to the lesson, after showing me the library, and then asked if they could come in and watch. They seemed sensitive to the situation (I am sure such a thing would not have been allowed had a local lecturer been teaching) and asked me to go and ask the lecturer if it would be all right. I did as they asked ... and he agreed. We sat in the front, on the left, to the side. I attempted to pull us all as far as permissible into the corner. I did not feel that it would have been done to ask my 'important' fellow observers to sit at the back. I sat between them and laid out my copy of the material on my briefcase for them both to see. I explained things to them while the students were doing group work, looking over things by themselves. The lecturer was also able to come over and talk to us at these times.

(Observation notes)

Several things could be noticed from this incident. It provided further evidence of the local caution about entering other lecturers' classes. It seemed that this caution had prevented the head of department from going to watch before, despite curiosity to see what this foreigner was doing with the students in the department. (There had never been a foreign lecturer in this faculty before.) Now that I was there, providing evidence perhaps that foreigners were not quite so cautious about classroom observation, the head of department and local lecturer took courage to ask if they could come into the lecture.

Supporting the notion of a resilient classroom culture was what appeared to be relaxed attitudes regarding the sanctity of the classroom. Although my two co-observers were very keen to ask the lecturer's permission to let them in, they seemed to have no qualms about my having to interrupt the lecturer, who had already entered the class, in order to get the permission. *I* certainly felt very nervous about having to do this. This apparent disregard for the sanctity of the lesson was made greater by the fact that my two co-observers had made me late for the lesson by insisting on showing me around the faculty.

3.4.5   Formality and casualness

The apparent casualness of the way in which this classroom culture received outsiders seemed in sharp contrast with other aspects of the culture, which seemed very formal. Again, the protocols underlying this distinction were deep in that they were difficult for the outsider observer to perceive. A particular example of casualness occurred when I was teaching and a local colleague came to observe. He:

> sat on my right and eventually came and sat right up next to me because he did not have his copy of the materials with him! This seemed a very normal state of affairs [in that] no-one seemed to think it was strange.

> (Observation notes)

There was a strong contrast between this and the formal image of the academic lecture which pervaded many classrooms. There were also other events which were particularly formal in nature. Visits to faculties to give demonstration lessons became formal showpieces:

> We were asked to sit in two of a row of wooden chairs squeezed tightly between a large table and a blackboard, facing the students, side by side with the head of department and some other lecturers in the department, as though we were a panel. We were placed to the left of the head of department, my colleague nearest the centre (in order of importance away from the head of English). The table

was laid with a cloth and had plastic flowers laid across, with the heads towards the students, spaced individually and evenly along the table. Three microphones stood on the table for the 'speakers'. On the blackboard were large, many coloured, chalk words welcoming the visitors from England, with flowers drawn around them as decoration. ... Both my colleague and myself were very surprised at the size of the occasion that had been made out of our visit, and that *all* the students who were majoring in English had been invited. ... The head of department spoke in low, charismatic tones to introduce us and what we were going to do.

(Observation notes)

Another aspect of formality was the significant degree of segregation between male and female students. The sketches, in Figure 3, are typical of the seating arrangements which show a tendency for blocks of seating according to gender. The front-back segregation (sketch A) was more common and occurred in cases where there was no central aisle. In these cases, the women were always in the front half of the room. The women on the whole seemed to get the best seats. In one faculty:

I noticed that the benches were marked with carved letters. One of the local lecturers explained that this demarcated seating arrangements for men and women.

(Observation notes)

However, this segregation did not prove restrictive in the majority of cases when students were asked to work together, and in some cases men and women were seen working together; the rules which governed this were of a deep action nature. In one of my own postgraduate classes I had had the class working in groups around all sides of the tables, men mixing with women, without any signs of opposition, for several months of the course. Because the room was badly in need of decorating, the students collectively paid for it to be redecorated. This meant that we had to use another room for a whole week. On returning to the original room on the first day after redecoration, I noticed that two out of the five tables, arranged along three sides of a rectangle as before, had pieces of material hanging down the sides facing into the room. This was to hide the legs of the women students who would now always sit at those tables. It also meant that, because of the material, one long side of each table could no longer be used for group work. There could be several explanations for this change in seating; but one possibility not to be ignored is that more important social standards deep in the classroom culture, connected to standards held by the wider community, had succeeded in reversing the innovation achieved over half an academic year.

45

Segregation was not always according to gender. One expatriate lecturer reported 'that at times of tension in Palestine, the blocking becomes Palestinians and Egyptians rather than men and women' (personal communication). (This event took place in the north of Sinai where there is a large Palestinian population, which has connections with the Gaza Strip over the border.)

Significant in these cases is the complexity of the key to what is considered formal and informal, and the different layers of preparedness for change or conservatism within the classroom culture which could be activated at different times. In the case of students reorganising their seating arrangement after redecorating the classroom, whatever the interpretation, there were elements hitherto submerged which could surface after unpredictable lengths of time to change the whole appearance of the classroom culture – or, to make one realise that the culture is in fact shifting and dynamic. The seating arrangements in large classes, illustrated in the diagrams in Figure 3, at once provide a purely surface mapping of what must be highly complex relationships between students beneath the surface.

The implication of the existence of a deep action, on the one hand, and the resilience of the classroom culture, on the other hand, for the design of appropriate classroom methodologies, within the curriculum project in which these phenomena were observed, were formulated in two hypotheses:

i)   The classroom culture is sufficiently hospitable and resilient to endure the trauma of change.

ii) The existence of deep action phenomena, which are difficult for outsiders to perceive, demands that, in the long term, innovation can only be effectively managed by insiders.

In Chapter 12 I shall show how hypotheses like these can become part of a gradually unfolding picture of a classroom environment in all its variety, and be central to approaching an appropriate methodology for that environment.

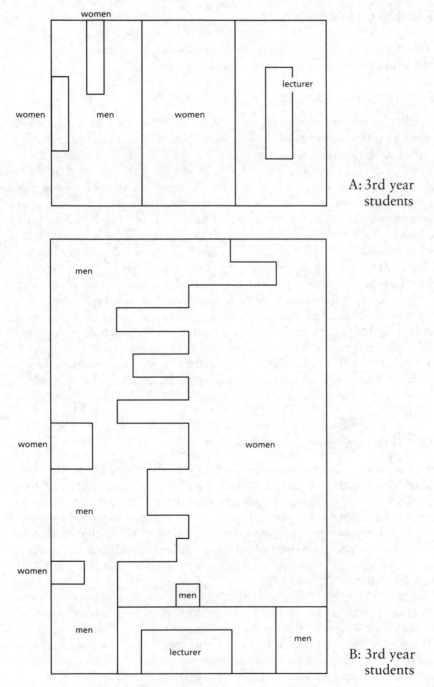

Figure 3 Gender segregation in seating arrangements

3.5   Need for caution

At this point it is necessary to be cautious about racing ahead with some of the lines of interest introduced in this chapter.

3.5.1   The use of typologies

Regarding the issue of typologies, much useful work can be done on looking at different types of classroom cultures to formulate typologies against which other classrooms can be measured. There is a large element of choice, however; and I would stress at this point that there can be as many typologies as there are different researchers. Typologies are nothing more than convenient ways of categorising what is observed. All the typologies to which I have referred (high or low pace and flow, teaching spectacles and learning festivals, large- and small-class cultures, *Gemeinschaft* and *Gesellschaft*, rational and traditional etc.) are descriptions of possible extreme cases. Real cases will fall somewhere between them, tending in one direction or the other, and will contain mixtures of the elements described in the typologies. The categories are therefore heuristic – notional standards against which to compare reality – and must not be taken as real. Typologies are thus 'ideal types' in the tradition of Weber – i.e. heuristic inventions against which 'real world' eventualities can be measured, and between which tendencies and movements can be traced. These latter, the 'forms' of 'transmission', are 'social facts' in the tradition of Durkheim (Bernstein 1971:49).

3.5.2   Reference to national culture

I began Chapter 2 by stating the dangers of overgeneralisation when talking about national cultures. However, as the cases cited in this section show, the influence of national cultures *is* important. What is needed is a systematic breaking down of what exactly we refer to when we talk about culture, and an attempt to define when a situation is created by a blend of national cultural and other cultural influences, particularly where these other cultures may transcend the boundaries of national culture.

The cases cited show that there is often an overriding cultural influence which may well be attributable to the wider society, governing, for example, the rhythm and movement of classroom groups [3.1], gender segregation [3.4.5], and the role the classroom plays in non-kin relationships [3.3]. However, there are also influences, as Figure 2 shows, from institutional or professional-academic cultures, which govern aspects of classroom cultures such as protocols and the formality of certain classroom events [3.4.2, 3.4.5]. These cultural influences are significant for two reasons.

First, there could well be a plurality of such cultures within the national context: the protocols and distinctions between formality and informality might well vary considerably between different types of institutions, such as primary, tertiary and private, and between the different types of professional-academic groups associated with them. The difference between small and large classrooms within one tertiary institution have already been noted [3.3]; these differences would be more likely to be between different types of institution. Ballard (in process) makes the important point that all societies incorporate a full spectrum of ways of doing things in education, and that what some people over-generalise as cultural differences are in fact dominant *tendencies* in one direction or another within individual societies. She refers to Australasian education as an example of this. Although the dominant educational culture tends to support an analytical, discursive, creative form of education, at primary and secondary level, a contrasting culture which supports a more reproductive approach can be found. Indeed, this type of plurality is a characteristic of 'modern', complex societies [2.6] to which all of the examples I am citing belong. Several early accounts, my own included, of working in 'Third World' countries take a particularly narrow view. For example, Britten and Sow (1981:23) suggest that teachers in Senegal suffer from a 'shortage of organisational skills (since relatively few people have had the exposure to complex systems to acquire such skills)'. The implications, which I consider to be false, is that 'Third World' and 'complex' are opposing concepts. Said (1993) observes that it is the legacy of imperialism which makes us fail to see the variety within other societies. The Western perception of other societies as unchanging and unvaried creates an image of backwardness [2.6]. As a profession, we now seem to be relatively happy with the notion that all languages are equally complex and developed, by virtue of *being* languages. It seems time that we saw all social groups as equally complex and varied, by virtue of *being* social groups.

Secondly, as I shall argue in Chapter 5, the professional-academic and institution cultures, because of their links with a wider professional-academic community in other countries, and with international educational cultures, channel into the local classroom strong influences which are not from the national culture at all.

3.5.3   *Cultural imperialism*

The cases cited above show that investigating classroom cultures for the purpose of designing and introducing new methodologies and syllabuses not only provides the data needed to solve the problem, it also reveals the immense complexity of the problem. The deeper one looks at introducing change in classrooms, the greater the awareness not only of the possibilities but also of the constraints. However, the deeper one looks, the more, too, one is faced with the issue of cultural morality. Coleman (in process) makes the point that we need to exercise caution before assuming that established English language teaching methodologies are or should be the ultimate aim for all classrooms.

Coleman (1987) found, during his observation of classes at Hasanuddin University, that although many local teachers and students had low expectations that 'learning' was actually going on in some classes, this was not seen as problematic as long as there was a harmonious teacher-learner relationship. Indeed, student respect for the teacher seemed a more important trait than that of the 'good learner'. An important implication here was that there were clearly different perceptions held by local and expatriate observers of the classroom. Although expatriate teachers and curriculum developers thought that the local classroom situation was highly problematic because learning was not going on, local teachers said that classroom behaviour was unproblematic. Importance was given by the local teachers to the physical environment of the classroom and the IQ of the student. As the latter was a quality brought to the classroom, it seemed unimportant that the teachers and the teaching process might be inadequate. Thus, a local concern with standards did not lead to concern with methodology and classroom interaction. This raises the whole issue of *cultural imperialism*, which will be discussed in detail in Chapter 6.

However, because of the link between the local classroom culture and professional-academic and other educational communities which extend beyond the national culture [3.5.2], the question of cultural imperialism cannot be seen simply in terms of national cultural conflict. It is not my concern to talk about cultural imperialism in terms of wide notions of East and West, of developed and developing. As I have shown [2.6], it is in the very nature of cultures, both large and small, to influence and invade each other in a constant state of conflict and flux. There is no such thing as a virgin culture whose boundaries need to be protected. Barrow (1990) argues that our fear of cultural imperialism is unjustified because it is a fact of life. I cannot, however, agree with Barrow's argument that some languages and cultures *are*, in reality, superior to others (1990:8–9). I see 'superiority' rather as a relative function of political ascendency and the cultural fashions of the time.

I shall argue in ensuing chapters that for the purpose of searching for appropriate methodologies it is more useful to look at the cultural imperialism of English language teaching methodology as projected by one particular professional-academic group within the wider profession – that which originates in BANA countries [1.2.2].

3.6   Summary

In this chapter, the following points have been made:
a)   Cultural variety in classrooms can be seen in several ways. Several writers observe relations between classroom culture and national culture, for example in Alaska (the type of movement in non-verbal behaviour) and Egypt (replacing certain village functions in urbanisation).
b)   Description of classroom cultural types can provide typologies and models which are useful when designing and introducing syllabus and methodological change. Such typologies include classroom as teaching spectacle or learning festival, as large-, or small-class culture.
c)   Evidence of a deep action in classroom cultures, which is difficult for outsiders to comprehend, shows the inadequacy of outsider curriculum developers.
d)   Investigations of classroom culture reveal not only factors which can help in syllabus and methodology change, but also the complex problems which have to be addressed, and the dangers of cultural imperialism. Classrooms often have functions other than the transfer of knowledge. Sometimes they represent ritual forms of behaviour.
e)   For the purpose of finding appropriate classroom methodologies it is more useful to look at the cultural imperialism of native speaker English language teaching methodologies, than at the more generalised conflict between national cultures.

3.7   Questions for discussion

1   In what ways are any of the classroom cultures described in this chapter similar to the cultures of classes you teach?
2   In what ways do the cultural features of the classes you teach influence the way in which you teach?
3   What examples are there, in the classes you teach, of interaction which has nothing to do with the lesson, but which has something to do with cultural forces outside the classroom?

4   To what extent do the methodologies you read about in books fail
     to address important aspects of the culture of your classroom?
     How far are these aspects connected to the culture of your country
     or region, and how far to student, institutional or professional-
     academic cultures?

4 Student groups

I have so far argued that the search for appropriate English language teaching methodologies necessitates looking at how interaction between people in the classroom is influenced by social forces outside the classroom. In Chapter 2 I considered the value of seeing these relationships in terms of the classroom as a culture. In Chapter 3 I demonstrated how this view enables us to appreciate that classroom behaviour may have social functions other than the transfer of knowledge and skills; and these functions will vary between different types of classroom culture. In order to be appropriate, English language teaching methodologies need therefore to be finely tuned to the various needs of individual classroom cultures: they need to be appropriate to local cultures in very specific terms.

In this and following chapters I shall look in more detail at various aspects of classroom cultures and how they can be understood by looking at the social contexts within which they are set. As with all cultures, classroom cultures contain different interest groups. An obvious division is between student and teacher groups. In this chapter I shall look at student groups, in Chapter 5 at teacher groups, and in Part B at how the interaction between these groups produces conflicts which need to be addressed if appropriate methodologies are to be found.

First I shall look at the notions of student group behaviour inherent in current thinking about English language teaching methodology, and how they produce a learning group ideal.

4.1 The learning group ideal

The search for universals in effective group behaviour has involved a detailed investigation of interaction, sometimes in clinical settings, independent of wider social forces. Most of the literature has concentrated on how group interaction might benefit learning (e.g. Slavin *et al.* 1985; Cortis 1977:1–36), and, more specifically, language learning (e.g. Wright 1987:36–45). This has been supported by research in management and social psychology (e.g. Handy 1985:227–82) and by second language acquisition research (e.g. Long and Porter 1985), and has had a major influence on modern collaborative classroom methodologies both in English language teaching and elsewhere.

As a *social psychology* of student groups, this literature is indeed of great value. In arguing that, in designing collaborative methodologies for the classroom, we are capitalising on existing, normal human work behaviour, it supports Breen's (1986) argument that there are natural features within the cultures surrounding classroom interaction on which classroom methodology should capitalise [2.1]. The overall impact on English language education has been the establishment of a notion of the optimum interactional parameters within which classroom language learning can take place. For the sake of discussion, I shall call this notion the *learning group ideal*. This learning group ideal sets the conditions for a process-oriented, task-based, inductive, collaborative, communicative English language teaching methodology. (I use 'communicative' here in the sense of having classroom activities which enable students to communicate.)

However, there are important things which this micro study of student groups does not reveal. In its search for universals in group interaction, it does not look at wider, *macro* social factors, and therefore does not consider how classroom cultures in different social settings might react differently to English language teaching methodologies.

4.2   The national cultural argument

At the *macro* level, there is a growing literature on the influence of cultural differences on the learning behaviour of overseas students in a variety of classroom contexts both in their own countries and in the countries where the target language is spoken (British Council 1980; Valdes 1986; Harrison 1990; Adams *et al.* 1991, Coleman in process). However, the emphasis is on national, or even wider-scale cultural factors, which, I feel, are overgeneralised and therefore distorting.

4.2.1   Learning group ideal as the norm

Most of this literature takes the learning group ideal as the norm; and the cultural backgrounds of students are seen as inhibiting the practice of this norm. Explanations are characterised by what Hawkey and Nakornchai (1980:70) refer to as 'cultural profiling', where an attempt is made to describe common characteristics of students from one particular country or region. Religion is a common focus in this profiling. Hence, Dudley-Evans and Swales (1980), Osterloh (1986) and Parker *et al.* (1986) describe the influence of Koranic attitudes to thought and language on the way in which students from the Middle East approach reading and writing, classroom authority and the whole business of learning. Similarly, Bowers (1980a) speaks of the influences of Buddhism in India on the study modes of students. In my own paper (Holliday and Cooke 1982:142), we use Berger *et al.*'s (1974) typology as a model, and describe basic cultural differences between Western and Eastern attitudes towards language and learning.

4.2.2   *Host culture as the norm*

Shamim (in process) makes similar generalisations about the cultural influences on her students in their opposition to her introduction of group work at the University of Karachi. Her article is significantly different, however, in that it is one of the rare accounts in the literature written from the point of view of an insider to the culture in question (cf. Kharma and Hajjaj 1985). She therefore speaks with considerable authority when she refers to the influence of 'the culture of the wider community' on her students' attitudes. This enables her to be more analytical in her references to culture, and also, to separate herself from, and therefore separate out, the *culture* of the English language teaching methodology which she introduces. Also, rather than looking at this innovative culture of the learning group ideal as the norm, she sees it as intrusive into the norms of the host national culture. It is indicative, in her account, that she begins with a feeling that there is need for improvement in the way English is taught in her institution, but she has to look to BANA-published literature for ideas. She tries these ideas intelligently, and finds that their implementation is highly problematic.

There are also outsider accounts of local national cultural norms influencing what happens in the classroom, which see the learning group ideal as intrusive – e.g. Coleman (in process) in Indonesia, and Miller and Emel (1988) referring to Pakistani secondary education. Miller and Emel go so far as to see this intrusion as cultural imperialism.

4.3   The need to consider smaller cultures

Following my argument in Chapters 2 and 3, I suggest that most of this literature overgeneralises the issue in attaching it to *national* or *regional* cultural influences. Looking back at the complex of different types of cultural influences in Figure 2 [2.7], we see that there may be a variety of cultural influences on student behaviour, such as classroom and institution culture, which it is important to consider in the search for appropriate methodologies, and which need to be considered differently according to their nature. Figure 2 shows that, although national culture can be a major overriding influence, professional-academic communities, which in turn influence institution and classroom cultures, partially transcend national cultural boundaries and are influenced by international education-related cultures.

The ways in which such diverse variables can inhibit or enable the practice of the learning group ideal can be seen in the Ain Shams curriculum development project. The classroom conditions which prevail in the classes described might seem extreme. However, they are not uncommon in many of the world's tertiary institutions; and how they stand up to the learning group ideal is therefore significant.

4.3.1   *National cultural traits or a lack of resources*

Observations carried out in classes where the learning group ideal had not been introduced revealed several things about student behaviour (Holliday 1991a:237–40). When I say, 'had not been introduced', I am however aware that there is no such thing as a classroom culture in Egypt totally unaffected by foreign methodologies. I have already commented [3.5.3], that there is no such thing as a virgin culture. This host educational environment, perhaps more than some others, was already being influenced considerably by expatriate English language teaching practitioners. These observations came five years in to a joint ODA-USAID-funded project. Egypt itself has a long history of cosmopolitanism. First of all, students appeared to prefer close proximity. This was particularly evident in one small class where:

> Two students arrived shortly after the beginning of the class. It was interesting that despite there being plenty of space in the room, all the students sat next to each other in the front row, in adjacent seats. On two occasions an arriving student sat on a seat without moving the bag and books of a student already seated in an adjacent seat, merely pushing them slightly to allow room to sit. This seemed evidence of close proxemics and lack of inhibition in sharing space.
>
> (Observation notes)

This ability to share space, and an overall gregariousness, seemed fundamental in the ways in which the students coped with large classes of between 60 and 450. In cases where there were not sufficient seats to go round, students were seen taking turns to sit down. This informal co-operation between students extended to arranging seating and the distribution of lecture notes. For example, in one class I observed that one student:

> was responsible for acting as agent in the distribution of the best copies of lecture notes to the other students, and therefore got hers free. She also organised seating and anything else that needed organising. The lecturer found it convenient to go through her for any dealings he had with the class as a whole.

(Observation notes)

This ability for informal group co-operation to cope with the crisis of scarce resources seen amongst students was also seen in the wider *institution culture*. Space sharing was observed where a seminar took place in a room which 'doubled as the office of the head of department, who sat at her desk' conducting business while the seminar was going on, and in the offices of university administrators:

> It is common for such people to hold audience with several different parties at the same time. If the office is large, and a large number of parties are present, one may have to wait a considerable length of time to get attention. Often, in such cases, waiting parties, or parties that have had their turn, may hold their own separate meetings in the same room simultaneously.

(Observation notes)

Within the wider *national culture* there was also the frequently seen example of informal co-operation in the face of crisis when seated passengers on crowded trams held the bags etc. of standing passengers, to whom they were strangers, and then passed them out through the windows when the passengers had alighted, because it was too difficult to carry them through the crush on the tram. On trams, too, when the crush of passengers was too great for the ticket collector to get to all the passengers, some passengers helped to collect fares.

The close proxemics, gregariousness and connected informal co-operation of students could thus be traced to wider cultural traits seen *both* in the host institution and the wider society. Close proxemics and greg-ariousness would therefore seem to be national cultural traits. There is research which connects proxemic behaviour with national or wider geographical cultural groups. An example of this is Watson and Graves (1973), who carry out a psychological experiment and find that 'Latin' and 'Arab' respondents prefer closer proximity than do Northern European respondents. Morain (1986:73) refers to the 'high contact cultures' of Arabs, Latin-Americans, Greeks and Turks as distinct from the 'low contact cultures' of Americans and North Europeans. However, the significance of close proxemics and gregariousness in the classroom may also have much to do with what might be regarded as an external, economic variable: the severe lack of resources in terms of space, acoustics, seating, books and materials and distance from the teacher (see Holliday 1993; Pett 1987). I do not wish to go into whether or not economic forces are external or internal to a culture; I simply wish to make the point that there were economic forces acting on the behavioural traits of students in this particular situation which were not peculiar to Egyptian, Arab or even Middle Eastern culture, but which are common through much of the developing world.

4.3.2 Responsibility and motivation

Also observed were the students' ability to take responsibility for their own learning and their motivation. In large classes of over 50, the physical distance between teacher and students meant that close monitoring of student work by the teacher was extremely difficult. The students, however, seemed to be used to this state of affairs and took responsibility (Holliday 1991a:297–300). This was exemplified in one class, where the local lecturer gave a half-hour lecture on half a set of rules in linguistics and then 'told the class that they would get the second half the following week and referred them to a book on generative phonology to read in preparation' (Observation notes).

Involved with this taking of responsibility was the students' motivation, in spite of the harsh classroom conditions. The proof of this motivation was the fact that they continued to attend, despite some lecturers apparently making 'little attempt to communicate with the students' and 'signs of student boredom' (Observation notes). It is important to add caution here, however, as I have already suggested that outsider observers would not necessarily be able to know whether or not, or what type of, communication was going on [3.4.1].

It would be erroneous to try and trace these traits directly to the national culture. As with student ability in informal co-operation, they could be traced partly to the force of economic conditions, and partly to an educational ideology, both of which were wider influences than the national culture. That students do not expect close monitoring by their teachers is not necessarily a result of scarce resources in large classes. Large classes themselves, as well as being common in the developing world, are also found in some countries in the developed world, such as Japan (LoCastro 1989, in process), and are not necessarily characteristic of scarce resources. Large classes might be permissible where prevailing educational ideologies do not see the role of the teacher as a monitor of learning, but as a fount of knowledge, which is delivered without any concession to students, and which students must struggle to attain. Indeed, this is an international educational norm found in the traditional British university. I shall deal with this issue in detail in Chapter 5, where I shall argue that English language education is in many ways unusual in being opposed to this norm. Thus if large classes in Egyptian faculties of education were in any way supported by educational ideology, this too, might not be traced only to a local Koranic attitude to education [4.2.1], but also at least partly to a more international educational ideology. Hence, although features of a local classroom culture, student gregariousness and responsibility for learning were at least partially influenced by factors that transcend the host national culture.

4.3.3 'Conservative' attitudes to education

In classes where the learning group ideal had been introduced, although there was evidence that students were well able to adapt to the innovation, which could be seen, after all, as just another crisis in the wake of all the others with which they had to cope, there was also evidence of deeper student attitudes which remained to a degree unconvinced. These attitudes could have been influenced by a variety of national and other types of cultural forces. They represent the conservatism characteristic of any culture undergoing the tensions of change referred to earlier [2.6].

In discovery-oriented activities, although the students generally seemed to take to them very well, they showed uneasiness. They seemed unsure about having to 'think' rather than reiterate what their 'teacher' had 'given' them. This insecurity implied dissatisfaction with the learning group ideal's insistence on a problem-solving rather than a didactic approach. Although often associated with national Koranic culture [4.2.1], this preference for didactic instruction rather than learning by discovery is also attributable to a common international view of education. In my own reading class, the students did not seem to appreciate what they had been doing, or why they were doing it in this part of the curriculum:

> At the end [of the class] I asked the students what they thought they had learnt. They said that they didn't feel that they had been reading. As in other cases ... several of the students said that it was not 'reading' because there was no reading aloud. They said that they never had anything like this normally (i.e. discussion and group work).

(Observation notes)

As trainee teachers, these students seemed to appreciate the fact that I was demonstrating something practical. They were sufficiently bright to see a connection between my methodology and a methodology they might use as teachers in the future; but silent reading for the purpose of finding information did *not* seem to be 'reading' to them. Their more normal expectation seemed to be to read aloud for their lecturer to monitor. (See the reference to students' expectation of reading as 'the word-by-word sounding of a text' in Holliday 1986b:25, 26n, citing observations by Silberstein.) They did *not* seem to think that I was teaching them to read. Whereas the learning group ideal tries to connect target skills with those outside the classroom in real life, the more formal attitude to education depicted here sees classroom skills as quite separate from real-life skills; and it may be that for these students 'reading' in real life, in the wider society outside the classroom, had a different definition from that promoted by the learning group ideal.

In another class, in which I gave a guest lesson, I was carrying out a very traditional (in my terms) essay writing lesson in which the students worked in groups to collect ideas and then were supposed to help me to compile an outline on the blackboard. However, presumably being unused to handouts, their first reaction to the worksheet which was handed out to them at the beginning was that it was an examination paper:

> Then I asked them to do the first activity without any help from me. They seemed to find this very difficult. Some students left; and one student at the front pleaded with me to explain what on earth I was trying to do (almost in those terms). They were clearly unused to this type of approach. I managed to get them on task after talking them through the first two activities. Then the same spokesperson told me that they were surprised that the essay style I was teaching them was so simple, with so few parts. I suspected that they had been previously lectured on several complex forms of the essay with little practical application.
>
> (Observation notes)

My supposition about the form their essay classes normally took 'was later confirmed by several local colleagues' (Observation notes). Barjesteh and Holliday, commenting on problems local students had adapting to the learning group ideal's inductive approach in grammar lessons, see anxiety about examinations as central, in that:

> Students, who seem to have been brought up on the deductive approach ... want superficial 'knowledge' [to learn] for the examination [through which] they want to move too quickly and are unwilling to discuss and explore.
>
> (Barjesteh and Holliday 1990:90)

These expectations on the part of the students, that a deductive methodology was most appropriate, and that an inductive approach might be interesting but inappropriate, reflected classroom cultural norms. These norms might have been in turn influenced by the *professional-academic culture* of their teachers, which I shall deal with in Chapter 5, and also the norms of the host *institution culture*, which, being a university, was not disposed to the teaching, by 'qualified' lecturers, of language skills, but rather the teaching of language theory. This point was exemplified in another class which I observed, where the students did in fact seem to be getting on with an inductive approach without any problems. Their local lecturer was an assistant lecturer – i.e. an MA holder. In the discussion after the class:

> I asked why the students seemed so willing to communicate and take part in informal discussion (he had also said that they were used to writing in class and working in groups) when other lecturers said that local students would never 'accept' this. He seemed surprised at the question. He didn't think his students were very different from those in other faculties or universities (elicited). Then, after more discussion of lecturer roles, he said that perhaps the students would accept this from junior lecturers but not from lecturers with PhDs. The latter would be expected to lecture more because they had more to give. (This was also borne out by a PhD lecturer who finds it difficult to get his students to accept him not lecturing.)

> (Observation notes)

Indeed, that the students derived considerable satisfaction from formal professorialism was illustrated in their insistence on calling all their teachers 'doctor'. This cult of the professor, and the desire for deductive learning which seems to go with it, is not restricted to Egypt, the Middle East, or even the developing world. It is also reported by Maley (1980) with regard to French students. Although it is impossible to verify the connection, it needs to be considered that that this attitude might be influenced by an *international* educational ideology [4.3.2] rather than be a product of Egyptian culture. (cf. Herrera's 1992:1–2 brief discussion of multiple influences, including French, on Egyptian education.)

4.4 The problem of appropriacy

Another area in which cultural arguments have sometimes been overgeneralised is that of the problem students from different countries have in acquiring the writing styles required in classes taught by native-speaker teachers, especially in English for academic purposes.

Dudley-Evans and Swales (1980) refer to a further 'cultural' problem with regard to Middle Eastern students – that of discourse style. They compare a text from an Arabic newspaper with an equivalent one as it would appear in an English newspaper, and show that they have very different rhetorical and organisational forms. This type of difference between Arabic and English text is verified by al Jubbouri (1984), where it is argued that in Arabic, poetic repetition and clausal and phrasal stringing is a predominant feature, whereas this is not so in English texts, where argument is staged, with introductions and conclusions setting and finalising the point, and clausal and phrasal embedding is the norm. (See also Sa'adeddin 1991.)

I do not deny that there is considerable truth in this argument, but again it comprises a generalisation which is not particularly useful. The form which a particular piece of discourse takes can be seen in terms of a discourse culture – corresponding to a discourse community. Some of the papers in Adams *et al.* (1991) begin to follow this line of argument. Bloor and Bloor demonstrate how students from a wide range of countries, European and elsewhere, have difficulties because of a 'false expectation that educational structures and systems do not differ internationally' (1991:2). They find it strange that in Britain, in writing academic assignments: 'The game is not to show the assessor that you know the facts, but to show the assessor *what you have read, and, moreover, what you think about what you have read* (Ibid.:2)'. This feature, and stylistic features such as hedging and acknowledging in academic writing, are not so much a product of national cultural differences as of differences between academic discourse communities with which students from different parts of the world are familiar.

A particular national culture will incorporate many discourse cultures; and at the same time many of these cultures will transcend national culture in the same way as professional-academic cultures can transcend national cultures. Thus, the discourse culture of science, which itself incorporates many smaller discourse cultures related to individual disciplines, may in many ways be *inter*national. I have already referred to Ballard's (in process) analysis of specialised educational sub-cultures within one society [3.5.2].

This might explain why, in my own multi-national Diploma TEFL class in Britain, with fifty per cent British students, *all* parties seemed to have difficulty mastering the academic discourse of English language education required by their assignments. Both the German and the Indonesian students in the class had problems with the requirement that the assignments should contain discussion, where they felt it was not their place, as students who should defer to their teacher's knowledge, to appear to negotiate this knowledge within the formal educational setting. Similarly, Bloor and Bloor (1991) argue that although students from many parts of the world find the British way *different* from what they expect, they find it different in many *similar* ways.

At the same time, my British students, approaching the academic discourse community of English language education from other British academic discourse communities such as literature, found it initially distasteful that their writing should be devoid, in their terms, of artistic expression – marred by headings which they felt broke the artistic flow, by hedging that to them showed lack of opinion, by the need to refer to what they had read, which to them showed that all their teachers wanted was 'regurgitation'.

The requirement by the professional-academic community of English language education that in assignments they should argue their opinions, but that these opinions should be constantly supported by very formalised references, either to their own experiences, expressed as 'case studies', or labelled 'personal observation', or to the literature, represents a finely balanced concept in writing which is extremely difficult for newcomers to the culture to learn. That there is an art in this form of academic discourse remains a mystery for the uninitiated. Many English language teachers, perhaps through adherence to principle, never succeed in appreciating this mystery; and these finer points of the discourse culture of English language education become a barrier that prevents them from entry to the 'secret society' of 'researchers' and 'writers' within the profession.

Certainly, it is where the student comes from – the already-learned cultures which she or he brings to the new learning situation – which determines, alongside individual motivational factors, the way in which the new culture is approached. The student's national culture will play a significant role here, but will not tell the whole story. The German and Indonesian students in my class came from widely different national cultures, but had been influenced by professional-academic cultures which seemed at least in part to have something in common. Indeed, I shall argue in the next chapter that it is the professional-academic culture of English language education which is eccentric, not only from the viewpoint of the developing world, but also from the viewpoint of other Western cultures. The British students had experienced a variety of other professional-academic cultures within Britain, and from these viewpoints found the culture of English language education strange. This is a further reason for arguing a BANA-TESEP rather than an East-West divide in English language education [1.2.2].

4.5   Non-pedagogic factors

Another important factor in considering the way in which student groups behave is that there are significant aspects of their behaviour, and of the way in which they interact with classroom methodologies, which are not pedagogic in nature. They have little or nothing to do with the learning process *per se*, but rather with other social relationships within the classroom that have direct relation with the forces of role, power and status in the wider society. One example already cited [3.3], is the way in which relations between students in large Egyptian classes restore a social cohesion function lost in the process of urbanisation.

4.5.1   Transaction and interaction

In the classroom culture, smaller groups interact as they would in any other culture. The teacher represents one highly significant power base; student groups represent others. These groups may have covert, *interactional* agendas other than the *transactional* participation in lessons which provides the overt *raison d'être* for the classroom (Widdowson 1987). The implication of this is that the student group and individual groups within the student body can have identities and agendas which are independent from the agenda of the lesson:

> They will quite naturally develop their own group dynamic and this
> will, just as naturally, be controlled by their own norms and
> expectations, and these will apply not to the role of pupil at all, but
> to the role of peer group member.
>
> (Ibid.:87)

I have already described how the peer and reference groups of students extend outside the classroom to other student groups, and beyond to groups outside the educational environment such as the family [1.4]. Within the host institution alone, individual students will take on a multiplicity of roles as they move from membership of one classroom group for one subject to another for another subject, as they move through different out-of-class groups such as clubs or informal groups for eating, playing, waiting in corridors for classes, travelling to and from school and so on. Within one particular classroom culture, they will be members of one group with one culture for one type of activity, and another for another activity. Each pair and group organised by the teacher will have its own culture; and there will also be informal groups within the classroom with non-pedagogic functions – playing, passing messages, taunting or supporting teacher, forming relationships and so on. Every single one of these groupings will have an umbilical cord linking it with pressure-, power-, play-, and gang-groups and so on far beyond the classroom and the host institution. Furthermore, whereas teachers may come and go, generations upon generations of students remain and transmit many of the cultural traditions, expectations and recipes for action which feed all of these groups.

Whenever a teacher attempts to organise a grouping within the class for the transactional purpose of learning, he or she immediately interferes with a powerful existing milieu. As the teacher moves from one class group to another, she or he is constantly re-entering, as outsider, an existing set of cultures, within each classroom culture, which has continued to develop, partly in reaction to the teaching styles of other teachers like her or himself. It is not simply a result of organisational logistics within many British secondary schools which keep teachers stationary within their own classrooms, while class groups move from room to room between classes; it is a way in which teachers can maintain a semblance of classroom cultural advantage, that of familiar territory. Unfortunately, new teachers are the ones who have to move also – perhaps as part of their initiation rite.

The exact nature of this situation will differ in different institutional contexts. The possible gap, or even conflict, between the transactional and interactional functions, which Widdowson (1987) argues, is likely to be greater in state education contexts, especially in secondary schools and in tertiary education in countries where education is available for all, where presence in classrooms does not necessarily correlate highly with the individual student's motivation towards transactional ends. In such cases, students may be attending for a variety of reasons other than the transactional – e.g. taking English degrees because they did not get sufficiently high secondary school scores to get into engineering or medicine, or because their families think it is good to get a degree before marrying, or taking university service English classes because it is a regulation that so many hours of English are a condition for registration on masters' courses. However, the gap will also occur in private language schools despite the existence of a business contract between institution and client: students who are sent by companies or parents may also be there for other than purely transactional purposes. But apart from these scenarios, the well-documented, complex and varied nature of motivation is such that there will always be an extra, social dimension to classroom attendance.

4.5.2 Coping strategies

As is evident in the case study of Egyptian undergraduates [4.3.1], one of the focuses of non-pedagogic student interaction is coping with classroom and host institutional conditions. Jackson (1968:10) describes how American high school students cope with three essentially problematic aspects of school life: having to live in a crowd, constantly having their 'words and deeds evaluated by others', and the 'sharp difference in authority' between teachers and students. These can be considered universals in the lives of educational institutions, and not only in developing-world situations such as that exemplified in the Egyptian case study. Although the shortage of physical resources may be a significant factor in developing-world situations, in all situations the educational environment can be one of continuing crisis for the student.

Political factors also have an influence. Chick (in process) describes how Kwazulu students' deference to their teachers reflects the position of their community in relation to an oppressive régime. He states that 'teacher and pupil collude in preserving their dignity by hiding the fact that little or no learning is taking place', a state of affairs which in turn contributes to a high failure rate in black South African education. He analyses the discourse of a 'good' mathematics lesson, which he chooses in order to exclude the variable of interference from in-service work in English language teaching, at the same time showing that the features he describes exist across the secondary school curriculum.

The teacher dominates the lesson by nominating one student at a time to answer a question. Chick sees the volubility which characterises the teacher's mode of delivery as a 'solidarity strategy', and the taciturnity of students as a 'deference strategy'. The other side of this interactional form is the chorusing of the students, which follows the question-answer exchange. He suggests that 'chorusing gives the pupils opportunities to participate in ways that reduce the possibility of the loss of face associated with providing incorrect response to teacher elicitations or not being able to provide responses'. In this way, the overall volubility of the lesson gives the outward impression of dynamism. The remarkably rhythmic manner of teacher-pupil synchronisation contributes to the false perception that learning is going on.

These interactional styles therefore serve social rather than academic purposes – to prevent loss of teacher face, reducing opportunities for students to challenge teacher. The importance attached to memorisation carries the same role – providing an impression of real learning. Chick makes the important point that these lesson traits are not so much features of ethnic or tribal culture, but of educational oppression. The asymmetry which marks this interaction in Kwazulu classrooms is connected to an asymmetry which is the norm in the wider community. He argues that this interactional form is consistent with interactional styles in encounters between Zulus and white English speakers, which are characterised by a particularly oppressive 'distribution of social power and knowledge'.

Overall, Chick makes the point which I repeat throughout, that in order to find appropriate English language teaching methodologies, it is necessary to look at 'how pervasive values, ideologies and structures in the wider society (macro context) constrain what takes place at the micro level'. The situation he describes is complex. It is important to understand that:

> When Zulus, who have low status, choose deferential politeness it is not because they like behaving deferentially, or that they 'feel' deferential, but rather because such behaviour is conventional.

(Ibid.)

They stick to these interactional forms despite the academic consequences. As with the interactional forms observed in small-class cultures in Egypt [3.3] and the teaching styles of Eskimos [3.1], this Kwazulu 'safe talk' is deep and traditional. Chick argues that the only way to fathom such characteristics is through *ethnographic* observation of lessons – a point which I shall expand upon in Part C.

4.6   Summary

The following points have been made:

a)   There has been much research into universals in the effective group behaviour of students. One outcome has been the establishment of a learning group ideal which provides conditions conducive to the methodological requirements of a communicative English language teaching methodology.

b)   However, this research has been largely micro, and has not considered wider, macro social factors and how they may affect the implementation of the learning group ideal.

c)   Research which has considered the macro context has concentrated mainly on national cultural differences of students, which overgeneralise and distort the influence of the wider social context. Much of this research is biased in its consideration of the learning group ideal as the norm. Relatively little of this research considers the host culture as the norm.

d)   It is necessary to look at the macro context not just in terms of national cultural influences, but also in terms of smaller cultural influences, such as those of professional-academic and other educational cultures. Some of these may transcend national cultural factors in significant ways.

e) Observation of Egyptian university students revealed how apparently national cultural influences on student behaviour may instead be due to i) lack of educational resources, creating cooperative behaviour traits, and ii) international educational ideologies, leading to the taking of responsibility for learning.

f) The students' reaction to innovation based on the learning group ideal, while showing their ability to cope and adapt, revealed a conservatism which might be universal, and a preference for didactic, teacher-centred ideologies which might be international.

g) Overgeneralised national cultural arguments have also been applied to the difficulty which many students find in achieving appropriate discourse, especially in academic English. However, these difficulties may also be connected to learning the language of smaller dicourse communities, which may also transcend national cultural boundaries, and which present problems to native-speaker and non-native-speaker students alike.

h) There are non-pedagogic factors which may be universal in student behaviour, generated by the sharing of power and status both within the classroom, between teacher and students, and in the wider society.

4.7   Questions for discussion

1   List features of the student cultures with which you are familar under the the headings transactional and interactional.
How far can these features be connected with the culture of your country or region, or with local classroom or institutional conditions which have little to do with national culture, or with aspects of student culture which may be common to students internationally?

2   In what ways does the learning group ideal conflict with or conform to classroom cultures with which you are familiar?

5 Teacher groups

In this chapter I wish to look at the ways in which teachers contribute towards the culture of the classroom, and shall argue that, as in the case of students, this contribution reflects wider cultural forces from outside the classroom acting upon teachers as groups. Teacher groups have long been a focus for the sociology of education. English language education has much to learn from this area of study.

First I shall look at how teacher groups form professional-academic cultures which get much of their status and tradition from the subjects which they teach. I shall then look at two basic types of professional-academic culture, which Bernstein (1971) describes as *collectionist* and *integrationist*. Then, by arguing that English language education is divided between these two cultures, I shall show how this division can help us understand some of the difficulties we encounter in finding appropriate methodologies.

5.1 The power of subjects

In Chapter 2 the professional-academic cultures of teacher groups were depicted as being a major source of influence within the classroom culture [2.7]. The concept of professional-academic cultures is not new in the sociology of education; it is referred to variously as epistemic and discourse communities, vocabularies of motive and communities of practitioners (e.g. Goodson 1988; Esland 1971; Kuhn 1970). A major orientation of these cultures is the discipline or subject with which teachers are involved.

Goodson argues that subjects themselves constitute cultures which begin to determine the attitudes and allegiances of teachers from the moment they begin their training:

> 'The most remarkable differences in attitude [of trainees and their lecturers] ... appear to be between subject specialists.' ... 'The subject sub-culture appears to be a pervasive phenomenon affecting a student-teacher's behaviour in school and university, as well as their choice of friends and their attitude towards education'.

(Goodson 1988:181, citing McLeish and Lacey)

For practising teachers, the subjects they teach continue to be central to their identity. At an instrumental level, they provide teachers with career structures (ibid.:193). They can also be seen as the basis for professional conflict:

> 'Academic subjects enjoy a socio-political entity in their own right. They represent powerful interest groups, legitimated and given sanction not only by the qualifications they award but also by the fact that the publishers' lists and library catalogues faithfully reflect the categories which they impose. The secondary curriculum can be seen as a territory, carved up and balkanized into a series of separate empires, over which the more powerful disciplines hold sway. Operating mainly from a series of bases within higher education they seek to colonize and inculcate the secondary schools with their values and their forms of thought'.

(Tomley 1980:41, citing Becher and Maclure)

Stenhouse provides a milder picture of this conflict: 'subjects are communities of people, competing and collaborating with one another, defining and defending their boundaries' (1975:10, citing Musgrove).

At an intellectual level, teachers trace the importance of their subjects to university departments where their research is carried out and the philosophies of their boundaries and methodologies are formed. Academic subjects thus represent a consolidated way in which knowledge is defined. This in turn provides the teacher group with an esoteric, specialised language which can be used to exclude other teacher groups:

> 'The disciplines of knowledge are not clearly described as areas of study or of knowledge, but metaphorically as communities of scholars who share a domain of intellectual enquiry or discourse. ... The group shares the precious resources of a specialized language or other systems of symbols which makes precision of definition and enquiry possible. ... The community has an inheritance of books, articles and research reports, and a system for communication amongst members'.

(Ibid.:10, citing King and Brownwell)

70

Researchers and academics in universities, who create and preserve the integrity of subjects, thus constitute reference groups to which the teacher looks for cultural identity [1.4]. Dominant professional-academic cultures, which survive longest and have the most influence, seem likely to be conservative, as their main function is to preserve the identity and status of their members.

At first sight, it might be difficult to place the English language teacher group in this scenario, especially as English language teaching is not normally seen as a player in the big E educational scene. However, as I have already mentioned [1.2.2], although the BANA side of the profession is largely working in the commercial sector, there *is* a large sector of the English language teaching profession working in TESEP in the rest of the world.

I appreciate that it is impractical to speak of TESEP English language teachers as one consolidated group – varied as they are between tertiary, secondary and primary levels, between rural and urban areas, and across a whole variety of countries. However, I wish to state that there is a strong tendency for this very large TESEP English language teacher group, which is involved very much in education with a big E, to be seen less as a leading part of the profession, and more as a *recipient* of the methodologies produced by the BANA group, and that this state of affairs is essentially problematic. I shall now demonstrate how this problem may be clarified by seeing the BANA and TESEP halves of the profession as belonging to two different professional-academic cultures which are potentially in conflict.

5.2   Collectionism and integrationism

Two basic cultures can be distinguished in teacher professional-academic groups in terms of how the subjects which they teach are perceived. A number of writers, both in the sociology of education and English language education, make this distinction. These writers all follow similar lines, but provide different emphases. To save a tedious review of literature, I have decided to use the typology which best suits my purpose, and which embraces most of the features of the others.

Bernstein presents a typology of two educational codes, 'collection' and 'integration', based on the way in which a 'society selects, classifies, distributes, transmits and evaluates' the boundaries of academic subjects (1971:47). Table 1 lists the features of these two codes. Being aware of the dangers of overgeneralisation, and that these typologies are no more than ideals, which represent extreme polarities, I wish to suggest that these codes represent two prototype professional-academic cultures.

5.2.1   The collectionist culture

Bernstein says that collectionism is common in the modern world, and draws examples from Western secondary level educational systems. The British 'A-level' system presents a specialised collectionist code in which pupils take a few subjects which are drawn from 'a common knowledge universe', with strong boundaries and high traditional status (ibid.: 51–3).

Table 1: Collection and integration

Collectionist paradigm	Integrationist paradigm
Separate subjects	Inter-disciplinary
Strong subject boundaries	'Blurred' subject boundaries
Didactic, content-based pedagogy	Skills-based, discovery-oriented, collaborative pedagogy
Rigid timetabling	Flexible timetabling
Hierarchical, subject-oriented, departmental structure	
Staff identities, loyalties and notions of specialisation oriented to knowledge of subject	Staff identities, loyalties and notions of expertise oriented to pedagogic and classroom management skills
Mainly vertical work relations between staff within their own subject	Horizontal work relations between staff in different subjects through shared, co-operative, educational tasks
Classroom practice and administration is invisible to most staff	Classroom practice can be team-oriented and is open to peer observation and discussion
Oligarchic control of the institution	Democratic control of the institution

(Based on Bernstein 1971:61–3, Reynolds and Skilbeck 1976:38)

He refers to subject boundaries as 'classification', and the degree to which teachers have freedom in interpreting the curriculum as 'framing'. Hence, the British system has strong classification but weak framing (i.e. more teacher freedom). Traditionally, at secondary and tertiary level, subjects are kept very separate, but teachers have considerable freedom over treatment. This however may be changing, with the advent of the National Curriculum, to stronger framing – the content of lessons being far more controlled at secondary level. The European system has strong classification *and* framing (i.e. less teacher freedom). Here there is a non-specialised, subject-based system, in which pupils can take a large range of subjects, but still with strong subject boundaries, although from different knowledge universes (ibid.).

The various types of integrated codes have low classification and variable framing. This is found in British primary education, where one teacher can teach all areas of the curriculum to the same class; and the American system has weak classification and framing at all levels, where subject boundaries are less sacrosanct (ibid.). (At tertiary level, instead of rigid subjects, there is a tendency towards various groupings of smaller 'courses'.)

I wish to argue that the professional-academic culture of the TESEP teacher group is essentially collectionist. There is a strong allegiance within this group to the disciplines of literature or linguistics, in which lecturers at the tertiary level might have to be 'specialised', with a doctoral degree, as I have already described in the Egyptian setting [4.3.3], and which I will look at in more detail. In teacher training, English language teaching methodology often becomes a discipline in its own right, and is taught as a highly formalised content subject, in which a lecturer is 'specialised' – a 'methodologist' – to doctoral level.

In secondary schools, teachers of English as a second or foreign language are also locked into the strong departmental structures of their host institutions. They have much in common with modern language teachers in Britain and as such derive much of their subject status from knowledge of the grammar and the literature of the language. Their concept of expertise and subject is however likely to be ambivalent: on the one hand they are likely to look to the universities in their own countries for reference, which, as I have just described are highly collectionist in nature, and which lead them to aspire to specialism in linguistics or literature; on the other hand, they are likely to look for practical methodology also to BANA sources, which, as I shall argue, are not collectionist. In Part B I shall explain how it might be this professional-academic schizophrenia which is at the heart of the difficulties in finding appropriate methodologies.

5.2.2 The integrationist culture

In contrast to collectionism, there are fewer examples of integration codes because, Bernstein argues, they are relatively recent phenomena in modern Western society. They tend to be found mostly in primary education, where subject boundaries are blurred because one teacher teaches all subjects. They are also found where several teachers 'team' teach either the same subject or different subjects. Here, the degree of integration depends on the number of subjects taught and the number of teachers involved (ibid.:53–4).

I suggest that the professional-academic culture of the BANA English language teacher group is essentially integrationist. In the last twenty years it has taken on a skills-based, and more recently a discovery-problem-solving, 'heuristic' approach (Breen 1987a, 1987b; Hutchinson 1989:27; White 1988), which the learning group ideal embodies.

5.3   The development of BANA English language teaching

The route by which the BANA English language teaching group has become integrationist is significant. The historical differences in the development of collectionist and integrationist groups are largely to do with the relative status of the subject cultures to which they are able to aspire.

5.3.1   A question of status

Various educational traditions can be related to professional-academic cultures of teacher groups. Tomley (1980) refers to a collectionist 'grammar-public' school tradition, and an integrationist 'elementary-secondary modern' tradition, which represent respectively more and less 'academic' streams in British education. Here, Tomley is talking about educational divisions common until the 1960s, where more 'academic' children went to 'grammar' and 'public' schools and the majority less 'academic' children went to 'secondary modern' schools. At that time, teachers in secondary modern schools, as well as in primary schools, did not need university degrees, but qualified with Certificates of Education which focused more on teaching skills than subject mastery. Tomley maintains that in the grammar-public tradition, teachers' status was motivated by a 'specialist knowledge of the subject, validated by the possession of an appropriate university degree' (ibid.:36). To use Bernstein's 'collection-integration' terminology, this tradition was therefore collectionist. In contrast, in the elementary-secondary modern tradition, there is:

> Less subject knowledge and weaker subject identity ... less in common with the 'pure' scientists ... [and] more emphasis to pedagogic skills, the needs of pupils and theories of mental development.
>
> (Ibid.:36)

This tradition was therefore more integrationist. Goodson (1988) likewise refers to Blythe's distinction between an academic and a pedagogic tradition. Consonant with the innovative nature of the integrationist paradigm, Tomley suggests that it was from the elementary-secondary modern tradition that the drive for new curricular approaches, which characterised the British educational scene in the 1960s, sprang, especially with integrated humanities projects. He argues that BEd graduates from teacher training colleges, especially in the humanities, were major subscribers to the elementary-secondary modern tradition. Because they did not have degrees in traditional subjects, which would carry the status of expertise in a particular content, they found a new professional-academic identity in integrationism. They were able to build a new esoteric knowledge base out of the social sciences and a learner-centred pedagogy (Tomley 1980:36).

I suggest that integrationism among BANA teachers is also due to their membership in a new, low-status discipline which has much in common with the old elementary-secondary modern tradition in that it does not have a long-standing academic tradition. Whether or not English language education does amount to a 'discipline' is not in fact clear. Its practitioners, in the British-based commercial sector at least, tend to have degrees in literature, modern languages, linguistics or a range of other humanities subjects, each of which only partly contributes to the discipline, and the major ideological support in university departments is in *applied* linguistics, rather than any 'pure' discipline.

5.3.2   Evolution of a discipline

The dynamism which is associated with integrationism may well have to do with the fact that the professional-academic culture is not satisfied with its basis on pedagogic skills rather than subject mastery. Whereas the collectionist group is essentially conservative, interested in preserving its strong subject boundaries and hierarchies, the integrationist group is up-and-coming and aspires to higher things. This would account for the rapid development of a strong pedagogic position found in the BANA community, which Phillipson (1992:48) refers to as 'professionalism' and to the rapid proliferation of professional and research literature. Of course, not all members of the BANA group would aspire to this trend. Many of them maintain a highly individualistic if not revolutionary stance. I am describing here the ideological superstructure of the group – the producers of its published technology – about which many chalk-face practitioners would undoubtedly complain. There are many conflicting subgroups within.

Again, the behaviour of the BANA professional-academic group can be compared with other initially low-status groups in British education. Goodson cites Layton's (1972) analysis of the evolution of science departments in secondary education in the nineteenth century:

> 'In the first stage: the callow intruder stakes a place in the timetable, justifying its presence on grounds such as pertinence and utility. During this stage learners are attracted to the subject because of its bearing on matters of concern to them. The teachers are rarely trained specialists, but bring the missionary enthusiasm of pioneers to their task. The dominant criterion is relevance to the needs and interests of the learners.
>
> 'In the interim stage: a tradition of scholarly work in the subject is emerging along with a corps of trained specialists from which teachers may be recruited. Students are [now also attracted] ... by its reputation and growing academic status. ... The internal logic and discipline of the subject is becoming increasingly influential in the selection and organization of subject matter.
>
> 'In the final stage: the teachers now constitute a professional body with established rules and values. ... Students are initiated into a tradition, their attitudes approaching passivity and resignation, a prelude to disenchantment.'
>
> (1988:184, citing Layton)

I would place the newly forming discipline surrounding BANA English language education somewhere between the second and final stages.

Another explanation for the dynamism of integrationist English language education might be that it represents a whole new educational paradigm, which itself represents a scientific revolution in the sense described by Kuhn. Such a paradigm displays 'universally recognized scientific achievements that for a time provide model problems and solutions to a community of practitioners' until an anomaly emerges and brings about a crisis that precipitates revolution (Kuhn 1970:viii). The paradigm is also a medium for communication in that it forms the basis for scientific discourse communities (Esland 1971:74, 81). The paradigm would thus embrace the ideologies of the new professional-academic culture, providing it with recipes for action and belief [4.5.1]. The 'frequent and deep debates over legitimate methods' which characterise a young, still forming paradigm (Kuhn 1970:47–8), are very much a feature of English language education:

The 'turbulent and iconoclastic period' in syllabus design which
Shaw identified with the early part of this decade has been one in
which the symptoms of paradigm shift were palpable.

(Breen 1987a:84)

Breen also cites Brown and Raimes who both refer to Kuhnian
paradigm change with regard to English language education.

The verbal elaboration and explicitness which characterise
integrationism may in fact be due to the temporary dereification which
Esland (1971:93) suggests takes place during paradigm transition when
'thinking as usual becomes unworkable' (Schutz 1964:96). Bernstein
says that subject boundaries are at their weakest at the onset of
integration (1971:53). Might not subject boundary weakness therefore
be a feature of the newness of integrationism rather than of
integrationism itself? Perhaps when the integrationist paradigm becomes
traditional there will be new groupings of integrated subjects, with
boundaries as strong as those of the collectionist subjects.

Indicative of this re-grouping is the movement in some university
departments away from the 'discipline' of applied linguistics towards
education, management and the social sciences (see Hutchinson
1989:29–31; Robinson 1989:146; White 1987, 1988:21, 1989b). Early
examples of this change in discipline were the Reading University MA
in English language teaching, and the English language teaching-related
MEds at Manchester and Leeds. There might also be a movement in the
opposite direction – as reported by Brown (1989) at the Centre of
English as an International Language at Cambridge University. This
might represent a polarisation within the profession, with 'applied
linguistics' concerned, more specifically than in previous years, with the
'*content* of English Language Teaching' (ibid.:169), and leaving the
concerns of curriculum development to the wider social sciences-
oriented courses which White (1988, 1989a) recommends.

5.3.3 The Mongols of English language education

The rapid expansion which has enabled BANA English language education to assert new statuses has depended on the existence of wide
stretches of territory ripe for conquest. It must be remembered that the
group did not originate in secondary schools but in teaching English as
a foreign language abroad. Unlike Layton's example from the
development of science departments [5.3.2], it has not therefore been
possible to develop within a home secondary school system. It is also
interesting that English language education is most active as an
innovatory force in foreign countries and foreign sponsored enclaves in
British universities, teaching foreign students. This may be because of

the strength of collectionism at home and a lack of realisation of the strength of collectionism abroad in less familiar circumstances (see Fullan 1982:48). This difficulty which integrationism has in establishing itself can be seen in Tomley's discussion of how this newly emerging tradition could only be fully legitimised at the primary school level. In the British secondary system, integrationism was left to flounder in the teaching of the academically 'lower' streams: the status of the BSc was unshaken by the emergence of the new BEd (1980:36).

The growth of a need for English as a foreign or second language in the rest of the world, partly stimulated by its dynamic enterprise, has been the fertile domain for BANA's advancing armies. The 'corps of trained specialists,' in Layton's stage two of departmental development, was first of all the teachers who staffed the English language institutes in the commercial sector both at home and abroad. It has attracted new followings in the lands it has passed through, especially with the advent of aid projects, which have sprouted new outposts in foreign state education; TESEP teachers and lecturers have been tempted from their existing departmental structures for similar training. In developing countries, where education has been expanding faster than its resources, and where English has become a technological and commercial necessity, the riches of the new BANA group have found a welcoming market.

My reference to the Mongols in the title to this section alludes to both a destructiveness and a nurturing of freedom and culture in their invasions of Asia and Eastern Europe (Saunders 1971). Although BANA integrationism claims a democratisation of language learning, its destructiveness of integrationism is also clear, where it insists on the breaking down of existing departmental structures and subject conservatism in its orientation to a skills-based, discovery-oriented, collaborative approach. Bernstein argues that integrationism:

> ... may tend to weaken the separate hierarchies of collection ... [and] may alter both the structure and distribution of power regulated by the collection code. Further, the administration and specific acts of teaching are likely to shift from the relative invisibility to *visibility*.

(1971:62–3)

This has happened in two main areas, which I shall deal with in more detail in Part B: where TESEP teachers come to BANA countries for training or higher degrees; and where aid-funded English language education projects plant integrationist centres of power within tertiary institutions and ministries of education abroad.

5.3.4   Aspirations to collectionism

The expansion of BANA English language education has also involved the adoption of existing, newly developed disciplines in the social sciences. Linguistics, socio- and psycholinguistics, and more recently, education and management studies, have become involved, with the effect of building the academic credibility of the new discipline. This has resulted in the gradual establishment of either departments or important parts of departments within universities and other tertiary institutions in the BANA home countries, with their own professors and masters and doctoral programmes. Furthermore, there are also lecturers in tertiary institutions, who are long-established members of the linguistics-related departments with which the BANA community is currently trying to merge, who are collectionist by tradition, but who are now adopting elements of the integrationist culture. Many of them have not been trained in BANA methodology. Gabriel (1991) describes university modern language classes where there is a surface concession to a 'communicative' learning group ideal, but where the classroom culture is still basically collectionist in the way in which teacher and student power are distributed. Indeed, the majority of classroom cultures within the BANA community are likely to contain elements of the collectionist practice, which after all represents the more established archetypical teacher role. See for example Nunan's (1987) account of so-called 'communicative' classroom practice retaining residues of 'teacher-centredness' – although this study is limited in that it refers only to spoken discourse and does not consider deeper classroom interaction [2.1].

The outcome is paradoxical – a professional-academic schizophrenia within the BANA teacher group which compounds the problem of finding truly appropriate methodologies (cf. my reference to schizophrenia in the TESEP group [5.2.1]). On the one hand the overall message is still integrationist in two important ways: tertiary institutions are highly influential in the dissemination of the skills-based, discovery-oriented, collaborative learning group ideal; the academic base cuts across several disciplines, and continues to integrate new disciplines into the fold. For this reason, it is still difficult to find a unifying *name* for the whole discipline. My own preference, as evident throughout this book, is English language education; but many would disagree with this choice.

On the other hand, many of the features of collectionist subject entity are already in place. Layton's final stage [5.3.2] is within reach. An 'internal logic' which is 'influential in the selection and organization of subject matter' is already in place. Tacit standards for the writing of postgraduate theses, journal articles, conference papers and books are beginning to emerge. These outward manifestations of the discourse community are already providing the means whereby 'students are initiated into a tradition'. What is lacking is a unifying name, and a final unification of a 'professional body with established rules and values'. (See, however, Coleman 1992b on the newly emerging British Association of TESOL Qualifying Institutions – BATQI.) The fact that the BANA sector of the profession depends on a wide international membership from TESEP English language teachers around the world, but has so far failed to find a teaching methodology which suits them, is central to the rift which prevents this unification.

5.4   Setting the scene for conflict

The contrast between collectionism and integrationism can be seen in the data collected in Egyptian university classrooms to which I have already referred. The examples given here are within the context of a curriculum project in which expatriates and local lecturers worked side by side, and indicate a situation prone to conflict between the BANA and TESEP branches of the English language education profession – a conflict which I shall look at in detail in Part B. I compare local and expatriate practice and attitudes in teaching similar university classes.

5.4.1   Linguistics or language skills?

An archetypal example of collectionism is the case of a local lecturer seen at a provincial faculty of education. The observation notes describe a lecture in theoretical linguistics:

> She was a very charismatic lecturer. ... She certainly caused a stir amongst her students. ... The explication of the list [of linguistic features] had the potential of being very monotonous, yet, with some use of the blackboard, she had the students very interested. ... I found the content impossible to follow, although the students seemed to be following with little difficulty, at least on the surface.

> (Observation notes)

The reader might wonder what this lecture has to do with English as a foreign language teaching. If this is the case, the reader is likely to be integrationist and a member of the BANA group. The point is that this lecture fell into that part of the curriculum which was called 'Linguistics', which in itself represented a basic difference in the way in which it was viewed by local and BANA teacher groups. Although both parties agreed that this was the place where essential language training for the students (trainee language teachers) should take place, despite the falling standards of English language competence among the students, there was a strong tendency for local lecturers to interpret this as lecturing on the subject matter of linguistics. The expatriate BANA personnel, on the other hand, interpreted this part of the curriculum as a place where language skills should be taught communicatively (Thomas 1985; Pett 1987).

The lecture followed one of my own guest lessons, which had been discovery-oriented and task-based. My observation notes reveal my bias as I use the terms 'monotonous' and 'surface'. From the other side, at the end of my lesson, the lecturer, who was watching, announced to the students that what I had done was 'the other [practical] side of the coin' (Observation notes). Despite my doubts about the theoretical lecture, 'the students seemed to enjoy the lecture just as much as my group had enjoyed practising intonation and listening' (Observation notes).

To return to my earlier point about the overgeneralisation of national cultural profiling [4.2.1], this example shows that the lecturer image may indeed be something beyond the exigencies of the local situation, which transcends national culture and is found in university departments generally. This local lecturer had an American PhD in theoretical linguistics, and as such was merely teaching her subject to pass on the knowledge she had gained through many years of study.

5.4.2 Theory or practical application?

Another contrast between the local collectionist professional-academic culture and that of my BANA colleagues teaching similar classes was brought home during a seminar in which a local lecturer gave a presentation on recent research work in the teaching of listening. Present were some MA students and some of my British colleagues:

> The first part of the paper was a technical review of recent research. ... This was followed by a practical example of [how to apply it in the classroom]. ...
>
> Questions from the floor fell into two distinct types: those from the local MA students, who asked for clarification of the finer points of the theory and theoretical justification of the practical application, focusing mainly on psycholinguistics, and those from my British colleagues, which addressed the application of the practical example in classroom situations, focusing on pedagogy. I wondered what the MA students must think of the very practical orientation of my British colleagues, which tended to open up the subject to yet more discussion, ever putting off the possibility of firm conclusions.
>
> (Observation notes)

In the discussion afterwards the lecturer:

> said that in his position it was expected by his peers that he should
> talk on a very theoretical level, that he had to be seen to be
> specialised in a theoretical body of *knowledge* related to his PhD
> research topic and to the department in which he was employed in
> the university, i.e. linguistics.

(Observation notes)

5.4.3 Professor or teacher?

All the examples so far have been of PhD-holders, where there might be
a special sort of confusion of roles between 'lecturer' and 'teacher'.
However, junior lecturers, who had neither doctorates nor masters'
degrees, who were expected to teach more elementary language skills to
first year students, also clearly aspired to collectionism. A revealing
example was seen with a newly graduated junior lecturer who had very
little teaching experience. In my biased view, she was playing what
she perceived to be the lecturer role so well that the students were not
noticing the shortcomings of the content and the methodology (in my
terms) of the lecture. Again, my account is highly biased:

> Good authority – manages to carry off the great academic act, good
> presence. True to this unworldly concept of a good lecturer. Totally
> inexperienced – seemed to be modelling herself on the head of
> department, ... with a foreign PhD and 'impeccable' English. ...
> Very lecturer-centred. Whole lecture consisting of the lecturer
> pacing the podium plucking sounds demonstratively ... from the
> air, asking the occasional question of a student to elicit an
> illustration of a point.

(Observation notes)

Significantly, the lecturer was supposed (according to expatriate
colleagues) to be using a coursebook whose objectives were the
communicative teaching of pronunciation, and had undergone many
hours of training in communicative English language teaching methodology at the hands of expatriate personnel.

5.4.4 Giving the lesson or managing learning?

Collectionism was also seen in the local lecturers' opinion that their
responsibility went as far as presenting subject matter to their students,
but not as far as managing their students' learning. This accords with
my earlier comments on students taking the responsibility for learning
[4.3.2]. The student must strive to reach up to the content presented by

the master lecturer, as can be seen in this account:

> The head of department later complained to me that other lecturers
> failed too many of their students because they could not write an
> examination which fitted what really happened in their classes, but
> rather examined something which they thought their students *ought*
> to have learnt.

(Observation notes)

This attitude, which again transcends national cultural boundaries,
explains why some teachers of very large university classes seemed
untroubled at being unaware of how much their students had learnt, or
of their initial linguistic level. That local lecturers did not see it as part
of their expertise to be classroom managers may also have contributed
to the cases [3.3] where lecturer-student rapport decreased as classes got
larger.

There was thus a tendency in collectionism away from involving
students in activities in the classroom. In the discussion following one
lesson, where the students had been asked to carry out exercises at
home, but did not do any in the classroom:

> I asked ... [the local lecturer] what she thought of introducing the
> activity process into the classroom through group work. She said
> she thought this might reduce the amount of work she could get
> through – which was true ... [but] It seemed that this concept of
> students doing activities in the classroom was strange to her, even
> though it was spelt out in the lecturer's notes to the material.

(Observation notes)

Also, in the discussion after the class of the junior local lecturer already
referred to, when I asked why the students had not been involved more
in the lesson: 'The lecturer was very interested in this; but said she
didn't think she was brave enough to let them do too much free work'
(Observation notes). One of the areas of concern, on the part of
integrationist BANA practitioners, regarding the collectionist practice of
not involving students in classroom activities, was that students were
not able to display their skills. For example:

> It was difficult to imagine that this was the same group as observed
> in [a previous expatriate's class where they were involved in
> activities]. ... As well as being quieter and less active ... the students
> were not displaying as much competence either in English or
> classroom process. ... [Their lecturer] apologised both before and
> after the class for her 'weak' students.

(Observation notes)

At the same time, the expatriate lecturer who taught the same students, again showing his bias, 'commented that his students often said that they were treated as though they didn't know anything by their other [local] lecturers' (Observation notes). Indeed, the perception of student ability presented by local lecturers was very much contrary to that observed in classes where students were given activities to do by expatriate lecturers. One such case was during a seminar, in which the video of students involved in group activities was shown to local lecturers and department heads:

> One of the heads of department said that he thought the lesson had been rehearsed, or that the students were not average, that they must have been taking extra English lessons privately.
>
> (Observation notes)

5.4.5   Learning without teaching?

One local lecturer threw considerable light on the local perception of the lecturer's role:

> [He] said that one reason why the discovery approach would be difficult for local students was that in Arabic the concepts 'teach' and 'teacher' are converses of 'learn' and 'learner': like 'buy' and 'sell', one cannot happen without the other. Whereas in English it is possible to say that one has 'learnt' something without having had a teacher, in Arabic one would have to qualify 'learnt' with 'by myself' to make the absence of a teacher clear. Whereas in English it is conceivable to be a 'teacher' without necessarily having taught effectively (without having students who have learnt) e.g. through incompetence, in Arabic, being a teacher implies that you have students who have 'learnt'.
>
> (Observation notes)

This argument can be found in Zikri (1979:199–212), and suggests one area where an international collectionist professional-academic culture is overlaid by a regional – Arabic-speaking – culture.

Evidence of the teach-learn relationship could be seen in a local junior lecturer's claim that her students were only prepared to take part in discovery learning – i.e. 'learning without teaching' – because they believed she was not sufficiently 'qualified' to be a real 'teacher' (Observation notes). Practice was thus considered inferior to theory.

The teach-learn converse puts lecturers in an extremely powerful role, in which their status and respect are high, as an indisputable component of the learning process. This point was exemplified on one occasion when I came across a local lecturer going through some students' essays in the staff-room: 'The students came in one by one and sat across the desk from ... [the lecturer], looking at their essay upside down while ... [she] went through it' (Observation notes). This may be an extreme example, but the implication remains, that as long as there is a 'teacher', the student must, regardless of any conditions, be 'learning'. Certainly, there must be an unspoken agreement of shared expectations between teacher and student, if the relationship is to exist at all. However, the degree to which the student has power in this agreement must also be variable. In the example cited here, I maintain that the student has very little power in this agreement, and has virtually become a prop to enable the teacher to acquire the status of being a teacher – or the necessary ritual spectator in Coleman's (1987b) 'teaching spectacle'.

5.4.6   Discovery or confusion?

On another occasion a lecturer came with me to observe the class of an expatriate, and was unhappy with the open-ended outcome of some of the activities in the lesson. In this lesson the students were asked to work out the definitions of a term by searching for examples of it in a text. The local co-observer, however, wanted the definitions to be given first and the activity to involve looking for examples:

> [He] seemed disturbed (we conferred in whispers while group work was going on) because clear *definitions* ... were not *prescribed* by the [expatriate] lecturer. It seemed to offend his integrity that the students could be allowed to create their own operational definitions.

(Observation notes)

After the lesson:

> There was a lot of discussion about how *open-ended* the lesson should be allowed to be. ... [The expatriate lecturer] said that although she was surprised at and unprepared for the students' innovative responses, she was happy about having to field them and didn't find it a problem ... [The local co-observer] held out however, and insisted that we should put concrete definitions of the categories in the lecturers' notes. This difference of opinion seemed to be a fundamental problem – perhaps a general difference in attitudes to education ... Neither ... [the expatriate lecturer] nor I had seen the categories as *content*, so much as aids to a *process*.

(Observation notes)

The attitude of the local co-observer can perhaps be explained in terms of the teach-learn converse described above. He was a fully qualified (i.e. PhD-holding) teacher. Therefore, his sense of professional expertise required that his students would not think they were 'learning' unless he was 'teaching', which implies giving factual information (i.e. definitions of the discourse features). The expatriate lecturer, on the other hand, did not have a PhD and, like the junior lecturer referred to above, got away with 'not teaching' because she was not seen by the students to be sufficiently qualified.

This locally held concept of 'teacher' and 'learning' is quite different from that required in the skills-based, discovery-oriented, collaborative approach represented by the BANA group. Inductive learning would tend to be seen as 'learning by myself', or 'learning without teaching'.

On another occasion I was criticised by the local lecturer of a class I was guest teaching for confusing her students by leaving activity outcomes open-ended, and leaving students with questions rather than 'right answers'. The local lecturer did not seem to think that this was teaching. Moreover, 'anxious to make a rapid exit' at the end of the lesson, she seemed embarrassed to be associated with me. With another class belonging to this local lecturer:

> [She] thought that I spent time on things that she did not spend time on. I felt this comment irrelevant and wondered why she did not see it more important to talk about the overall methodology instead of the content.

(Observation notes)

In another case, where a local lecturer watched me teach:

> [He] did say out loud to another senior staff member present in the room that she thought I was doing something new that the students had not had before, and which they needed: getting them to solve problems. But there may have been a touch of sarcasm when he said that I confused them intentionally to make them think.

(Observation notes)

These contrasts in practice and perceptions between collectionist and integrationist professional-academic cultures working within the same institution were instrumental in creating serious conflicts which greatly inhibited the procedure towards appropriate methodologies being found, which I shall look at in more detail in Part B.

5.5   Implications for the social context

The discussion so far in this chapter has several implications for the way in which teacher groups bring issues and influences from a wider, macro social context to what happens between people in the classroom. In many ways, what teachers do in the classroom is an acting out of their preoccupations outside the classroom.

5.5.1   *Factors in methodological effectiveness*

First of all, there are a wide range of factors which affect teachers' decisions about what they want to teach, and whether or not they should adopt methodologies. Many of them – perhaps to do with school politics and personal professional considerations – which are not strictly pedagogic (Kelley 1980), are rooted in their professional-academic cultures. Kelley cites the example of the Nuffield Schools Council projects in Britain in the 1960s. Despite an otherwise 'conducive innovation climate', enthusiasm for the new curricula failed to comply with the non-pedagogic real-world factors, such as 'self-image, personal characteristics' and 'relationships with colleagues', which lead teachers to adopt new methods (ibid.:71–2). (Woods 1984:51 and Hargreaves 1984:65–7 report how teachers set survival in less than perfect work situations at higher priority than pedagogic concerns. Shipman *et al.* 1974 list many similar factors.)

A very early example of this can be seen outside English language education in Armstrong's attempt to introduce a 'heurism' into the methodology of elementary science teaching at the turn of the century in Britain (Eggleston 1980; Atkinson and Delamont 1984:36–7). Very much in line with the *learning group ideal*, pupils were to learn by discovery, and the new approach was to be evaluated by trying it out. Armstrong's results seemed to him to be conclusively in favour of the new approach; initial trialling satisfied him that the new methodology did indeed enable more efficient learning. However, teachers who had not been trained in the new methodology did not succeed in making it work.

It was not so much the teachers' pedagogic incompetence as their unwillingness to involve the pupils in classroom activities, because to do so would run against the traditions of their collectionist professional-academic culture. As Eggleston puts it, the failure of Armstrong's experiment derived from the 'academic', 'professional' and 'political' 'discourse communities' which govern what is acceptable in current forms of knowledge, teacher practice and educational aims respectively (1980:92). He suggests that:

> Perhaps 'heurism' failed to be implemented rather than failed when
> implemented. ... I would speculate that the 'heuristic method'
> applied to science teaching in schools in the late nineteenth century
> was at variance both with the intellectual climate in science, which
> was increasingly dominated by theory building, and the social
> function of the education system, which was concerned with
> upward mobility.
>
> (Ibid.:91)

Although he does not use the terms, Tomley (1980) argues that failures
in educational innovation can be brought about by a resistance by
dominant collectionist professional-academic cultures to integrationist
innovation. The collectionist tradition does not take easily to curriculum
change which is motivated by a learner-centred approach, which, in its
emphasis on pedagogic skills plays down the teachers' hard-earned
academic expertise.

Hence, as with the Armstrong experiment, when science teachers
who had supposedly adopted the Nuffield O-level Biology course,
which stressed 'pupil-centred enquiry', were observed, the majority
'were found to teach didactically so that many of the higher aims of the
Nuffield course were not translated into practice' (ibid.:40). Although
there was much interest shown by science teachers in the new Nuffield
syllabus, it was mostly an interest in content rather than methodology
(ibid.:41), and in the fact that the course material provided an excellent
source of data upon which teachers could base their lessons (ibid.:40).
Tomley is citing Kerr, and Monger's (1971) report on the implementation of the Nuffield course.

5.5.2 The culture argument

A further consideration is that the professional-academic cultures to
which teachers belong largely transcend national cultural boundaries, as
do many of the factors governing student behaviour referred to in
Chapter 4.

There might be *tendencies* for a predominance of one type or another
of such cultures within a particular society. Bernstein (1971:67) sees a
tendency towards integrationism in 'advanced' societies where there is
less prescription on what constitutes 'knowledge' and where there is
more complex division of labour. Cortazzi (1990:58) relates a
'*transmission* view of education' (which is close to collectionist) to
'cultures stressing continuity, stability and group identity', and 'the
more *innovative* view that learners creatively build up knowledge and
concepts through activity' (close to integrationist) to the West's
'emphasis on individual development and personal experience'.

However, these *can* only be tendencies. Talking of whole societies in this way is dangerous. An underlying chauvinism is sensed in Bernstein's use of the word 'advanced' when referring to societies where integrationism is more common (1971:61). I have already referred to Ballard's (in process) argument that all societies contain elements of all educational traditions [3.5.2], which further erodes the case for profiling what happens in classrooms totally in terms of national culture [4.2.1].

Some educational sociologists link the educational ideologies that characterise teacher groups with political systems. Bernstein discusses how different educational codes are the products of differing forms of order and control and the distribution of power in the wider society (1971:47). Young (1971) cites Williams' 'neo-Marxist' analysis of how 'curricular changes have reflected the relative power of different groups [in the wider society] over the last hundred years'. For example, the educational policy which promotes the 'non-vocational', the 'educated man' and an 'emphasis on character', and which seems consonant with collectionism, is powerful when the liberal-conservative ideology of the aristocracy-gentry is dominant. Likewise, 'higher vocational and professional courses' with 'education as access to desirable positions', which seem more consonant with integrationism, are more common when the bourgeois ideology of the merchant and professional classes is dominant (ibid.:29).

Young presents a similar connection in Weber's analysis of the dominance of the Confucian literati in the ruling bureaucracy of ancient China. There, the curriculum which nurtured the 'cultivated man' was highly conservative:

> Any change in the curriculum would have undermined the
> legitimacy of the power of the administration whose skills therefore
> had to be defined as 'absolute'... The 'non-bookish' were for the
> purposes of the Chinese society of the time 'not educated'.

(Ibid.:30)

He thus sees a movement in Britain away from a relatively collectionist 'psychometric' educational paradigm, which reifies knowledge, alienates the child as a deficit system, produces a false consciousness' (ibid.:89), is 'answer oriented' (ibid.:98) and in which:

> Access to the 'mysteries' of the [academic] subject is controlled by,
> and made through, the teacher, and is delayed until the child is an
> accredited member of the subject community.

(Ibid.:89)

Esland suggests that in Britain there is a movement towards a relatively integrationist 'epistemological' paradigm which is child-centred, discovery-problem-oriented and based on a 'dereified ... socially-approved and socially-distributed' knowledge (1971:94,98), which is a result of 'economic nationalism ... technology ... [and] industrial needs' (ibid.:101). Current changes towards a national, highly structured curriculum [5.2.1] might change this prognosis.

All of these explanations need to be approached with caution, and may be as dangerous as overgeneralisations regarding national culture profiling. The collectionist educational systems in some of the countries where TESEP English language education seems to be strong (e.g., in Eastern Europe and the Arab World) have been through socialist or communist periods, which goes against Young's and Esland's Marxist association between collectionism and the right, and integrationism and the left. On the other hand, the systems prevalent in these types of societies might be residues from previous times. There are arguments that see collectionism in some developing countries as products of colonialism. (See Britten and Sow 1981:23, referring to Senegal, Brumfit 1980 regarding Tanzania and Hyde 1992:2 referring to Morocco.)

Nevertheless, all of these different types of explanations suggest that curricular content and what is considered worthwhile knowledge are realities constructed by particular elements within societies, whether ruling classes or dominant teacher groups, rather than by national cultures (see Esland 1971:74).

5.5.3 *Methodologies as socio-political constructs*

The influence of professional-academic cultures in the choice of teaching methodologies supports the notion already expressed [3.3.3], that these methodologies are in themselves *ethnocentric*, not in terms of national cultures, but in terms of groups of teachers or political interest groups. These methodologies are constructions on reality created largely to satisfy the needs of the professional-academic cultures of teacher groups. They represent paradigms which provide these cultures with recipes for action, rather as scientific paradigms provide recipes for action for scientific groups [5.3.2]. Hence, the maintenance of these methodologies is essential for the cohesion of the teacher group, and provides the standard for the group's identity.

5.6 Summary

In this chapter, I have made the following points:

a) A major orientation in the professional-academic cultures of teacher groups is provided by the subjects which they teach. They provide ideological, hierarchical and economic structures.

b) There are two basic types of professional-academic culture in teacher groups. Collectionism has strong subject boundaries and presents a subject-oriented, didactic approach to education. Integrationism supports a breakdown of subject boundaries and a skills-based, discovery-oriented, collaborative approach to education.

c) Two branches of the English language teaching profession correspond to these two cultures. Teacher groups in state education(TESEP) tend to be collectionist; groups in the commercial sector (BANA) tend to be integrationist. This produces a rift in the profession which contributes toward the difficulty of achieving appropriate methodologies.

d) Like other initially low-status disciplines, the BANA teacher group has used integrationism as a means for expansion. Because it isbased abroad, this expansion has been partly into the territory of TESEP English language education.

e) There is a confusing schizophrenia in the integrationism of the BANA group, as it aspires to the higher status of collectionism.

f) Important implications are that: i) teachers' adoption of methodologies is influenced by non-pedagogic factors generated by the politics of the professional-academic culture; ii) the professional-academic cultures to which teachers belong transcend national culture; iii) methodologies are themselves ethnocentric constructs of professional-academic cultures.

5.7 Questions for discussion

1 Describe the professional-academic group to which you belong. In what ways would you say it is either *integrationist* or *collectionist*?

2 How far do the descriptions from the Egyptian case study relate to situations with which you are familiar?

3   Put a score of 1–10 (*not very much* to *very much*) against each of the following, according to how much they influence your choice of teaching methodology: *pedagogic principles, career, membership of a professional group, professional or academic status, peer pressure, expectations from your students, other reasons.*
    Do you agree that most teachers' choice of methodology has more to do with other factors than with pedagogic principles?

4   To what extent can English language teaching methodologies really be said to be *ethnocentric* – i.e. motivated by the preservation of a particular professional-academic group?

Part B Sources of conflict

6   Technology transfer

In the previous chapter I suggested that English language TESEP teachers (working in state tertiary, secondary and primary education in many parts of the world) are the *recipients* of English language teaching methodologies produced by a separate BANA branch of the profession (instrumentally oriented in Britain, Australasia and North America) [5.1]. These methodologies are oriented to a learning group ideal which derives from universals of effective group work [4.1]. The technology transfer between two branches of the profession is problematic because the educational environment within which BANA methodologies are designed and implemented is very different from those of TESEP English language education. In this chapter I shall look at some of these problems.

6.1   The special needs of state education

English language teachers who work in state education have special needs which have to be taken into account if appropriate methodologies are to be achieved. Whereas BANA teachers are often more able to concentrate on the intricacies of methodology, upon which their expertise is based, TESEP English language teachers may have other, wider social preoccupations and responsibilities which can overrule their choice of methodologies. Their role in state education demands that they comply with wider educational principles set by the institutions within which they work. TESEP English language teachers also need to consider how they fit within the structure of a host institution; and where this is itself collectionist in orientation, departmental membership and mastery of subject content becomes the wider measure of professionalism and status.

93

Another important difference is with regard to the process of *socialisation*. Teacher groups within the context of state education are a primary source for socialisation (Bernstein 1971:64; Stenhouse 1975:9), which is in turn a major contributor to the stability of a society. TESEP teachers have a responsibility as role models in the process of socialising their students into membership of the wider society. Here, the purpose of education is *primarily* not only to teach language skills according to the learner's sociolinguistic needs, but also to take students or pupils through a complex process in preparation for life in their society (e.g. LoCastro in process, with regard to Japan). In contrast, BANA English language education is likely to see socialisation in the far narrower terms of preparing students to be language users or as participants in the learning group ideal (e.g. Allwright in process).

In this respect, in the case already cited [5.4] where my own Egyptian university class in practical oral skills was contrasted with that of a local lecturer teaching linguistic theory charismatically, the latter might have been far more meaningful:

> [The] students waved at [the local lecturer] … in admiration as we left the faculty. In a sense, what she was doing was effective in socialising the students into the academic culture – much more so than what I was doing.

(Observation notes)

Despite these differences, technology transfer is frequently attempted in a variety of ways: i) in BANA-sponsored English language projects, where the aim is to introduce methodological innovation at a curriculum level, often requiring TESEP staff to adopt the technology; and ii) where BANA writers and publishers are involved in the introduction of new textbooks. In the latter case, the BANA connection may seem tenuous, but the lines of influence are still there. The publishing house may be locally owned, but with a franchise of advisors from a BANA publisher. BANA co-operation may be at ministry level, but the ministry's centralised control over what teachers do will indirectly carry this influence into every classroom. This distance between the BANA influence and the classroom may enable an indigenisation of the technology; on the other hand it could amount to a distortion. Technology transfer takes place iii) at a more piecemeal level whenever BANA teachers teach in state institutions in other countries; and iv) directly, when BANA personnel train TESEP teachers or teacher trainers in other countries. A further important way in which technology is transferred is v) when TESEP teachers go to BANA countries for training and higher degree courses related to English language education.

Indeed, although the technology transfer is initiated by both sides, it provides a major source of income, employment and status for the BANA professional-academic group, and maintains its expansion [5.3.3]. The rest of the English language teaching profession is to a greater or lesser extent dependent on this transfer.

6.2   The political power of language teaching

The wider social implications of what TESEP teachers do in the classroom both underline the need to look beyond the classroom at more macro influences, as has been argued in Part A, and give some idea of the complexity of problems likely to arise from technology transfer. From the BANA viewpoint, the transfer of technology might seem simply to be of a superior, well-developed methodology which is characterised by the learning group ideal and by integrationism. However, in reality, it might involve a form of social engineering, the extent and effects of which are not fully understood.

Particularly in countries where educational institutions are relatively new and have overtly primary roles in holding nations together, the effects of technology transfer could be destabilising – especially where the focus is *language*. The following discussion will make this point clearer.

6.2.1   Socialisation

The process of socialisation needs to be looked at more closely. Cortazzi makes the point that 'the process of acquiring adult roles, internalising the beliefs and values of society' also involves socialisation in the ways in which language is used in society (1990:56). Indeed, language becomes a powerful means of socialisation. The way in which work is organised is a powerful tool in any classroom; and this is 'doubly true of the foreign language classroom where the target language is at the same time both the *content* and, usually, the *medium* of learning' (ibid.:57–8). Cortazzi suggests that although it is becoming increasingly evident that 'children *are* socialised', teachers 'may not always be conscious ... of [how] the tightly structured nature of much classroom interaction' influences students' attitudes about 'rights, rules, roles and unspoken assumptions about how to learn and what is worth learning' which in turn influence their attitudes to society as a whole (ibid.:57).

6.2.2 The democratic factor

BANA proponents of the skills-based, discovery-oriented, collaborative approach implicit in integrationism might feel that one of its intrinsic values is the freedom it allows the individual, and the 'democracy' it therefore brings to the classroom. This notion is problematic, and perhaps a little too naive for several reasons.

The democratic nature of the ideal BANA classroom, based upon the skills-based, discovery-oriented, collaborative learning group ideal [4.1] might itself be questionable. Although claiming to be learner-centred, the learning group ideal demands considerable control of classroom interaction on the part of the teacher. Since the days of the direct method, there has been a liberalisation in notions of how students should behave. When I did my teacher training examination in 1973, it was expected that the students should not say anything which was not elicited by the teacher; and the whole class was conducted rather like an orchestra. Now, in the 'communicative' classroom, students are allowed to express themselves, and the degree to which students initiate utterance is one of the measures of lesson success (cf. Nunan 1987). (I hesitate over the label 'communicative' as there are several interpretations, which I shall discuss in Chapter 10, only one of which is probably within the common BANA perception.) Nevertheless, the form of control which the teacher maintains is subtly pervasive. Although the students are free to express themselves, they must do so within the framework of complex activities which are designed by the teacher in such a way that the form of student behaviour is carefully monitored. There is carefully managed control by the teacher, which is based upon an implicit 'training' of student learning behaviour. The term 'learning how to learn' is often heard. This type of classroom is like a so-called democratic society in which the behaviour of its subjects is carefully, though perhaps unconsciously, brought to conformity through tacitly educating media. Students are thus socialised, not to be members of the society outside the classroom, but to be members of the learning group ideal. It is not my intention to place a value or judgement on this image of the ideal BANA classroom, but to describe its natural social forces.

Bernstein throws a different type of doubt on the democratic nature of the integrationist classroom. He argues that whereas the strong subject boundaries of collectionism, upon which, after all, much of British middle-class education has been based, breed the strong values necessary for a democratic society, the apparently democratic nature of the integrationist classroom may produce a type of anomie which makes the student vulnerable to the forces of totalitarianism:

> Order created by the integrated codes may well be problematic. ...
> The openness of learning under integration may produce a culture
> in which neither staff nor pupils have a sense of time, place or
> purpose.
>
> (1971:64)

In his view, whereas integrationism, despite its modernity, might be symptomatic of 'moral crisis' (ibid.:67), collection codes breed considerable personal freedom and privacy of action within the confines of strong subject boundaries (ibid.:64). Students are thus given a sense of security in what is being learnt, and a firm feeling of what constitutes 'knowledge'. The teacher teaches the subject matter and leaves the students to fend for themselves. The degree of responsibility which students must therefore take [4.3.2, 5.4] generates a degree of freedom; and at the same time they have a clearer understanding of what they must agree or disagree with. There is a firm foundation of authority against which they can measure their own thoughts. Furthermore, the institutions of knowledge set up by subject boundaries provide a buffer, as do other intermediate social institutions such as family, peer and pressure group, against would-be totalitarian ideologies.

Bernstein's argument may or may not hold water; but it exemplifies how the introduction of integrationist BANA methodologies into classrooms which have been collectionist in tradition needs to be looked at very carefully. There are likely to be effects on student attitudes, beyond the classroom, and on teacher authority and status, which have not been calculated. (A fuller description and critique of Bernstein's argument can be found in Holliday 1991a:89–93.)

Whatever the nature of the ideal BANA classroom, the type of social order which it represents might not be appropriate for state education within certain social settings where socialisation may be tuned in other directions. A society into which a BANA integrationist approach is to be imported might already have a dominant collectionist educational code which carries out the job of socialisation effectively in the terms of that society, and which creates a completely different type of social order within the classroom. Indeed, the régime of the 'communicative' classroom, where a certain type of student behaviour is demanded, is generally not very adaptable to other classroom cultures.

6.2.3 *Language and political supremacy*

The political nature of educational codes has already been discussed [5.5.2]. Education is a powerful force within any society – a point which is well appreciated by many governments. Holly has a lot to say on this subject:

> The most widely-held notion of learning sees it as a handing-down of knowledge, an encounter between the inevitably powerful and the inevitably powerless. In this context the 'secret language' metaphor seems to make sense.
>
> (Holly 1990:12)

He reminds us of Illich's 'hidden curriculum' argument, that education involves a 'covert process of subtle – and sometimes not-so-subtle – repression' (ibid.:11).

The teaching of language *per se* is a powerful force within education:

> In relation to native speakers, the question of language teaching is everywhere highly political. The intention of teaching a language to those who already have that language is, quite clearly, regulatory.
>
> (Ibid.:13)

The introduction of language teaching from outside a society, coupled with a different educational approach, might therefore have complex effects, especially where the language is as internationally powerful as English, which, Holly argues, is 'the social vehicle, *par excellence*, of imperialism – old-style *and* new-style' (ibid.:11). He suggests that 'all human language necessarily carries a cultural charge' (ibid.:14), and goes on to argue that:

> If the learning of any other language can result in a general alienation from other cultures and, as I argued, the promotion of xenophobia, the learning of especially high-status languages associated with cultural empires – which tend to outlast political ones as Latinate cultural hegenomy outlasted Roman imperialism – can result in 'ideological colonization' ... a hopeless sense of inadequacy in the face of vaunted excellence.
>
> (Ibid.:15–16)

English is 'the language of the dominant political-economic system of the modern world'. Through the power of Wall Street and the City of London, 'the unspoken curriculum of English ... is the cultural baggage of entrepreneurialism and commercialism' (ibid.:15–16).

6.2.4   Linguicism

Phillipson (1991, 1992) goes further and argues that English language teaching professionalism itself implies a global 'covert political agenda' beneath its 'overt technical agenda'. At the centre of his argument is the notion of 'linguicism', which is defined as:

ideological structures and practices which are used to legitimate, effectuate and reproduce an unequal division of power and resources (material and immaterial) between groups which are defined on the basis of language. Linguicism is affirmed in similar ways to racism. In linguicist discourse the dominant language is glorified, dominated languages are stigmatized.

(1991:27)

He explains how linguicism is carried out at the *macro* level in postcolonial societies where 'IMF structural adjustment policies involve a continued emphasis on the learning of the former colonial language' (ibid.:27). English linguicism is part of a cultural imperialism which involves the 'establishment and continuous reconstitution of structural and cultural inequalities between English and other languages', through, for example, Anglo-centric professional and technical training (ibid.:27). (Phillipson describes six interlocking types of imperialism: economic, political, military, social, communicative, cultural. Cultural imperialism is further subdivided into media, educational, scientific and linguistic imperialism; ibid:27.)

At the *micro* level, linguicism is served by 'the tenets which served as pillars of the rising ELT profession'. Phillipson states that these tenets were presented 'at a key conference at Makerere, Uganda in 1961' (1991:27). He asserts that they are based on five fallacies: the *monolingual* and *subtractive* fallacies, that the mother tongue should not be allowed in the classroom, and the learning of other languages will inhibit English language learning; the *native speaker* fallacy, that non-native speakers cannot be effective teachers; the *early* start and *maximum exposure* fallacies, that effective learning must start at an early age and involve maximum exposure (ibid.:27–8).

Phillipson's point of view might seem extreme, and implies a conspiracy view of English language teaching which is over-simplistic and naive. Bowers (1991:29), in his reply to Phillipson, takes umbrage at the idea that English language teachers and curriculum developers from the BANA group – which he refers to as 'core English countries' – are in any way involved in such conspiracies. He refers to the prestigious Ain Shams University project in Egypt, about which I shall say more later, and asserts that 'there was never in fact any danger that the fundamental decisions regarding educational policy would be outside the control of national politicians and administrators' (ibid.:30).

Nevertheless, the danger of linguicism is there, and is very real in the minds of many members of the TESEP community. Hyde reports a paper by Saber at the 1991 MATE (Moroccan Association of Teachers of English) conference, in which English language education is seen as something close to a pernicious disease, where:

'English language heads a subversive cultural imperialism,
destroying traditional values and replacing them with alien ones.
Moroccan youth are corrupted through their knowledge of English.
… Students should be given a warning before they begin to study
English.'

(1992:3)

Hyde suggests that Saber's delivery 'betrayed, I feel, a deep anguish'.
Saber warns of the danger of English for specific purposes 'using "us"
for specific purposes', and stresses that it should rather be '"us" using
English for specific purposes' (ibid.3). Not everyone holds such a
negative opinion, however. On a more positive note, Abou-Talib, at the
same conference, dismisses the need to worry about cultural imperialism
'by stating with a wave of the hand "the French colonized us, we
colonized the Spanish, who cares"' (ibid.:3).

There are clearly many sides to the question of English language
education as a form of technological transfer; but from whichever side
one looks, English language education is a powerful and dangerous
commodity in three senses: i) it is in demand world wide; ii) in its 'at its
best' BANA form, it carries with it an educational approach, which
involves a classroom methodology that might be in conflict with
indigenous educational approaches; iii) it implies excellence, which
implicates complex notions of what Holly (1990:15) calls 'ideological
colonization' of one type or another.

The last point is significant. For the TESEP teacher, a notion of
excellence might well apply not only to the English language itself, but
also to what is conceived as the ideal in English language teaching
methodology. However, if this methodology is unattainable in the sense
that it is felt to be inappropriate to the teacher's educational
environment, what Holly (ibid.:15) refers to as 'a hopeless sense of
inadequacy' might be impossible to overcome.

I feel that this problem is at the root of difficulties encountered in
achieving appropriate methodologies. On the one hand, the dominant
(BANA) branch of the profession builds its status and expertise around
a technology which is not universally applicable, but which depends for
its status and expertise on international dissemination. On the other
hand, the less advantaged (TESEP) branch of the profession looks to the
BANA group for a superior technology, which amounts to denying its
own, indigenous intuitions.

6.2.5 *The destructive nature of integrationism*

A further factor in potential conflict is the possibility that the
integrationism which the BANA professional-academic group attempts

to import into largely collectionist TESEP institutions is in itself destructive. Bernstein argues that integration codes are both innovative and disruptive by nature:

> A move from collection to integrated codes may well bring about a disturbance in the structure and distribution of power, in property relationships and in existing educational identities.
>
> (1971:62–3)

This can be seen in many English language projects, especially at tertiary level. There is more than an occasional lack of respect afforded by BANA practitioners to the collectionist subject boundaries and didactic approach of TESEP English language education. Although linguistics and phonetics are accepted as valuable input to the TESEP profession, the learning group ideal rarely includes them as a valid part of the English language lesson. Often considerable project energy is spent either on fighting for the independence of service English courses from the influence of the resident English department (Cooke and Holliday 1982:28–9; Lilley 1984:186,189–92), or on infiltrating xisting English department courses with skills-based, discovery-oriented, collaborative approaches. Cooke and Holliday (1982:29) and Coleman (1992a:5–6), in projects at Damascus and Hasanuddin Universities, found that the only way to maintain project influence was to by-pass the (in their view) entrenched senior members of the English department as far as possible. Zikri (1992:17) reports conflicts with the English department at Ain Shams University, Cairo. Furthermore, the issue of 'attitude change' away from 'traditional' educational attitudes runs through much literature on English language curriculum design (e.g. Kirwan and Swales 1981; Britten and Sow 1981; Andrews 1984; Maley 1980; Kennedy 1987). I shall say more about conflict within English language projects in Chapter 7.

As collectionism in Britain has sometimes been thought of as alienating less able pupils from a middle-class education (Esland 1971:89; Bernstein 1971:57–8), integrationists in English language education may be motivated by what they consider to be signs of student alienation or lack of participation in collectionist lecture-style language classes (Bowers 1980a:109–10; Holliday and Cooke 1982:134; Holliday 1988:165, 1989b:11) and falling standards (Andrews 1984:176; Coleman in process) in the developing world. However:

> The conventional patterns of behaviour which we encounter in an academic institution have valid functions ... however exotic some of those behaviours may appear to be to the outsider. Although our attempts at reform may be admirably well-intentioned, our

> missionary zeal to do away with behaviours which are apparently
> inappropriate may actually have unforeseen repercussions elsewhere
> in the ... eco-system.

(Coleman in process)

This quote from Coleman makes the point that what may appear
educationally inappropriate, I would suggest from an integrationist
point of view, may also seem 'exotic' because it originates in a host
educational environment which is generally opaque to the outsider
English language curriculum developer.

6.3   A responsibility to understand

In the discussion so far, I have argued that the degree to which the act of
introducing a new methodology into a classroom culture, depending on
whether or not it is in accordance with the prevailing professional-
academic culture, can have a resounding effect which is wider-reaching
than the classroom or even the host institution. In the case of English
language education, where the new methodology may well be of a
totally alien nature, coming from outside the local educational
environment, the impact may well have a complex ripple effect
throughout the whole host ecology of cultures, as discussed in Part A.
At the same time, the success of the innovation will depend on a deep
understanding of this ecology. There is therefore a socio-moral
implication in trying to introduce BANA integrationism into TESEP
institutions in other people's countries, with possible effects that go far
beyond the management of learning a second or foreign language.

There is a grave danger of teachers and curriculum developers, from
both the BANA and TESEP groups, naively accepting BANA practice as
superior, and boldly carrying what are in fact the ethnocentric norms of
particular professional-academic cultures in English language education
from one context to another, without proper research into the effect of
their actions. TESEP teachers who adopt BANA practice without really
understanding it or its consequences are in particular danger:

> Unexplained violations of the expected norm by teachers
> enthusiastically embracing communicative approaches may lead to
> the diminution of their status and percieved competence in learners'
> eyes.

(Cortazzi 1990:59)

The outcome can be what Savignon (1991:271, citing Kleinsasser) refers to as the uncertain and routine teaching, characterised by a heavy reliance on the textbook with few opportunities for spontaneous, communicative interaction, of teachers who have adopted a new technology without deeply understanding it. Allwright looks more positively at a situation where teachers only partially adopt a communicative approach. It is possible to adopt a non-communicative syllabus (e.g. traditional grammar) together with a communicative process (1982:2). He argues that state school systems might need a less communicative syllabus because of the need, for their own socio-cultural purposes, for linguistic description; and a more communicative description is used only as a supplement. Communicative activities, which would be of the 'weak' transfer and pre-communicative type (citing Littlewood and Savignon), would therefore be restricted to the practice stage of the lesson. Allwright suggests that these are easy to adopt but the whole practice stage is also easily abandoned by the teacher who needs to finish the textbook (ibid.:4–7). The responsibility is, however, clear. English language practitioners need to see beyond their methodologies to the social effects of what they do.

The responsibility needs to be taken by both sides. I am not suggesting that TESEP English language practitioners around the world are helpless in their acceptance of BANA technology, but that both they and BANA practitioners need to be more aware of the wider socio-cultural implications of the commodity with which they are dealing. A very positive note from the TESEP side is described in Abou-Talib's paper, 'The teacher as a sophisticated learner', cited by Hyde (1992). Abou-Talib explains how teachers never stop learning, that there are many ways to teach, and that teachers must continually experiment. However, rather than looking to BANA technology, much of the knowledge required for such self-investigation is:

> 'under all Moroccan noses in their own culture and literature. ...
> Only a person knowledgeable about his own culture, and secure in
> that knowledge, is capable of making value judgements about ideas
> from the rest of the world.'

> (Abou-Talib, cited in Hyde 1992:3)

He goes on to make 'continual reference to Arab writers from the past', which, in the conference, were 'contrasted startlingly with other people's use of references from modern American and British linguists' (Hyde 1992:3).

Very few reports of the effect of BANA innovation are published by their TESEP recipients. There is a double bind here. When the skills-based, discovery-oriented, collaborative methodologies which characterise the learning group ideal and integrationism are criticised by TESEP practitioners, it is often through their own lack of real understanding, looking from a collectionist point of view. In the literature, TESEP writers can therefore be partisan and over-negative. On the other hand, the methodologies about which they complain are likely to have been implemented under the influence of BANA teachers or advisors who lack understanding of the TESEP educational environment. Confusion is thus compounded by lack of understanding from both sides – of how a 'communicative approach' might work on the part of TESEP recipients, and of how to make it work in the TESEP environment on the part of BANA promulgators. The latter is not helped by the BANA group's own confusion resulting from the rapid change which the profession is undergoing [5.3.4].

When BANA teachers, who have been used to a particular host educational environment in the commercial sector, go and work in state education alongside TESEP teachers, they need to learn about a whole new host educational environment, and about the very different professional-academic culture of their new colleagues. They cannot rely simply on their methodological expertise. This is a source of much conflict at the interface between the two types of professional-academic cultures. This interface is critical in many work situations, especially English language aid projects in the developing world, where BANA personnel are sent to develop the professional skills of TESEP personnel. Such conflict situations will be the subject of the next three chapters.

English language curriculum developers may argue that it is not within the confines of their job to consider the effects of their work on the wider society, especially when this society is not their own. I would answer this claim by saying that understanding better how their work interacts with the wider society, first at the level of the host educational environment, will enable them to be more effective within the scope of work which is allotted them.

6.4   Transferability of the learning group ideal

A key factor in the transferability of BANA technology to TESEP situations is how far the learning group ideal, given its claim to be based on well-researched universals in how people learn [4.1], can be successfully implemented in those situations.

6.4.1   Transfer as disruption

I have argued that the learning group ideal is in itself ethnocentric in its inception [6.3]. This is illustrated in Figure 4, which shows two macro contexts – A, a host educational environment within a BANA-oriented scenario, and B, a host educational environment within TESEP state education in the rest of the world. In context A the learning group ideal is supported by the commercial sector, through the host educational environment. However, when an attempt is made to transport it to a state institution (context B), it is not supported by the host educational environment of the state sector, and disrupts all around it.

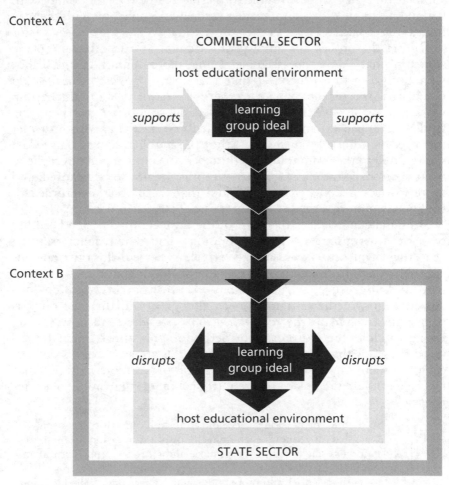

Figure 4 *Relative positions of the learning group ideal in different environments*

This disruption is described very well by Shamim (in process) when she attempts to introduce group work into her university class in Pakistan [4.2.2]. The outcome is a disruption of the 'etiquette of interaction' within the classroom culture. Unhappy with the way in which she had been teaching, after 'a one-year training programme' doing an MA in Britain, during which she had 'search[ed] for an alternative approach to teaching in books and articles on ELT methodology', she chose a small class of ten postgraduates, believing that they would be sufficiently adult and handleable, to try out a new skills-based, discovery-oriented, collaborative methodology. She told her students that they would be able to discuss the new methodology with her and negotiate different outcomes if they were unhappy with the way things were going.

During the process of innovation attendance was often poor, the students often did not do assignments and, moreover, told her that they were not going to do them. Despite this open opposition, they would not discuss the reasons why they were dissatisfied. She found group work impossible. When she approached the groups to give help, the students stopped talking; when she tried leaving the classroom to let them get on with it by themselves, they did nothing. It was only when she resorted to the more traditional teacher role of 'watching over them' from the front of the class, that her authority seemed to be restored, and more work was done. She then found that the more she returned to traditional authority, the better everything got.

Shamim acknowledges that part of the problem might have been her own lack of training in the methodology, and that teacher training generally might be a key issue. Nevertheless, her conclusion from this experience, and from looking for ideas for methodological improvement in BANA literature, is that student reaction is rarely taken into consideration in the design of methodologies, and that the onus is nearly always put on the *resocialisation* of teachers, rather than on trying to close the gap between methodologies and student needs. (Shamim states that Nolasco and Arthur 1986 are an exception to this claim, in their emphasis on learner training programmes.) Acceptance by clients should take place before introduction of innovation. She cites Krasnick:

> 'In the ESL profession as a whole almost all our effort has been expended on refining teaching techniques and revising teaching materials. The overall effect is more and more to refine cultural and interactional issues out of existence by focusing on problems which are perhaps easier and more convenient to approach. The fact that cultural and interactional forces do not call attention to themselves

does not mean that they do not exist. It may simply be that we do not recognise their existence.'

(Shamim in process)

Commenting on the disruption which her attempt at innovation created, she suggests that:

Once the teacher broke the contract, as it were, by stepping out of her traditional role and changing the routine structure of the classroom event, this seemed to provide sanction to the learners to indulge in forms of behaviour that would be termed deviant in the framework of a traditional classroom.

(Ibid.)

She goes on to describe the macro social influences on the classroom, in terms of authority, home and family, and, like Coleman [3.2], draws attention to the fact that classes, as other forms of meetings, have social as well as academic or administrative functions, which are rarely acknowledged in the literature that describes BANA methodologies.

6.4.2   *Putting macro 'constraints' first*

The relationship between the learning group ideal and the educational environmental factors which might inhibit its realisation can be likened to the relationship between ideal syllabus specification and what Munby (1978:217) describes as the cultural, sociopolitical, logistical, administrative, psycho-pedagogic and methodological 'constraints' placed upon it (see also Swales 1980:70, 1989:83; Bowers and Widdowson 1986:9 and Robinson 1988:147).

Munby (1978) recommends that these constraints be dealt with after syllabus specification, as and when they arise. Swales (1980) takes the opposite line and accuses those who put off dealing with the constraints until as late as possible of 'calculated procrastination'. The same could be said of those who put off dealing with the cultural variables which inhibit the learning group ideal. Although I do not think that this is their intention, Swales later comments on how many American researchers who carry out the '"micro" investigations' characteristic of second language acquisition research:

are somehow unconcerned with field experiences, with ESL policy at home and abroad, with ESL lessons from history or geography, or with the uncertain status of the profession.

(1989:79–80)

Indeed, there does seem to be a degree of naivety in current thinking about English language teaching methodology, which presumes that ideally, despite certain psychological differences in individuals, if one puts most students into a given learning situation they will behave in the same way as they would in any other learning situation. At the same time, the more macro British studies, which do consider wider cultural influences [4.2], tend to see these factors as thorns in the side of sound methodological practice. The implication is that these thorny cultural problems need to be understood so that they can be diminished, in order that the learning group ideal can follow its prescribed path. Understanding them for the purpose of accommodating them is not really on the agenda. Swales (1989:90) also cites Bowers' (1980b:71) account of 'war stories and romances' as seeing many of these macro accounts as anecdotal, lacking adequate criteria for furthering a real understanding of the macro context.

In contrast to this thinking, I wish to argue that the various cultural influences on students, which work against the learning group ideal, are extensive outside the instrumentally-oriented educational environment within which BANA English language education operates, and present a very varied *normality* in student behaviour. I am not suggesting that the methodological principles of the learning group ideal are not valid, but, rather, that the cultural conditions which have so far allowed them to become realities in actual behaviour tend to be restricted to the commercial environment. In TESEP state education in much of the world these conditions rarely exist.

The problem which I wish to address is how to develop a more adaptable learning group ideal which can work within the varied and complex environments of TESEP English language education. This has to be through finding ways of seeing local environmental factors, not as inhibiting, but as *central* to the design of appropriate teaching methodologies. As with the case of syllabus design, appropriate methodology design needs to consider the so-called 'constraints' within the macro environment, not as constraints, but as essential features. The existing learning group ideal might remain an ideal, but in the sense of an ideal typology, to be used as a heuristic, designed essentially to be adjusted. In other words, we should not treat the learning group ideal as the operational norm, and cultural factors which inhibit its operation as problems; we should treat the cultural factors as given, and how to make the learning group ideal appropriate to these factors as problematic.

6.5   Summary

The following points have been made in this chapter:
a)   There is a technology transfer between the BANA and TESEP branches of the English language teaching profession. This is

problematic because of the different needs of the two branches, and because the learning group ideal, the core of the technology, is designed only for educational environments found in the BANA sector.

b) The special needs of the TESEP branch include consideration of the wider social influences of the curriculum, institutional norms and the responsibility to socialise young people into society.

c) Socialisation is particularly at issue within the context of language teaching because of the political, cultural and economic power of language.

d) Collectionism and integrationism have different socialising influences; and an integrationist BANA technology transfer into a TESEP host educational environment which is already collectionist will therefore be problematic.

e) Integrationism is destructive by nature. This is seen in English language teaching projects, which often attack host collectionist structures.

f) Both BANA and TESEP branches of the profession therefore need to take a greater responsibility in understanding the wider social effects of technology transfer.

g) The learning group ideal needs to be taken as a hypothesis for optimum methodologies, which need to be validated and adapted in the light of real socio-cultural situations.

6.6   Questions for discussion

1   How conscious are you of socialising your students?
In what ways do you try to socialise them?
Do you agree that if you are a TESEP teacher socialisation mainly concerns preparing your students to live in society outside the classroom; and that if you are a BANA teacher it mainly concerns teaching your students to conform to the learning group ideal?

2   Is the learning group ideal a fixed, unchanging concept?

3   Is the classroom within which you work 'democratic'? How far does your teaching methodology support this?

4   How far is the English language teaching with which you are involved linked with any form of cultural or linguistic imperialism?

5   Think of an example of when you or a colleague resisted technology transfer.
What type of cultural factors (e.g. national, institutional, classroom) influenced this resistance?

7　　The politics of projects

Chapter 6 discussed the problems which arise when there is a technology transfer – a transfer of English language teaching methodologies – between the BANA branch of the profession and TESEP institutions in the rest of the world. A specific scenario in which this transfer occurs, in a focused, organised manner, is in English language projects. I have already referred to some of the issues arising out of projects, talking about how destructive the integrationism inherent in BANA approaches can be within the context of traditionally collectionist host institutions [6.2.5]; and in several places I refer to a case study which is taken from an English language teaching project at Ain Shams University, Cairo.

This and the next chapter will be devoted to this one aspect of a wide variety of English language education activities, because within project work there is a range of issues which are relevant to other activities within the profession. In this chapter I shall be looking particularly at the problems which arise when expatriate project personnel belonging to the BANA professional-academic culture need to work closely with local teaching and administrative staff who belong to the TESEP professional-academic culture; and in Chapter 8 I shall discuss the difficulties which arise when BANA practitioners fail to find out about and appreciate deep elements in the TESEP educational environment.

7.1　　Culture conflict

My first reference is not from an English language project, but from Shipman et al.'s (1974) account of the Keele Integrated Studies Project which sought to introduce integrated social studies across the humanities curriculum in British secondary schools during the late 1960s. Their project base was the Institute of Education, Keele University. Funding was through the Schools Council. The team were to act as project 'co-ordinators' – in direct contact with a number of different schools in the area in which innovation was to take place.

110

Although the Schools Council and the Keele University Institute of Education were the instigators of the project – as a result of negotiations with other bodies – the project team were the day-to-day agents of innovation. I refer to their experience because I wish to show how the problems which occur in English language projects are not due to but only exacerbated by national cultural differences. This will reiterate the point I have made elsewhere [4.2.1] that it is misleading to explain problems in terms of national culture profiling, and that distinctions between professional-academic cultures are more useful. I wish to show, too, that the conflict between integration and collection, discussed in Chapters 5 and 6, is not specific to the BANA-TESEP division in English language education, between instrumental and state scenarios, but represents a more universal educational conflict, where innovation is by nature integrative, and collection by nature respresents an educational status quo.

According to Shipman *et al.*, the Keele project was fraught with conflicts between 'diverse groups each pressing ... reasonable and legitimate views':

> Reconciling the different perspectives of the Schools Council, the university, the local authority and trial school teachers, [and] the compromises that resulted will exasperate those who yearn for rapid centrally directed change and those who support change through initiatives in individual schools. ... This context for curriculum change at the local level consisted of diverse groups each pressing what seem to those involved to be reasonable and legitimate views. The Keele project could only be launched after these interests had been contacted, consulted and reconciled. Even after launching, the need to reconcile contrasting interests delayed getting the project under full steam.
>
> (1974:2)

This view is consonant with my description of an educational environment constructed from a variety of interconnected cultures [2.7]. Figure 5 illustrates the scenario within which English language projects operate. The project itself is a cultural entity interacting with target professional-academic, classroom and institutional cultures. Whereas the target cultures constitute an established ecosystem, the project culture is a temporary newcomer which brings an intrusion of change. The relationships between the target cultures are established, but the project has to build new relationships with them.

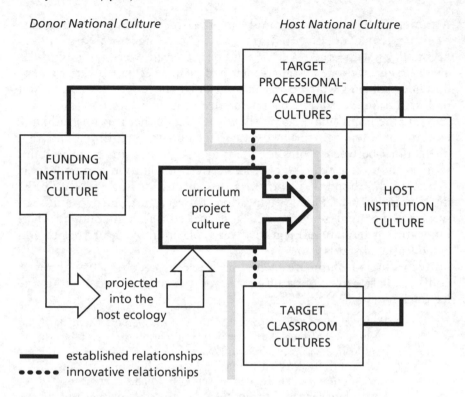

Donor National Culture   Host National Culture

Figure 5 *Curriculum project as intruding culture*
(taken from Holliday 1991a:112)

A significant difference between this scenario and that of a project within a single national culture such as the Keele project is that this scenario is split between a host and a donor national culture. The funding institutions and the curriculum project are within the latter. This makes the project's business of forming relationships with the target cultures more difficult because they are *foreign*, and have to be negotiated across a national cultural divide. Nevertheless, the problems are similar to those encountered in the Keele project in that, even within a single national culture, the target cultures are sufficiently *new* to make communication difficult. I distinguish between *new* and *foreign* in the following way. A new culture is the culture of a class group, a job, a group of colleagues or an institution that is approached by a newcomer. A foreign culture is within the context of a foreign country. Both can be sufficiently strange to require much learning on the part of the newcomer; but in the case of English language project personnel, the cultures of the host educational environment are *both* new *and* foreign.

The position of the funding agency is also significant. Although it usually belongs to the same national donor culture as the project, it has a relatively established, international relationship with the host cultures. Although funding institutions instigate change, they are distant from it. I shall describe in more detail later [8.4] that, as established institutions, their roles are essentially routine and non-innovative. They therefore have to sub-contract the actual job of innovation to the curriculum project, which, due to its essentially transient, dynamic nature, *is* disposed to innovation.

These relationships are extremely complex, whether working across a national culture divide or within the same national culture. Indeed, Shipman *et al.* (1974:169) conclude that 'many of the problems that overtook the Keele project were caused by the under-estimation of the difficulties involved'.

7.2 'Real world' problems

The project team arrives in the host educational environment and has to begin to form relationships with host teachers and administrators. This is immediately problematic because, just as when anyone joins a new institution and new groups of colleagues, when changing job or department, these teachers and administrators already constitute an established milieu, with its own complex network of statuses, interests and issues about which the newcomer has to learn. I have already referred to how these factors are basic influences on how teachers and administrators receive curriculum innovation [5.6.1]. Kelley (1980:65) explains that although curriculum innovation may be planned and put into action through official means, actual curriculum development and implementation is 'a form of social action', and, as such, 'involves a variety of social and personal behaviour' (ibid.:79). The work of any project can therefore only be effective if realisable within this existing 'real world' of its target personnel. The first task is therefore to learn about and appreciate the real world of relevant parties within the host educational environment. In Holliday (1992b:405), citing Swales (1980), I argue that failure to do this has been a major cause of failure in English language projects. (Swales also refers to the real world of students. This has been dealt with to some extent already [2.6, 4.2], and I shall take it up in detail in Chapter 9 in my discussion of conflicts between teachers and students.) How problematic this task can be is illustrated in Shipman *et al.*'s (1974) account of the Keele project, which shows how learning about the real world of a new culture is a two-way, reflexive process. One learns about others through monitoring how they respond to one's own actions. The project is an agent in a process of change, and must begin with action, with a process of making contact with target personnel. The reactions of local personnel are the first signs of the real world which their reactions represent. Ideally, these reactions must be observed and responded to: they are the bases of the data which the project needs to inform its own action. I shall discuss the procedural aspects of this reflexive process in more detail in Part C. The examples from the Keele project are of this process going wrong.

7.2.1 'Ivory tower'?

From the beginning the Keele project team had difficulty producing a consistent and consolidated 'public image' in the eyes of local target groups (Shipman *et al.* 1974:18). There were many factors involved here. The project team were inexperienced, teachers themselves, who had been seconded for the period of the project. The funding agency also demonstrated lack of experience in projects of this type, which resulted in false starts (ibid. 1974:18–20). There was resentment on the part of local teachers, who saw the project as belonging to the 'ivory tower' with which the 'university' was associated, out of touch with the 'battleground of the classroom' (ibid.:22). On the other hand, some teachers, who were attracted to the academic prestige of the university, were disappointed to find that all the team members had to offer was 'folk wisdom'. One of the teachers interviewed stated that:

> 'It was cheek, really. All we got was drivel about logical development. We knew they were not really teachers but they should have stopped telling us how to do our jobs. What I wanted was, I don't know, inspiration, something to tell me what I was supposed to be doing. I've been to a university and I expected to be treated as part of it again. We got a royal visit and a few kind words after we joined [to co-operate with the project] but nothing we could get our teeth into.'
>
> (Ibid.:22)

Between the lines, this was a resentment at the project team's apparent lack of appreciation of the teachers' own professional-academic culture. This is seen again in an interview with another teacher who says, 'I still see myself as a very academic English teacher; my first question is, "What is in this pack [of new materials] for the English teacher?"' (ibid.:104).

7.2.2   Face to face

An early attempt to form a relationship with the schools took the form of conferences in which the team tried to present the project objectives and introduce the idea of integrated studies. The outcome was:

> A serious communications gap. Questions from the floor consisted largely of complaints about jargon and lack of concrete advice. ... Curriculum theory is a relatively new area of study. It has rapidly developed a language of its own. But this is not the 'language' used by teachers. The attempt to interest the teachers ... failed. The teachers, supported by local authority advisors, responded with vigour and scorn.
>
> (Ibid.:26)

However, 'members of the team felt they had a responsibility to put basic issues before the teachers to ensure that the implications of introducing integrated studies were understood' (ibid.:27). The only alternative would have been 'for the project to do its conceptual thinking in private' (ibid.:41n). There was also difficulty in getting the teachers to feed back, due to the extra work this would require – filling in feedback forms – but also because of a 'rejection by the teachers of the value of the sort of information that was being requested by the team' (ibid.:28).

7.2.3   Cargo culture

The 'communications gap' with the teachers also led the team to exotic perceptions of the target schools and teachers as foreign cultures. Shipman *et al.* comment that 'the relationship of the project to its trial schools is a novel social relationship'. To cope with this, the team rationalised the relationship through 'guiding metaphors' such as 'reciprocal obligations', and 'exchange of gifts'. They also stored stereotypical comments from teachers, such as, 'We're not a trial school. Just helping out', which members of the team construed to be a cover-up for instrumentalism in cases where the teachers were really looking for new curriculum material to take away with them (ibid.:98–100).

These metaphors did not help real understanding. There were cases where the culture of the project committed sins against that of the teachers. It attacked professional privacy (ibid.:107) and existing authority structures within the schools, and manipulated 'the reference orientations of the teachers' to their established professional-academic cultures (ibid.:98).

On the other hand, the project team also felt that the teachers had exotic images of the project, represented by another metaphor, 'cargo cult'. In social anthropology, 'cargo cult' signifies:

115

> The reaction of primitive communities to a contiguous highly
> technological culture. Cargo cults have in common a reaction to
> 'culture shock' expressed in bizarre beliefs about cargo.'
>
> (Ibid.:117)

It was felt that the teachers saw the project as a cargo boat arriving
from a distant land with 'curriculum materials, electronic gadgetry,
dust-free chalk, stationery, individual study books, display material etc.'
(ibid.:117).

However, it was felt that the cargo boat provided more valuable
things than equipment. More important for many teachers, who were
dissatisfied with their own work situation, was the outlet through
contact with a foreign entity, which the cargo boat provided. Such
teachers would express their loyalty to the project with comments like,
'I like to feel in the front line in the fight for integrated studies'
(ibid.:109). The project team soon realised that 'the absence of physical
resources was unimportant compared with the enthusiasm of staff' as a
motivating factor for co-operation with the project (ibid.:130).

Whether in terms of poor physical resources or professional
dissatisfaction, 'the cargo culture metaphor places the school firmly
within the culture of poverty, and the teachers' behaviour is based upon
a frank recognition of this fact' (ibid.:118).

7.3 Local perceptions

I can do no more than hypothesise that states of affairs similar to the
one described in the Keele project are not uncommon in English
language projects, where the cultural distances are made larger by the
foreignness to the project of the host environment. Evidence of this type
of conflict is not often reported. My own experience from the Ain
Shams University project in Egypt, in which I was involved with a team
of American and British advisors in developing the teacher education
curriculum in faculties of education throughout the country, led me to
believe that the local lecturers who worked closely with the project had
perceptions of the project which were quite different from my own and
those of colleague curriculum developers (Holliday 1991a:371–84).
These differing perceptions were not always apparent until they were
highlighted by specific events, of which the following observations are
examples. They indicate that the project was not really synchronising
with the real world of local lecturers.

7.3.1 Who are the experts?

The first example is when I took a local co-observer, Dr Anwar, with me to visit Beatrice, an expatriate lecturer who was working with a new language laboratory at a provincial faculty of education. Dr Anwar was interested in developing materials for language laboratories, and I felt it would be useful for him to see what other people were doing. I describe the confrontation which took place between this local colleague and the expatriate lecturer concerning the latter's attitudes towards local regulations in Holliday (1992a:225). Beatrice had broken the university regulations by using the language lab after normal working hours (8.00–2.00) to give her students extra tuition. Her priorities had been her students' education in what she considered a deficient educational situation. Dr Anwar, quite rightly, felt this sort of behaviour was not developmental because it did not produce techniques that could be developed by local lecturers. Despite this confrontation I nevertheless found the visit professionally enlightening in that many of the issues involving the use of language laboratories in the local context were aired. However, on the way back, Dr Anwar:

> said that his time had been wasted and that he had learnt nothing and that he had been brought on the visit under false pretences, that he had been led to believe that ... [the expatriate lecturer] was an expert.

(Observation notes)

This reaction was repeated when Anwar was introduced to Chris, another expatriate lecturer who had considerable experience with language laboratories and who had collected a lot of material which he was prepared to share.

On both occasions, perhaps erroneously, I perceived Dr Anwar to be a recipient of useful ideas as a result of meeting the expatriate lecturers. However:

> [Dr Anwar saw] himself in each case as the consultant and expert, a perception not shared by the expatriate lecturer[s], who felt that ... [they] had been asked to the meeting[s] to advise.

(Observation notes)

I interpreted Dr Anwar's misconception (in my terms) regarding the aims of our professional relationship as a difficulty on his part in accepting practical experience as valuable. I felt that he saw himself as already expert because of his PhD, and was only prepared to learn from somebody with more theoretical knowledge. The credentials of Beatrice, who overtly played down what she knew, very much putting forward the image of 'amateur tinkering' (Observation notes), were not sufficient in Anwar's terms. Chris had produced a very comprehensive and detailed list of materials and procedures which he felt appropriate to the local situation; but it did not contain any theoretical points. Here was a direct confrontation between the local collectionist professional-academic culture, which appreciated theoretical expertise, and the integrationism of expatriate personnel which laid more value on the ability to solve problems and develop solutions on the spot.

Further light was thrown on the nature of this conflict of viewpoints when Dr Dahlia introduced me to her students. I had been invited to guest teach her class. She 'announced over the mike at the beginning that she would change a class in three weeks' time so that "we" could go on a "visit" together', and then, 'no formal introduction of myself' (Observation notes). This apparent casualness in maintaining scheduled classes, although common in the data, may well have been a show of lecturer power – the important academic having other more elevated things to do – but using the project as a prop for this power. Perhaps Dr Dahlia wanted the status of going on visits with an expatriate curriculum developer, but not at the expense of fully accepting him as an expert – hence her not introducing him as such to her students. This lack of introduction, especially of someone who was about to teach the class, was significant in the light of the marked hospitality seen elsewhere in the classroom culture [3.4.3].

7.3.2 Territory and status

On another occasion, I and two local co-observers, Dr Ezzat and Dr Fadia, who had co-operated in the development of new course material, went to watch a local lecturer, Dr Ghassan, use the material at another provincial faculty of education. I was pleased that Ghassan had taken an interest in the project's materials development activities and had attended some of the committee meetings. These meetings were voluntary. Local lecturers were nevertheless encouraged to attend on a regular basis to take part in the design and writing of the new materials. They were then supposed to trial the materials in their own classes and report back (Holliday 1991b:302; Zikri 1992). Dr Ezzat and Dr Fadia were key members of the committee. Although Ghassan had offered to trial materials previously produced by the committee, he did not use them exactly as they had been designed. Nevertheless, he was introducing considerable innovation into his classroom by using part of the material. However:

> On the way back, ... [Ezzat and Fadia] showed considerable anger
> at the fact that ... [Ghassan] had 'stolen' our material and misused
> it, and felt that I had been far too soft with him. They felt that
> there was very little of merit in what they had seen, that their time
> had been wasted, and that it would not be worthwhile for them to
> visit his class again. I tried to explain my point of view – of the
> importance of developing the lecturer and not just the material,
> and of the material being a catalyst for development rather than an
> end in itself – but they would not take this point; and we had to
> agree to differ, although I felt considerably professionally deflated
> at this.

(Observation notes)

Dr Ezzat and Dr Fadia thus did not seem to share my appreciation of
the process of development in which I believed Ghassan was taking
part. They seemed to be more concerned with the preservation and
status of the product which they had helped to make. There was an
indication that they were being territorial in the defence of their
expertise. It did not, however, seem to be a problem to Dr Ezzat that he
was not actually using the material he was being so defensive about
(Observation notes). I shall say more about this later [7.3.4].

Territorialism was also evident in a seminar presentation, reported in
Holliday (1992a:226, 229), which I made jointly with two local
colleagues, Dr Hassan and Dr Jamila, to introduce project materials to
local lecturers. My integrationist motives in organising the seminar had
been to involve local lecturers in the curriculum discussion and
development process – the area of expertise upon which the project was
capitalising. Hassan and Jamila had seemed keen to take part in the
seminar, but perhaps for different reasons. To me, the seminar seemed
fraught with an apparently clumsy vying for territory. Hassan felt that
Jamila had stepped on his territory; and I found it difficult to obtain the
territory I needed for my part of the presentation. For both local
presenters and participants it seemed to be an arena for asserting
professional-academic status. It was as if the project had provided a
further arena for the acting out of their own micro-politics.

7.3.3   Sabotage

The occasion in which Dr Dahlia did not introduce me to her students
when I was about to teach them as guest lecturer could also be
interpreted as sabotage of the project. Although Dahlia had been
working with me to develop the materials I was going to teach, and was
supposed to have been using them already, or, at least, was supposed to
have given the students the materials necessary for my lesson:

> Essential materials for the ... session (the activity sheet) had not been photocopied. This may have had more implication than I at first imagined (I was left to work without a concrete plan in the students' hands). I had to insist to have the missing material photocopied after the beginning of the lesson.

(Observation notes)

This was the class in which Dahlia disapproved of my inductive approach [5.4.6]. On reflection, I wondered:

> Was the fact that the activity sheet had not been given out some sort of unconscious sabotage? Although the lecturer had insisted on it in the planning session, she didn't seem to think that not having it was important. She obviously believed that the lecture lacked structure, yet did not acknowledge that this may have been due to lack of activity sheet. Lesson structure is clearly seen to be the lecturer's responsibility. Is putting the activity sheet between the lecturer and the students a threat to lecturer status?

(Observation notes)

The same thing had happened in another case, where Dr Kamal, a local lecturer, whose class I was teaching, was supposed to have given out the activity sheets the lesson before and had not. Because it was impossible to teach without them I had to 'ask him to go and photocopy the activity sheets (which he had omitted to give the students during the first session)' (Observation notes).

On the other hand, this apparent sabotage could have been nothing more than the local lecturers not appreciating the technology necessary for the integrationist approach, as has already been observed elsewhere in the classroom culture (Holliday 1991a:303–5).

7.3.4   Apparent duality

Dr Ezzat's admission that he was not in fact using the new materials, although he was a co-author [7.3.2], and Dahlia's and Kamal's apparent sabotage of the innovation process, reveal an apparent duality in their behaviour. This was seen elsewhere in the Ain Shams project. The committee approach to materials development worked only on the surface. Although attendance on the committee seemed popular with many local lecturers (Zikri 1992:27), and some of them participated significantly in the production of materials, observation of classes revealed that there were very few cases in which they actually used the materials (Holliday 1991a:377–80, 1991b). (The apparent success of committees, known throughout the project as 'working parties', was not only in the production of new materials for undergraduate language classes – on which I report here and in Holliday 1991a – but also for literature and methodology materials (Hawkey 1986; Kowitz 1986). The 'working party' ethos was a mainstay of the whole curriculum development project.) However, the duality might not have been so much in the behaviour of local lecturers, but in the gap between the perception of the curriculum developer and the local lecturers with respect to the whole curriculum development process.

This duality is expressed in the soft systems models in Figure 6. They throw light on how local lecturers could take part in the materials writing committees set up by the curriculum developer, but with viewpoints and motives very different from those of the curriculum developer.

Activity system 1
A CD- and T-owned system to increase student participation so that English language teaching can be more effective.

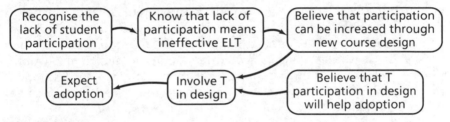

Activity system 2
A T-, T-profession- and student-owned system to improve the teaching-learning situation in ways that will protect teacher respect and survival.

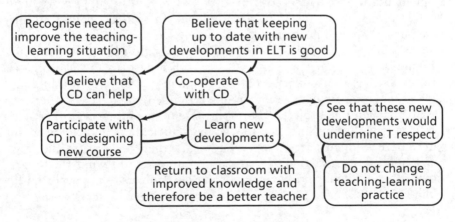

T = local lecturer   CD = curriculum developer

***Figure 6** Dual perceptions of curriculum development*
(adapted from Holliday 1990:79)

In Activity system 1 (top of figure) the curriculum developer, who sees herself in charge of the situation, and imagines herself to be working alongside and on behalf of local lecturers, has followed a train of thought which seems logical to her. From the premises that there is need for change in the course design and that involving local lecturers in the design process is worthwhile, collaboration takes place. However, Activity system 2 (bottom half of figure) shows that the local lecturers themselves do not see their collaboration in the same way: they have completely different motives. They begin with the premises that, yes, there need to be changes in the teaching-learning situation, and that it is professionally useful to keep up with new developments in their field. They also consider their students, with whom they share the classroom culture. Their corporate train of thought is more complex than that of the curriculum developer. It is emergent rather than designed – reacting opportunistically to the arrival of the project. The outcome is that although the local lecturers go through the process of collaborating with the curriculum developer, the purpose, in their view, is for them to learn new developments, and not what happens in the classroom. At the same time, these new developments would be counterproductive if put into practice. Hence, without announcing it to the curriculum developer, they return to the classroom with improved knowledge but the same practice as before.

A collectionist-integrationist distinction is again evident. Whereas the integrationist curriculum developer sees importance in practical application, and the development of a materials writing and implementation *skill*, the collectionist and therefore subject-oriented local lecturers see learning new developments in a *subject matter*, in this case pure or applied linguistics, as an end in itself.

This state of analysis is not uncommon in English language projects. The analysis in Figure 6 was not just with regard to the Ain Shams project, but also to similar scenarios in Sudan and Sri Lanka (Holliday 1990:77n, citing Saunders and Thomas). Kennedy (1987:164), referring to the Tunisian ESP project, reports the case of local teachers who could not reconcile their real needs with the new curriculum, and followed an alternative 'hidden curriculum'. They said they were using the new curriculum, but in fact, subversively, continued to do what they were doing before. Similar problems at Damascus University are reported in Holliday (1988).

7.4   Intercompetence

This last example of the development of a hidden curriculum underlines the two-sidedness of the conflicts set up in curriculum projects. It is not just a matter of an invading technology failing to understand the real worlds of a local ecology. The invading technology has its own reality and its own culture. As I have already suggested, the problem is two-way [7.2]: the difficulty which expatriate project personnel find in understanding and appreciating the real world of local personnel, and the problems local personnel have with the project culture, produce a cultural interface which creates unusual behaviour in both parties. This unusual behaviour can be termed 'intercompetence' – an intermediary behavioural competence in the process of learning a new culture (parallel to interlanguage in language learning) (Holliday 1991a:409, 1992a). (The term 'intercompetence' was originally coined by Terence Cooke, at Damascus University in 1982.) The confusion of roles characteristic of intercompetences further confounds the problem of learning a new culture.

Several examples of intercompetence are cited in Holliday (1992a), on the part of both expatriates and local lecturers: the failure of Beatrice, the expatriate language lab lecturer [7.3.1], to conform with local protocols, upsetting local colleagues; in the same situation, Dr Anwar apparently also trampling on local protocols by interfering in the conflict between Beatrice and local lab technicians in someone else's faculty of education; the confusion of roles of myself and the two local lecturers in the joint seminar [7.3.2], which led all of us to behave clumsily and out of character; two junior lecturers seen smoking at the back while I was being videoed teaching a demonstration lesson with their students (ibid.:226).

Possible explanations for this anomalous behaviour are suggested (ibid.:227). i) The seminar is a case where the very different professional-academic cultures of the expatriate (integrationist) and local (collectionist) personnel are trying to operate within the same event. ii) In the situations set up by the project, such as visits to other faculties, lesson observations, demonstration lessons, the use of video, and joint seminars, which are not normally characteristic of the host institution, local lecturers become outsiders and suffer from an inverted culture shock. iii) As a result of ii), distinctions between formality and informality in the project culture are misinterpreted by local lecturers.

I make the point in Holliday (1992a:230) that intercompetence, if not addressed, can lead to conflict. This can be seen in Dr Anwar's and the local technical staff's reaction to Beatrice's failure to conform to local regulations [7.3.1]. Another example of this is reported by Pociecha in her open letter to the Peace Corps, and any other organisation involved in sending volunteer English language teachers and teacher trainers to Polish teacher training colleges. She argues that the expatriate volunteers' refusal to conform to the local system, and their belief that 'whatever is familiar (e.g. – "the way we do it in America") is automatically right, good, appropriate in the new situation' represents a 'defence mechanism' against an 'unfamiliar situation (such as a foreign country, such as a new job, such as both of these at once)' (1992:13). Pociecha expresses a local anger at this expatriate attitude, similar to that shown by Dr Anwar, when she asserts that:

> Polish teacher training colleges are not – and aren't meant to be – imitations of American Liberal Arts colleges; nor are they language schools devoted to providing practice communicating with native speakers. ... Although the Polish education system is undergoing radical changes, it *does* exist, and the colleges are part of it. ... It *does* have aims, standards, procedures and regulations. These are not obvious to many volunteers and must be explained to them. Volunteers, in turn, should try to understand and adapt to the system. This doesn't mean that volunteers aren't entitled to question and criticize the system (like everyone else), but it does mean, among other things, that volunteers ... shouldn't expect to overhaul the entire ... system, [and] should comply with existing procedures and regulations (usually).
>
> (Ibid.:13)

Of course, this goes wider than intercompetence. That the volunteers are insufficiently qualified and experienced to carry out their work to the 'high standards' required by the colleges is not the fault of the volunteers, but of the agencies that send them (ibid.:12–13), which might be bad management, lack of funds, or a general failure of these agencies to appreciate that the BANA technology of 'American Liberal Arts colleges' or 'language schools devoted to providing practice communicating with native speakers' does not fit the needs of TESEP colleges of education. I shall look at the problems created by hyperrational funding agencies failing to understand local realities in the next chapter [8.4.2].

7.5   Summary

a)   The conflicts which occur in English language projects are common to those in many other English language teaching situations.

b) These conflicts can also be found in curriculum projects which take place within a single national culture. Integrationism is inherent to innovation; collectionism to established educational structures. Curriculum projects are therefore by nature integrationist. National culture barriers in English language projects merely make this conflict greater.

c) Conflicts are created when projects arrive in and disrupt the established relations between cultures in the existing educational environment.

d) The newly arriving project has great difficulty finding out about and understanding the real world of local institutions and personnel, and vice versa.

e) Project events can therefore be seen in very different ways by the expatriate and local parties who take part. This can result in a clumsy intercompetence on both sides, where each becomes the outsider to the other's world.

7.6   Questions for discussion

1   Do you think the types of conflict described in this chapter are inevitable?
    Is it inevitable that members of different professional-academic cultures will have conflicting perceptions of the same situation?

2   What advice would you offer teachers and curriculum developers in the conflict situations described?

3   Think of a similar conflict from your experience.
    What were the reasons for the conflict?
    Was the conflict solved, never solved, or tolerated? What were the reasons for the outcome?

4   How might you act differently in a conflict situation as a result of reading this chapter?

5   Think of examples of intercompetence from your own experience.
    What were the two conflicting cultures which caused the intercompetence?
    Who became outsider to what?

8   'Calculated procrastination'

The potential failure of expatriate project personnel to understand and take account of the real world of local personnel clearly inhibits the effectiveness of English language projects, and therefore presents serious implications for project management.

8.1   Implications for project management

I have already referred to a core problem in the transfer of BANA English language education technology to TESEP spheres as 'calculated procrastination' – a term used by Swales (1980) to refer to a preference not to address complex local constraints and realities [6.4.2].

8.1.1   'Busy work'

In projects generally, development personnel can very easily pursue accessible 'busy work' in areas with which they are professionally familiar rather than tackle complex local problems. Shipman *et al.* (1974) argue that failure to understand the real world of target teachers and administrators in the Keele project resulted in a breakdown of communication between them, which in turn resulted in the project team's own identity crisis.

It was therefore largely to avoid 'the less accessible problems of definition and research' into what they ought to be doing, that the project embarked on the more accessible work of in-service courses, materials production and project centralisation, which Shipman and his co-workers later felt to have been therapeutic and cosmetic, serving the project's self image but in actual fact counterproductive (ibid.:154).

The in-service courses were held within the university, and detracted from developmental work with schools (ibid.:21); the materials production was later seen to alienate target teachers who found it too difficult to participate in, and produced sharp tensions over production issues among the team (ibid.:59). The move to centralisation was to make it easier to tie up the work on time and to get materials published, to show a quantifiable product (ibid.:53–5). This was later seen to be counterproductive because it involved specialisation among the team members (ibid.:59), and made them less effective in detecting and reducing problems with the schools (ibid.:44). It was on the whole ironic that while the target education system was being urged by the project towards change, in the direction of a more integrationist code, the project, due to a need for a therapeutic cultural consolidation, was moving in the opposite direction. (See the discussion of a similar tension in the BANA English language teaching profession generally [5.3.4].)

Morris, in his rather severe critique of a range of aid project work in Yemen, comments that aid workers were largely 'unequipped to cope with the discrepancy between image and reality'. The result was that:

> When they fail to achieve the goals set them they may become
> consumed by guilt, attempt to disguise their enforced idleness
> by a charade of hard work, immerse themselves manically in
> diversionary activities, hoard information in order to inflate their
> own importance.

(1991:4)

Returning to English language education, Swales reports how the failure of expatriate staff at Khartoum University [7.2] to consider the real needs of local parties was connected with their tendency to pursue their work in a direction which was largely independent of the real needs of the local situation. They satisfied their own professional standards through 'quality materials', 'intra-departmental efficiency' and 'hard-working staff'. They thus achieved a validity which was *internal* to the world of the project; but they failed to achieve *external* validity, in the terms of the host institution (1980:62).

In Holliday (1992b:405) I list two areas which have been seen to suffer as a result of a break in project action away from the real world of its recipients: staffing and the status of institutions set up by the project. Regarding staffing, expatriate project workers are 'recruited by methods and criteria different from those normally adopted in the [host] institution' (Swales 1980:64). Similarly, local staff are recruited by the project, to work in the centres which they set up, with professional abilities which are suitable in their terms, but without the formal qualifications which will enable them to survive in the wider host institution once the project has departed (Barmada 1983). Projects are often interested in training local staff to take over the management of project-nurtured centres. This frequently takes the form of sending people to Britain or the USA to get their MA degrees. It rarely seems to be realised that many host collectionist institutions will accept nothing less than a PhD for such a position; and project time-scales and funding rarely allow for training to this level. This under-qualification of local staff in turn contributes to the difficulty many such centres have in achieving permanent, independent status (Lilley 1984; Holliday 1991a:185).

8.1.2 'Bogus co-authorship'

Bowers states that there are:

> clear procedures ... for engaging local authority, making project aims and processes subject to local constraint, and ensuring through both training and structural means the local ownership and sustainability of a project.
>
> (1991:32)

He refers to management procedures which have become a common focus in English language project design. C. Kennedy (1987:164–6) recommends normative-re-educative strategies, which aim to involve local personnel in project design and development work. (See also Hoyle 1970, Straker Cook 1986 and White 1987.) The intention is that they will thus be educated in the principles of curriculum development and attain a sense of ownership of what the project wishes to do.

I wish to argue that, while the democratic intention behind a normative-re-educative approach might be sound, it will not in itself cope with the deep-rooted differences between the curriculum project's integrationist stance and the real world of local personnel, as described so far in this chapter and in Chapter 7. The fact that local lecturers participated in and in some cases initiated the design of the new courses in the Ain Shams project, yet did not teach them or deeply appreciate their methodological aims and potentials, illustrates this point. The normative-re-educative approach, which was the basis of curriculum development through committees at Ain Shams, failed to deal with the existence of a hidden curriculum [7.3.4].

There is a grave danger in adopting textbook management strategies without fully considering the real world of local personnel. A normative-re-educative strategy which does not do this could result in the type of 'bogus co-authorship' described by Jenkins (1986:223–6), which involves a 'rhetorical con-trick' to give local participants the impression they have influence in the change process when in fact they do not. The situation in English language projects has the possibility of being a *double* rhetorical con-trick. The curriculum developer is also under the impression that the local participants are supporting the new courses, when in fact they are using the situation for professional advancement, as shown in Figure 6 [7.3.4]. However, I must stress that this interplay is not necessarily as Machiavellian as it may at first look. I do not believe that the rhetorical con-trick is on either side intentional, rather that it is the result of a tacit adherence, on both sides, to conflicting paradigmatic standards. The curriculum developers believe in the sincerity of the normative-re-educative approach as much as the local lecturers do in the educational benefits of developing expertise in a subject matter *per se*.

8.2   Deep action

The difficulty which project personnel have in understanding the real world of local personnel implies that the latter exists at a deep, tacit, opaque level of the local cultures. In Table 2 I distinguish three spheres of deep action, psycho-cultural, informal order and micro-politics, and show how they contrast with an official, formal order.

The *psycho-cultural* element is rarely described in English language education. It has already been referred to with respect to classroom cultural features in Egyptian faculties of education, such as hidden communication, tacit protocols governing classroom instructions, sanctity and hospitality, formality and informality [3.4], and the ritual aspect of classrooms described by Coleman [2.3]. It is very much at issue in the difficult job which teachers – and more so expatriate teachers – have in learning the culture of the classroom, which will be discussed in detail in Chapter 9.

My description of *micro-politics* in Table 2 comes from Hoyle (1988). It constitutes the internal politics of schools and departments – some of the personal professional considerations referred to by Kelley (1980) as being major factors in teachers' decisions to adopt innovation [5.5.1]. It is at the core of the workings of professional-academic cultures as described in Chapter 5, and local perceptions regarding project events described in Chapter 8. Hoyle suggests – I think over-negatively – that it is 'a dark side of organizational life'. Although everyone is aware of it and to a greater or lesser extent takes part in it, it is rarely the focus of academic study, and one needs to go to 'television serials, films, plays and novels' to see it represented (ibid.:256). I suggest that it is not a 'dark side' as much as normal human endeavour to achieve natural aspirations, rights and allegiances within the confines of the work of the people involved. Whereas psycho-cultural deep action represents the unconscious foundations for group behaviour, micro-politics represents the conscious dynamism of group behaviour.

Table 2: Deep and surface action

Surface action	Deep action
Can be plainly seen, documented and reported	Cannot be plainly seen, undocumented, not reported
The official, administrative and executive aspects of the organisation	**Psycho-cultural:** Tacit rules governing cultural behaviour
Manifested in official agreements, contracts, job descriptions and official responsibilities, attendance registers, textbooks, teaching hours, examinations and student assessments	Unspoken recipes and traditions, for everyday behaviour Derived from national and group cultural features **Informal order:**
What should happen	Unofficial, non-professional, practical
Respectable, professional, according to management principles	What actually happens Motivated by unsatisfactory institutional and physical conditions **Micro-politics**
	'Organisational mafias', 'hidden agendas', 'playing politics' and 'Machiavellianism'
	Interest

It is certainly a bias of my own focus that my description of the Ain Shams project concentrates on the micro-politics of local personnel and says little about project personnel. Bernstein (1971) suggests that the collectionist code is particularly prone to micro-political intrigue, although he does not use the term. His argument is that the mainly vertical departmental relations of teachers within the collectionist code [5.2], coupled with the 'invisibility' of classroom and administrative practice, encourage 'gossip, intrigue and a conspiracy theory of the workings of the organization' where teachers become territorial and defensive of departmental boundaries (1971:61–2). In the collectionist code, horizontal work relations across subjects are largely limited to senior staff, or are non-task based. However, I am not sure that this is any less the case in integrationist communities. Morris (1991) includes graphic descriptions of the micro-politics of aid workers.

Informal orders are referred to in the sociology of work (Wadel 1979:5) and directly or indirectly in some literature on English language projects, as will be described later. Examples cited in Holliday (1992b) include: unofficial deals between teachers and students over the weighting of examination scores (Swales 1980); reading lists and libraries, presented in official documents as evidence of English language resources, in fact unused because lecturers felt their students' English too poor (Coleman 1988, 1992a); official claims to English medium lecturers, whereas in reality English was rarely used (Andrews 1984); books and syllabuses actually in use completely different from those stated in official documents (Cooke and Holliday 1982:22,27); lecturers teaching far fewer hours than timetabled due to time spent commuting, and effective teaching time reduced by poor acoustics (Holliday 1991a:222–34). Another example, referred to earlier [7.3.4], is that of teachers claiming to trial and later use new materials and courses, and in fact not doing so.

My division of deep action into these three spheres is purely for the sake of argument. In reality, they are difficult to disentangle. I would say that Coleman's reference to informal orders in fact refers to all three:

> An intangible network of personal relationships, shared knowledge, unwritten conventions, ethnic rivalries and internal political considerations ... [which] runs sometimes in parallel with and sometimes in conflict with the formal overt structure of the [institution].
>
> (Coleman 1988:157)

It is also important to note, as Hoyle (1988:256–7) suggests, that deep action has a symbiotic relationship with surface action, the two are largely shaped by each other. (Hoyle is speaking about micro-politics. I am taking the liberty of applying his words to deep action generally.) Hence, 'a proposed innovation which threatened the territorial interests of a teacher might well be resisted by mobilizing "professional" arguments' (ibid.:257). It will be the surface action professional arguments which are presented to the project personnel.

Deep action is the basis of what I have been referring to as the real world of the host institution and its personnel, which is mostly not stated, but which absolutely must be understood if appropriate change is to take place. Hoyle (1970) maintains that successful educational innovation does not normally take place as a process of official adoption (surface action), but rather through the more personal 'individual response of heads and teachers', which does not necessarily follow the official decrees of the institution (deep action). Hence, local personnel have to be seen as *people*, rather than as operatives who will comply with official directives. At this level, argues Hoyle, curriculum planning must consider the host institution as a 'social system' (ibid.:2).

The crux of the problem is that success at the surface action level does not necessarily guarantee success at the deep action level; any failing at the deep action level will render all apparent successes at the surface action level null and void. Coleman (1988:158) sums up the situation – 'in actual day-to-day decision-making this impalpable network is frequently of much greater importance than any formal organizational structure'.

There have been several examples of projects changing direction as a result of finding out about and appreciating various aspects of deep action, thus reducing the gap between project action and the real worlds of local personnel and institutions (Coleman 1992b; Andrews 1984; Cooke and Holliday 1982; Holliday 1991b). The problem is in finding out about deep action elements sufficiently early to make projects work within their limited lifetimes. (I shall look at the restrictions of hyperrational objectives laid down by funding agencies later [8.4.2].)

It is important to make the point again that deep action phenomena exist equally, although perhaps realised in a vast variety of different ways, in *all* types of institutions regardless of society or national culture. I have already referred to the duality of the problem of both expatriate and local personnel failing to understand the realities of each other's worlds in project scenarios [7.2, 7.4]. Part of this problem is expatriates failing to see and account for deep action phenomena in local cultures; but part of it is also expatriates failing to appreciate how their own project or technology culture has its own deep action phenomena. On the one hand, expatriate 'experts' may have the very misguided impression that 'irrationality' is only a feature of local systems, and that this is a reason for their needing 'help'. On the other hand, they may have the equally misguided impression that their own systems do not contain any 'irrationality', and that this is what makes them 'superior'. It is unfortunate that most of the data which I cite in this book consists of BANA failing to understand the deep action of TESEP situations, giving the false impression that deep action is a feature solely of TESEP situations. It would have been nice to have an account, for example, of a TESEP teacher's problems in unravelling the deep action of a BANA institution where she or he was doing an MA or diploma in English language education. One example of informal order which such a person might discover is how allocation of teaching hours between staff, rather than expertise, can influence who teaches what.

8.2.1 Information collection

I deal with this problem of collecting information about deep action phenomena in some detail in Holliday (1992b). It is a fact of organisational life that project managers, and the consultants who precede them, begin, in their search for the information they need, by communicating with the host institution at the formal, official, surface action level. As I have suggested [8.2], they are more likely to hear about the official line upon which the institution is supposed to operate than about what really happens. This is especially true when they already have their own strong agendas, which create in them 'a sociological blindness' toward the local situation, which misinterprets local rhetoric (Morris 1991:3). Furthermore, if they do begin to look into the deep action of the host environment, the information they collect seems too sketchy and impressionistic to be easily dealt with, and there is no systematic means for obtaining it.

For a variety of complex reasons – obscure, deep action phenomena themselves – either the information is simply not available, or local informants are reluctant to reveal it, or do not appreciate its significance. In some cases, the need to collect information of this nature is itself characteristic of the project's integrationist problem-solving approach, and conflicts with the local view, which considers informal information improper and unimportant. I remember an instance in a university staff room in Egypt, where an expatriate colleague, Don, was asking a local lecturer, Dr Layla, questions about the courses, timetabling, teaching loads etc. Don was one of several lecturers working in Egyptian universities as part of the Ain Shams project; they had all been given a questionnaire to fill in, through interviews with local colleagues, so that the project could build up a data base of relevant information about the institutions. Later on, Layla confided in me that what she had told him bore little relation to reality, but that she had not wished to disappoint him by telling him that she could not answer most of the questions.

An interesting example of inaccurate formal information having been collected can be seen in Seymour and Bahloul's discussion of the Tunisian ESP project. They report how project plans for the continuance of its work after expatriate departure although 'sincere' was a 'miscalculation of the Tunisian reality at tertiary level' (1992:4). The project's institution of local advisors – [cf. 8.1.1] – a resources centre, a newsletter and seminars, although practical while under foreign sponsorship, would not have the legal standing to operate without this sponsorship. Local advisors were acceptable while they were assistants to foreigners, but were not acceptable as experts in their own right as soon as the foreigners departed. Their colleagues, after working hard and satisfying stringent qualifications to achieve their positions, would reject help or advice from these new local experts, who had been appointed by a project committee which contravened local union regulations (ibid.:5). The ability of the project to produce anything that was sustainable after its termination thus became less credible; and Seymour and Bahloul argue that it could only really survive if *more* foreign support were provided (ibid.:6).

However, in some of the cases cited in Holliday (1992b), ethnographic approaches to information collection, involving wide-ranging observation of classroom culture and informal interviews, are tried with a degree of success (Andrews 1984:175; Cooke and Holliday 1982:6; Coleman 1992:228). A description of these will follow in Part C, where it will be argued that investigation of deep action phenomena does not have to be sketchy and impressionistic, but that through a systematic *means analysis*, it is possible to address this problem during the course of project work. Furthermore, despite the qualitative nature of deep action phenomena, they do present behaviour which is as open to the formulation of sociological and anthropological rules as any other sphere of human behaviour (Holliday 1992b:413).

8.3   Tissue rejection

I have argued elsewhere that the conflicts which are set up between the project and the established host educational environment, as described in Chapter 7, can result in project failure resulting from 'tissue rejection' (Holliday 1991a, 1992b). Hoyle (1970:2) takes the term from medicine, where it is used to describe failure in organ transplant, and uses it to describe what happens when curriculum innovation 'does not become an effectively functioning part of the system'. The curriculum innovation is thus seen as a new, implanted organ; the host body is the institution into which it is introduced.

In English language projects, the implant often takes the form of courses or materials, or of a fledgling institution such as a language centre or department, which the project attempts to set up. Tissue rejection takes place when the implant does not survive as an integral part of the host institution, once project support is taken away. Further implications for project management can be connected to this notion, with regard to the surface-deep action division.

8.3.1   *Over-ambitious surgeons and inexperienced immunologists*

Within the organ transplant analogy which 'tissue rejection' evokes, the surface action corresponds to the *surgical* process of physically sewing in the new organ. The parts to be cut and connected, the thread, the instruments, the cleanness of the incision and the final scar, are all plain to see. There are no visible signs within the context of the surgical operation which can give clues as to whether or not tissue acceptance will be complete.

In contrast, an *immunological* concern is with the eventual acceptance of the new organ by the body's immune system. Immunology, unlike surgery, deals with an invisible, opaque world which corresponds to deep action. Much literature on project management (e.g. Brumfit 1980; Bowers 1983, 1991; Rea 1984; Adams-Smith 1984; Roe 1980; Chamberlain *et al.* 1978; Maley 1980), although concerned with making curriculum and curriculum project design comply with the host educational environment, does not explicitly report outcomes interpretable as tissue rejection. As far as their papers report, they are mainly concerned with the surface action of the host environment.

In terms of the transplant analogy, they are mainly concerned with the quality of the surgery. Like the surgeon, these writers are concerned with the operation stage, and leave the immunological stage to take care of itself. They seem, like many writers in the field of education (Hoyle 1970:2, citing Bhola, Carleson, Rogers and Miles), more preoccupied with planning and setting up than with the actual process of implementation.

On the other hand, some of the literature cited in this chapter (Swales 1980; Barmada 1983; Lilley 1984; Andrews 1984) is concerned with the far more problematic deep action phenomena within the immunological sphere. These papers concern the effects of the transplant, after the operation has taken place or during its later stages. Therefore, they appreciate the imminence of tissue rejection. However, although they appreciate the importance of immunology, they are not trained in this profession and feel ill-equipped to prevent tissue rejection when they see it. Lilley (1984:190) comments that 'turning to the literature on ESP, we found nothing at this "macro" level to help'. Smith (1989:3) similarly remarks that there is 'inadequate research into the process of change in third world educational systems'.

8.3.2 Creating 'new webs of reciprocity'

As described in Figure 5 [7.1], the relationship between the intruding project and the established cultures of the host environment has to be negotiated. Shipman *et al.* explain this relationship in terms of the organ transplant analogy:

> A sociological perspective on organ transplantation suggests that completely novel social relationships throw a peculiar strain on all participants. Organ transplantation cannot be considered simply as a problem in medical technology, as it raises issues about what appropriate social framework unites donor or next-of-kin and the recipient. Social relationships are governed by a web of reciprocity that evolves over time. The absence of cultural norms and expectations poses problems of what behaviour is 'appropriate'.

> (1974:98)

The 'peculiar strain' which is placed on all parties has been illustrated by the misunderstandings within project contexts reported in Chapter 7. The local intercompetence observed in the Ain Shams project exemplifies how project action not only causes conflict between expatriate and local personnel, but can also create situations which upset existing, established 'webs of reciprocity'. Dr Anwar tramples (in my view) on local protocols by interfering in someone else's faculty of education [7.4]; two local lecturers create a disturbance (in my view) on someone else's territory by confronting students in a particularly belligerent way (Holliday 1992a:225–6); in the joint seminar [7.3.2] a violent (in my view) argument breaks out between my local co-presenters and their peers from several faculties of education and arts over a video of an expatriate lecturer doing skills-based, discovery-oriented, collaborative work with undergraduate students.

The strain of upset and reforming webs of reciprocity is clearly multi-directional and hinged on deep action phenomena strange to the outsider project worker. Thus, the issue is not simply one of innovative curricular elements which need to be made to fit the surface needs of the host institution, if tissue rejection is to be avoided: the whole mode in which these innovations are introduced has to be *culturally* appropriate at a deep action level.

Shipman *et al.*'s reference to 'what appropriate social framework unites donor or next-of-kin and the recipient' (1974:98) emphasises the multi-directional nature of tissue acceptance or rejection, and also the fact that the process of matching has to be two-way. A donor with the appropriate potential for tissue acceptance has to be found. In English language curriculum development terms, during the pre-project stage, when initial consultancies take place in response to host government requests, careful matching of existing resources with host needs has to take place. This also is essentially a deep action process, for it is not the documented sociolinguistic and educational needs of host learners which are critical in avoiding eventual tissue rejection, but rather a matching at a deeper, more subjective, cultural level. Fullan comments that 'educational change is a process of coming to grips with the *multiple* realities of people' (1982:113). Fullan also comments:

> Neglect of the phenomenology of change – that is, how people actually experience change as distinct from how it might have been intended – is at the heart of the spectacular lack of success of most social reforms. It is also necessary to build and understand the big picture, because educational change after all is a sociopolitical process.
>
> (Ibid.:4)

However, it requires not only a phenomenology of change, but also a phenomenology of the requirements of change.

Description of the phenomenology of school life is a common focus of ethnography in general education research (Delamont and Hamilton 1984:3), where the emphasis has been on 'what *actually* goes on in schools rather than ... what *ought* to go on in them' (Wolcott 1982:71) – 'lived experience' and 'the subjective interpretations of curricular reality made by pupils and teachers' (Whitty 1985:70) – 'the complex social reality of everyday life in institutional settings' (Atkinson and Delamont 1986:239). I shall argue the importance of ethnography in the search for appropriate methodologies in Part C.

8.4   Isolation of the project culture

An important factor in the failures which are common in project design is the relevant isolation of the project culture.

A project, by nature, has only a limited lifetime in any given location, and as such must have a project team either employed specially for the purpose or brought from projects in other locations. In whichever configuration, the culture which the project takes on is likely to be alien to the ecology of local cultures, simply by virtue of its being brought in from outside. However, the project is outsider not only to the local environment, but also to the workings and expectations of the funding agency.

8.4.1   Outflanked

Figure 5 [7.1] shows that there are established international relationships between the host ecology and aid agencies, similar to those between the host ecology and universities and other educational institutions abroad [2.7]. These relationships will in a sense outflank the curriculum project. *Before* the arrival of the project, a source of the professional-academic identity of target personnel will have been directly (in the case of tertiary) or indirectly (in the case of secondary) through links with traditional collectionist departments in linguistics and literature in Western universities. Certainly, in the case of the Ain Shams project, many of the local lecturers had received doctorates in theoretical linguistics or literature in Britain or America; and more junior local staff aspired to the same source of development. *After* contact with the project, the lecturers who become involved will find themselves working with integrationist project personnel whose influence will tend to alienate them from their own dominant professional-academic reference group; and the retraining they will get through the project will be in supposedly technologically appropriate, but low status, applied linguistics, which will be of use to them only while the project remains to give professional support. This type of conflict contributes to the staffing problems of project-nurtured centres after project departure, where staff will have been created who are not considered qualified by the host institution (Barmada 1983 [8.1.1]). Other local teachers and lecturers not yet involved will simply be put off and not co-operate.

The conflict between the integrationism of the project and more established institutions was also seen in the Keele project, where the materials produced by the project team were not of interest to the publishers who had 'difficulty coming to terms with the principles of integration developed by the team' (Shipman *et al.* 1974:63). See also Tomley (1980:41).

8.4.2   Meeting hyperrational objectives

Funding agencies are by nature bureaucratic, conservative, 'hyperrational', and distant from the innovation process (Daft and Becker 1978:3–4; Fullan 1982:81 citing Wise). The difficulty which established aid agencies have in setting up projects is exemplified in Shipman *et al.* (1974:3–11) who report several changes in direction and false starts in the Keele project. The objectives which they set and the reporting which they require often do not fit the realities of the situation. Smith makes the point that there is a trend in British funding agencies to insist that the English language project becomes a 'management task involving conversion of inputs to outputs'. He suggests that this emphasis on short-term quantification rather than long-term quality is restricting the freedom of traditional professionalism which has been previously characterised by 'an acceptance of uncertainty and the need for flexibility' (1989:2–4).

Hence it is difficult for project personnel to report the qualitative aspects of deep action phenomena which I have argued are fundamental to project design and management, and therefore difficult to incorporate these factors in arguments surrounding the meeting of the objectives set by funding agencies. It is partly for this reason that the deep socio-cultural aspects of the host environment have not achieved high status in discussions and literature. They appear too sketchy and impressionistic to be reportable [8.2.1].

The subsequent need to serve two masters – the realities of the local situation and the hyperrational requirements of the funding agency – add to project failure in meeting the needs of the local real worlds. This is a contributing factor to the common indulgence in 'busy work' referred to [8.1.1]. One of the reasons for the Keele project embarking on counterproductive materials production and centralisation was to effect an early tidy finish to ensure the meeting of objectives.

Another aspect of the hyperrationality of funding agencies is their reluctance to fund evaluation. This represents a general fear of allowing projects to continue without concrete evidence of a 'worthwhile' product – failing to see that an evaluation stage might provide such evidence (Shipman *et al.* 1974:44).

8.5   Cultural imperialism?

I return once again to the question of cultural imperialism – an accusation often levelled particularly at English language projects. The rationale and philosophy behind the way in which expatriate innovators are placed in other people's countries are problematic. I have already described Phillipson's argument which sees aid projects as instruments of a 'covert political agenda' centred on linguicism [6.2.4]. Speaking of 'developmentalism' generally, Morris:

> questions the wisdom of imposed development which answers no [locally] felt needs and is incapable of inducing changes in perceived needs. ... Aid agencies delude themselves if they talk of fostering self-reliance while excluding beneficiaries from the most vital stage of any development programme – the determination of aims and plans.
>
> (1991:2)

He reduces the policies that promote this type of aid to a means for assuaging 'the collective guilt induced by the legacy of our colonial predecessors' (ibid.:1) – 'a peculiarly Christian insistence on the ultimate triumph of altruism' (ibid.:3) – and recommends that help to developing countries would be much more effective if more support was given to 'ongoing, locally initiated schemes' (ibid.:2).

However, such warnings of cultural imperialism are often too vague to be helpful. For the purposes of this book I take it as given that aid programmes *are* organised in such a way that expatriates *do* find themselves in situations where they have to make the best of imported aid systems. I do not wish, here, to concentrate criticism on the way in which projects are conceived and initiated at government level, but to suggest ways in which specialist practitioners in the field may reduce, through greater sensitivity to local cultures, possible negative effects of what they are doing, and work to achieve maximum benefit for local people. An understanding of why tissue rejection occurs will, I hope, heighten the appreciation of a need for greater sensitivity. Reducing tissue rejection may achieve greater local benefit, despite misconceived beginnings, and may help to nurture the 'locally initiated schemes' to which Morris refers.

Furthermore, Morris's argument may be unduly negative in some respects. Readers who have worked on aid projects will surely recognise that imported aid schemes very often do produce highly locally appreciated outputs, often at a grass-roots, interpersonal professional level, perhaps as unexpected offshoots to initially intended objectives. Moreover, I do not believe that the issue of aid can be seen as clearly in the 'us' and 'them' terms implicit in Morris: at one level all participants are dealing in a complex market place which travels beyond straight cultural or national boundaries.

8.6   Summary

a)   Inability to come to terms with the hidden real worlds of local personnel can lead project personnel to embark upon work whichsatisfies internal validity in the terms of the project and funding agencies, but which can be counterproductive in local terms.

b)   Textbook management strategies such as normative-re-education are ineffective if they do not respond to local real worlds.

c)   The difficulty expatriates have in understanding and coming to terms with local real worlds is largely caused by these real worlds existing at a particularly opaque deep action level.

d) Collecting information about deep action phenomena is highly problematic. An ethnographic approach, which would help to address the problem, is not currently a recognised part of project expertise.

e) Failure to address deep action phenomena can lead to tissue rejection – rejection of the project action by the real world of the local situation.

f) The problem is exacerbated by the hyperrationality of funding agencies which do not easily digest the more qualitative aspects of project work.

8.7 Questions for discussion

1   Draw up criteria for distinguishing counterproductive 'busy work' from productive project action.

2   Think of an example of 'calculated procrastination'.
    What were its causes? In whose interest was it?

3   In what ways can the notion of 'bogus co-authorship' also be applied to English language teaching methodology?

4   List deep action phenomena within your own institution which might be difficult for outsiders to perceive.
    From your experience, are informal orders more a feature of some societies or institutions than others?

5   Do *all* project managers really *need* to address deep action phenomena?

6   Why are good management techniques alone unable to solve the problems posed by deep action phenomena?

9 Teachers' and students' lessons

In the previous four chapters I have been looking at various aspects of the conflict between two professional-academic cultures within English language education. In this chapter I shall look again more closely at what happens between people in the culture of the classroom, at what the teacher on the one hand, and the students on the other hand bring to the classroom, and how these are irrevocably in conflict. In my analysis, I shall draw upon what has been learned about teachers and the groups they belong to in the previous four chapters, and about students and the groups they belong to from Chapter 4.

9.1 Two lessons

I wish to argue that classroom events incorporate not just one lesson, but many lessons – one which the teacher plans and administers, and one for each student taking part. Table 3 shows this distinction. Because it is not my intention to go into the psychology of individual students, I shall deal with the students' lessons as one, group agenda.

The table shows that the different lessons are marked by different agendas, which are influenced by a mixture of the respective expectations of teacher and student groups and individual abilities and preferences. These are in turn influenced by deep action phenomena – psycho-cultural, informal and micro-political factors which are often hidden from outsider view [8.2]. In the case of the classroom, the teacher is at least partially an outsider to the culture of the students, and the students to the culture of the teachers.

The influences on each agenda within the classroom derive from the variety of forces outside the classroom depicted in Figure 2 – the professional-academic cultures of teachers, students and institutions [2.7]. I have already described how the student culture, with all its constructs on what should happen in classrooms, is formed both inside and outside the classroom through successive generations of students [4.5.1].

Table 3: Teacher's and students' lessons

Teacher's lesson	Students' lessons (one for each student)
Teacher's agenda, expressed in a lesson plan:	**Student's agenda**: what each student wants to get out of the lesson:
• what teacher would like to happen • organised according to teacher's ideas • a fine production	• what each student actually gains from the experience of the lesson • organised according to each student's learning style
Influenced by:	*Influenced by:*
• conventions of methodology • textbooks • teacher's and institution's expectations about student and teacher roles, and what should happen in lessons • conventions for organising academic subject matter	• student expectations about student and teacher roles, and what should happen in lessons • conventions for responding to lesson events (answering questions, drawing attention, taking turns etc.)
• teacher's personal needs, abilities and motivation	• student's personal needs, abilities and motivation
Influenced by:	*Influenced by:*
Deep action • tacit rules within professional-academic culture for teacher and student behaviour • institution micro-politics and informal order	**Deep action** • tacit rules within student culture for teacher and student behaviour • student micro-politics and informal order

The significance of seeing what happens in the classroom in these terms is that the teacher's and students' lessons *are* inevitably *different*, and are very likely to be in conflict. The students want one thing out of the classroom process, and the teacher something else.

9.1.1 'The curse of Caliban'

This notion is inspired by Widdowson's (1984:189–200) allegory about Caliban not learning what Prospero wishes to teach in Shakespeare's *The Tempest*. To cut a long story short, Prospero attempts to teach Caliban, whom he perceives as linguistically uncivilised, how to speak properly. Caliban learns; but he does not learn what Prospero intends to teach. Caliban has his own, student's agenda, and, to Prospero's astonishment, learns instead how to curse.

The moral of Widdowson's rendering of Shakespeare's story is that teachers should not expect their students to be slaves to their lesson plans. Widdowson is really aiming his comments at English for specific purposes (ESP), which, at the time of writing, was still recovering from the narrow discipline set on it by Munby's (1978) needs analysis régime [6.4.2]. The sociolinguistic needs of the target situation, in which the student would eventually use her or his English, would be defined in terms of language functions. These language functions would form the syllabus. The student, on mastering these language functions, would then presumably be able to operate in the target situation. Two problems with this were: i) there are other things going on in target situations than the utterance of prescribed language functions; and ii) students often have far wider aspirations than to be able to operate in limited target situations. This type of linguistically narrow ESP, Widdowson argues, sees students as slaves to syllabus design and implementation, for they are not allowed to learn beyond its specifications. My reference to Saber's fear that ESP might be 'using "us" for specific purposes' [6.2.4] takes on a clearer meaning in this context.

9.1.2 Deferred versus immediate outcomes

In one case at Lancaster University, with a group of Iranian trainee ships' engineers and a local, native-speaker teacher, it was observed that conflict was caused by a serious rift between the students' desire for spontaneity and the teacher's need to follow a prescribed lesson plan (Holliday 1984:38–9).

Table 4 shows how this conflict was manifested. Some of the interpretations in the table are less well founded than others. They are the result of observation of classes and interviews with teacher and students, who, by the way, were all keen to resolve the conflict. However, whether or not the interpretations are fully accurate, there was sufficient evidence to suggest that i) there were widely differing viewpoints held by the various parties, ii) the conflict was influenced by events outside the classroom, and iii) there was a degree of alienation or

even anomie, on the part of the students, due partly to ii), and partly to
the course purposes, which were too complex and different from what
they had been used to.

This situation supports some of the hypotheses I have presented earlier.
The micro events of classroom interaction need to be seen in terms of
wider macro influences from outside the classroom, and also in terms of
the differing viewpoints of the actors. These viewpoints are such that
there is clearly a student *real world*, created partly by circumstance and
partly by a deeper culture, to which the teacher is outsider. Concerning
the latter point, this teacher was eager to understand but found it

Table 4: Classroom conflict example

Teacher behaviour	Student behaviour
Follow step-by-step procedure: i) show slides of a dockyard while students take notes ii) students write a report	Disrupt, talk in own language
Teacher view	*Student view*
The course is 'communicative' in that it addresses student sociolinguistic and learning needs, provides authentic tasks and language data and allows student participation	Want to learn, but frustrated by the way in which the teacher's lesson plan defers the lesson pay-off. The slides are fascinating. Need to talk about them immediately
Students' lack of co-operativeness due to belligerence - 'the students don't care - talking about other things, don't want to learn'	Teacher's failure to appreciate this view due to dislike of students
Background	*Background*
Student reputation for belligerence on campus	Loss of traditional generalised respect for teachers
Local nervousness with regard to early events in the Iranian revolution	Confusing 'liberating' effect of the 'communicative' course which held teacher-student 'negotiation' as one of its overt principles
	Unsettling effect of events at home – especially with regard to traditional authority structures

extremely difficult to fathom what was going on in the students' real world. The research which succeeded in demystifying the situation, at least sufficiently to enable action to be taken, was carried out by a third party, employing an ethnographic approach – although it was not labelled as such at the time – the subject of the next chapter.

The outcome was arbitration which resulted in a change to a more open-ended methodology that allowed both students and teacher to negotiate what they wanted within the lesson. At the same time, to provide a greater feeling of security for the students, the course was given more structure (Holliday 1984:8–9). The examinations to which the students had been exposed were of a particularly esoteric kind (e.g. highly abstracted problem-solving tasks in which they were assessed on behavioural criteria which were not explained to them), and had not provided a structure of assessment they could recognise.

The 'communicative' régime of the course had insisted that the students should develop an understanding of what it was all about as part of a process competence at which the course aimed. Ironically, their revolution against the course, which their apparent belligerence in effect represented, followed by the change that they later negotiated, meant that the students had succeeded in acquiring sufficient process competence to be highly critical of what was being done to them, but in their *own* terms, rather than in the terms set by the course. Or, perhaps what this process competence really amounted to was a stage in learning the strange culture of the course, to the extent that the students would be able to see its inadequacies. The course had failed to learn *their* culture, despite claims that the 'communicative approach' acknowledges what 'learners bring to the situation' (see Breen and Candlin 1980:93); and it was only when research to investigate the nature of the conflict began, and the two cultures were presented to each party by the third party, that each side began to appreciate the sincerity of the other – the 'want to learn' and the 'want to teach', which had been hidden by anxieties and suspicions – and that the way was paved for reconciliation.

9.1.3 'Anglos' and Eskimos

I have already referred to Collier's (1979) study of the rhythms of movement within the classroom [3.1]. Although these were not English language classes, the research provides insights into the conflict between teachers' and students' lessons from which we can learn.

Different classrooms with 'Anglo' American and local Eskimo teachers are compared, both with primary level Eskimo pupils. The rhythm of movement of the Eskimo teachers blended with that of the young students – 'things took longer and the transitions between activities were less sudden and distinct'. However, the rhythm and movement of the Anglo teachers was very much in conflict. 'Anglo teachers generally ran their classes on a schedule that gave relatively short periods of time to each activity' (ibid.:43). Indeed, the conflict was severe:

> The fast pace and aggressive, linear style of movement of many teachers was deadly. In every case, the students responded with confused behaviour indicative of the failure of the communication process. In extreme examples, the students froze up; the harder the teachers tried, the worse it got.

> (Ibid.:48)

As with the British teacher and Iranian students above, the Anglo teachers were following agendas which related to their own image of how a lesson should be constructed and carried out, which might have been highly sophisticated and rationalised in terms of methodology, and appropriate to their own professional-academic culture, but were failing to learn the culture of the students.

This appropriateness to their own professional-academic culture at the classroom level might indeed reflect a defence mechanism against the uncertainty of the foreign culture of the students. This parallels the 'busy work' defence mechanism of expatriate staff faced with the uncertainty of local realities in English language projects [8.1.1]. Hence, the 'calculated procrastination' which this represents in project work can also be seen in classroom teaching.

Within the context of project work, Swales provides an example of the failure on the part of expatriate personnel to understand and adapt to the real world of students from the Khartoum University project to understand and adapt to the real world of local students. When the project introduced foreign teaching and examination styles, which bore little relationship to their previous experience, the students underwent 'educational shock' as well as 'culture shock' (1980:64). However, the expatriate teachers were unable to address this problem. The outcome was not so much the alienation of the students, but an overall failure of the project 'to convince the students that we were a serious department' (ibid.:66).

9.2   The myth of expatriate success

Because teachers inevitably fail to lesser or greater degrees to address the portion of the classroom culture that belongs to their students, preoccupied as they are with the technology of their perceptions of *their* lessons, much of the 'success' of these technologies is in effect mythical.

147

This can be seen expecially in the case of expatriate lecturers teaching Egyptian trainee teachers in the Ain Shams project.

9.2.1 Short-term effectiveness

During the course of the Ain Shams project I saw many examples of expatriate lecturers coping masterfully with difficult classroom conditions, displaying state-of-the-art BANA methodology in producing the learning group ideal (Holliday 1991a:324–36). Furthermore, an integration of language skills and methodology for the Egyptian trainee teachers, who are the students, was admirably achieved. A particular example was of students purposefully and successfully being given responsibility to do classroom tasks, un-monitored, in the class of about 50:

> The [expatriate] lecturer displays excellent classroom management. She ... successfully has the students working in highly organised groups, doing sophisticated group activities, in two rooms at the same time, during which time she withdraws except as a monitor and achieves decentralisation. ... The students have to (1) look at blackboard diagrams which indicate a division of labour within each group concerning what they have to do with an authentic extract from the textbook which they will use on teaching practice. They then (2) have to go into groups, men in one room, women in an adjacent room, and prepare sentence types (a different type for each member of the group), which they have to (3) write up on the blackboard and (4) peer teach, the women to the men in their room, and then the men to the women in their room. ... (5) Students have to copy *all* the sentence types into their teaching practice notebooks before leaving the room. ... Local students are not supposed to be used to writing in class at all, never mind finishing something completely in class.

(Observation notes)

(The descriptions of this and other lessons in Holliday 1991a are supported by photographs.) The final comment in the notes underlines the sense of achievement felt by the expatriates in completely changing indigenous classroom behaviour, away from collectionist lectures. To use Coleman's (1987) terms, the students had been converted from being the audience in a 'teaching spectacle', to being participants in a 'learning festival'. At least, this is the surface perception an observer might get; but how deeply 'successful' was this change?

Despite this apparent success, there is in fact a grave danger here of expatriate lecturers unconsciously disregarding local protocol because of their highly rationalised forms of classroom control. I have already referred to possible inappropriateness in the way in which expatriate lecturers constantly gave explicit classroom instructions [3.4.3]. One factor which has to be considered here is that the expatriate lecturers were immune to some of the conservative forces within the local classroom institution which influenced local lecturers. This point was actually made by some local lecturers who saw this immunity as an unfair advantage on the part of expatriate lecturers, enabling them to accept the project's 'unnatural' approach (Holliday 1986a:10). The notion of immunity to local cultural forces grows out of the observation that despite these insensitivities – albeit unconscious – expatriate lecturers *could*, through their rationalised approach, be effective in the short term. In other words, expatriate lecturers could get away with trampling over local protocols in the short time that they were in contact with them. This was all the more possible because of the resilience and hospitality of the local classroom culture [3.4.3–4]. This point is also made strongly by Hawkey and Nakornchai with regard to Thai students' apparent adaptation to foreign methodologies:

> We should beware, however, of over-simplified = equations between what is traditional and expected and what is difficult to accept because it is new. A foreign teacher in Thailand may well find that students revel in the opportunity to be creative and to work independently if they offered it, just *because* it is novel.

> (1980:73)

Consider another expatriate lecturer's class. He is grappling with his second week in a provincial university, with no previous experience of teaching either in a university or outside Britain:

> British school teacher, down-market clothes, books in ethnic bag (commented on by senior local lecturer colleagues) – a long way from the local PhD image. Refuses to allow janitor to carry things for him (a little embarrassing when he had a *lot* to carry, clearly couldn't manage elegantly, even with my help). Clearly a good teacher, but mechanical authority, constantly asking the students to be quiet. Small voice, therefore had to shout, but no more than necessary. Very cool despite having quite a hard time (janitor dropped 150 x 4 photocopies on the floor, so that he had to spend twenty minutes picking up and collating [without allowing the students to help], at the same time as myself, the head of department and another senior lecturer came in to watch with only one minute's warning). Sweating brow keeps turning into a ... smile – 'It's like a zoo in here; but they're so nice aren't they'. ... Eyes absolutely fixed to him. The lecturer uses his foreignness to show how he can make sense of the Arabic text (included to demonstrate similarities with English) despite his inability to 'read'.

> (Observation notes)

Although he did not conform to the local lecturer image with his casual appearance and willingness to carry things by himself, he was carried through by his students' fascination and hospitality, and by the novelty of his approach. Although his teaching style was *mechanical*, and his approach did stimulate some complaint on the part of the students regarding the 'unstructured' nature of the skills-based, discovery-oriented, collaborative approach this teacher employed, the students were:

> very careful to say that he was a marvellous teacher, especially for his keenness to turn up to every lecture for the full time. They were very concerned that their criticisms would not be taken as being against him.

(Observation notes)

Moreover:

> It was significant that ... [he] had very little time to sit and talk because he was teaching three classes in six hours, and was being conscientious enough to attend on time. ... [My two local co-observers] seemed very impressed with the pace he was able to keep up

(Observation notes)

I wish to suggest that, despite hard work and a genuine concern for the students, the 'success' of this lecturer's highly rationalised approach was largely a myth maintained by the novelty, likeability and the respect for being clearly devoted and hard-working afforded him by his local peers and students. This is reminiscent of the way in which the hospitable Egyptian lecturer gave her expatriate colleague information that would please him, rather than upsetting him with the reality of the situation [8.2.1]. In fact, the *apparent* acceptability of expatriate lecturers was in sharp conflict with private conversations I had with the local teaching staff, who seemed to find it hard to take seriously the expatriates' lack of seniority, lack of formal qualifications, lack of university experience, and lack of ability to appreciate and get on with local protocols, regard for the sensitivities of local colleagues and so on.

An interesting case is reported by Szulc-Kurpaska (1992). An evaluation of language and methodology courses for trainee teachers in Poland revealed dissatisfaction on the part of students with regard to the degree of informality practised by expatriate lecturers both in and out of the classroom. Despite the initial attractiveness of this behaviour, students were becoming confused and uneasy over the blurred definitions of teacher and student role. They wanted to know where they stood, and were happier with local lecturers who managed to blend friendliness with a traditional social distance. Szulc-Kurpaska found that although students could go to her home to discuss work, they knew where they stood because she insisted on being addressed by her title and family name and did not extend friendliness beyond the work relationship (personal communication). It took years of experience and knowledge of local protocols to be able to manage such a balance.

9.2.2 Dealing with student attitudes

One area where expatriate lecturers in Egyptian faculties of education could not be immune was in dealing with local student attitudes. The ease with which their intentions could be misconstrued by the students is illustrated in one case where:

> One expatriate lecturer who had tried the 'Vegetarian' text in a provincial faculty had complained that the students had accused him of trying to corrupt them with Western ideas – naturally, he suspected, they had identified him too much with the interactants on the recording.

(Observation notes)

This text was a conversation between two vegetarians about their diets. The expatriate lecturer believed that the students thought he was suggesting they should become vegetarians – a sufficiently eccentric concept within the local national culture to be considered 'Western'.

The problem was not so much that the text content might have been inappropriate to the so-called national culture, which would have been a dangerous overgeneralisation, but that the expatriate did not know sufficient about the real world of the students to understand their reactions, which seemed confusingly varied and unpredictable. On several occasions, texts in the project materials were criticised by local lecturers on the grounds of being potentially corrupting; but it was difficult to achieve consensus among local lecturers because of widely differing opinions.

Examples of outsiders to the student culture receiving confusing signals can be found in the following three cases. In an essay class which I was observing:

> I was asked to comment on the introduction of one male student. When he said that 'poor people' were an evil which had to be solved, I assumed that he wanted to say 'poverty' was an evil, and not 'poor people'. The more I tried to make my point that what *he* said sounded as though he wanted to eradicate the people rather than their condition, I began to see that he *did* intend the former, and that it was not a language problem that made what he said seem strange but a marked attitude difference that I had not expected. In the same way, when the class began to discuss

possibilities for the next essay assignment on the effects of divorce
on women, and a female student remarked that society inflicted
great suffering on divorced women, I assumed that she meant this in
a negative way, and that she was making a plea for women's
liberation. However, I soon got the impression that she, and all the
others, felt that the women's suffering was a *positive* thing because
it was a disincentive for women to get divorced in the first place.
Divorce was *bad*, and *women* should not do it, no matter what. The
progressive end of the class were the ones who accepted that
divorce was common in their society, albeit bad; the conservative
end would not accept this and said that women in their society did
not choose divorce except in rare, and presumably criminal, cases.

I was guilty of ... grave misinterpretations. I had assumed that
the statements by the students were eccentric because of language
difficulty rather than because their underlying attitudes were
different to my expectations. I did not have the experience of the
culture outside the classroom to accurately perceive what was going
on.

... [Their local lecturer] said that he too was sometimes shocked at
his students' attitudes.

(Observation notes)

This case illustrates how the attitudes of students are very different from
what one expects, and easily misinterpreted. My first reaction to this
event was that the local students were conservative in their attitudes.
However, this hypothesis was not substantiated in another essay class:

The students seemed outspoken, the [local] lecturer seemed to be
provoking them. The subject matter may have been considered
sensitive by an expatriate. There were several references to
manwoman relationships in co-ed schools. One woman said that if
women found out about men's mentality in co-ed schools they
would never marry them, and that normally women never found
out about men until marriage because in university they kept apart
and at work their roles were very separate. Several men said that
they had to be careful of what they said when they got to university
(after single-sex schools) because women were there. The lecturer
asked if he meant bad language and he giggled. Two women said
that they preferred single-sex schools because they could sit on the
floor and not care about anyone else. Several women said that at
university they did not communicate with men. Some said that men
kept away from them because they didn't like to admit that the
women were not inferior academically. Some men said that they
didn't know how to behave with women after single-sex schools
and that they felt that this was a lack. One man said that women
were superior academically and that he couldn't have known this
had he been to a single-sex school.

(Observation notes)

In both cases I felt that the issues being discussed with the local lecturer would have to be too sensitive for me as an outsider to handle, that these were areas in which I was out of my depth in an inscrutible student culture, within the context of the classroom where the expatriate lecturer cannot afford to be misconstrued.

In a third class, in which I was giving the guest lesson:

> At the end of the lecture some of the [students] ... asked how they could learn better English. The women said they watched the foreign serial (which came on the television every night), but found the present one *The Foundation* (a British TV business drama) difficult because everyone talked so fast. I agreed (in fact the acting does seem quite bad and everyone does seem to talk quite fast). One woman asked why I didn't seem to be like the people in *The Cedar Tree* (another British serial about an upper middle class family between the wars). She said that they seemed very conservative and cared too much about traditions. I thought it impressive that she had picked this up (although there *are* Arabic subtitles). I explained that it was set a long time ago and about a very upper class family, not dissimilar to old Egyptian films set in the 40s and 50s.

(Observation notes)

Later, in a discussion with one of the students' local lecturers:

> We talked about the interests of the students in the TV and radio. I mentioned the business of *The Cedar Tree* ... and asked if they listened to a particularly well-known radio local English language broadcaster and disc jockey. She said that although this broadcaster was very popular with the students in the capital, in the provinces she was considered too 'Western' and was not listened to. This didn't seem to fit with the students' talk of *The Cedar Tree* being too conservative.

(Observation notes)

These apparent contradictions in student attitude exemplify how far student attitudes are part of a complex deep action within the student culture, and that it is not helpful to explain these things away by referring to national cultural traits.

It was no less confusing to consult local lecturers on the question of text appropriacy. One local lecturer complained vehemently about a text in which there was a 'report on Saudi women's education with reference to a man at the gate keeping men out of the school' (Observation notes). She:

> said that the project's essay and reading comprehension course was
> completely inappropriate because of the content of this particular
> text. I had defended myself and the course by saying that several
> local colleagues had vetted all the texts during the selection process.
> The head of department had said that these people could not be
> relied upon. I had also had a similar reaction from another eminent
> member of an English department who had seen the reference to
> alcoholic pilots in one of the texts. ... [He] said that the texts in the
> course encouraged anti-Western feeling among students by showing
> a bad side of Western culture.
>
> (Observation notes)

It was hard to get consensus however. Another local colleague, who had
watched me use the text without difficulty, said that the text was ideal
(Observation notes); and other 'local colleagues who had helped select
the texts still maintain that the items mentioned are not inappropriate'
(Observation notes).

The issue of text appropriacy was not therefore just a matter of
inscrutable student culture, but of a wider complex of cultures within
the institution and perhaps beyond – a deep action involving perhaps
micro-political, political or religious conflicts beyond the sight of the
outsider.

9.2.3   Counterproductive tinkering

There were cases where expatriate lecturers did not get away with
their rationalised approach. I have already referred to Dr Anwar being
unimpressed at Beatrice's expertise in the language laboratory and
attitude towards the local system [7.2.1]. Despite (in my view), her
ability to make the language lab lessons work, in terms of the learning
group ideal, she was also missing important things about the culture of
her students and how they related to other personalities. She failed or
refused to understand that a lab technician was available to see students
to their places and help them operate the machinery (Holliday
1992a:224). Furthermore:

> The technician and the lab assistant also said that they thought
> Beatrice was unprofessional in the way in which she favoured
> particular groups of students who were nice to her and invited her
> to their homes at weekends, by giving them special classes, and that
> *these* students would be the ones she would give special sessions to
> in the lab. They felt that this was not a valid reason for wanting to
> break regulations by having a personal key or for asking them to
> work overtime – the only alternative.
>
> (Observation notes)

In this way, rationalisation brought to the situation by the expatriate lecturer, oriented as it was to the learning group ideal, failed to either perceive or appreciate other important features of relationships within the local educational environment. Using Widdowson's terms [4.5.1], the quality of the relationship between teacher and student might not be dependent simply on the quality of the learning *transaction* which is taking place, but also on the quality of a wider set of *interactions*. The social perceptions of teacher and student roles, not only by the teacher and students, but also by other involved actors (e.g. the lab technician), although appearing to have little to do with pedagogy, had also to be right. Returning to my insistence on referring to 'student' rather than 'learner' [1.3], a large part of Beatrice's problem, and of the alienation of many teachers from the culture of their students, was her apparent assumption that her students were there only to *learn*. She might have rationalised her methodology on an understanding of how 'learners' learn, but not on how *students* interact with their world and all the complex social factors surrounding why they are in the classroom.

9.3 The possibility of integration

There were, however, cases which proved that the intrusion of expatriate lecturers did not have to be counterproductive. Although Collier suggests that outsider Anglo teachers in Alaska were unable to work to the natural rhythms of their students, he did find an exception to this rule in the case of one teacher, Mr Scout, who 'broke away from the standard Anglo pattern' (1979:48):

> Many activities [in his class] ... were group activities in which he was only marginally involved. The pacing of these activities was largely in the hands of the children ... [and this teacher] is highly sensitive to non-verbal signals.
>
> (Ibid.:45)

Significantly, Mr Scout created a 'classroom environment ... in which it was possible for him to learn the movement patterns of the children and them to learn his' (ibid.:40). Collier further speculates that the ability of this teacher to integrate with the culture of the class might have been connected with the fact that he was from a marginal immigrant background (ibid.:33). One might assume that being an experienced marginal person by nature would permit the cultivation of an ability to observe and adapt to other cultures.

Such an ability was also found in the lessons of an expatriate lecturer, Dawoud, in an Egyptian faculty of education. In the first place, he too was able to create a learning environment which put activities in the hands of the students, enabling them to express and capitalise on their natural gregariousness and ability at small-group organisation [4.3.1], and which also gave scope for observation of their behaviour. Secondly, he was a member of an immigrant minority in the United States, and brought up in the Middle East in a culture cognate with the one in which the project was taking place:

> Dawoud was born in the Middle East, and has a PhD in linguistics ... [thus] his undergraduate educational background is culturally more similar to that of local lecturers and students than that of any of the other expatriate lecturers. ... Several students were carrying flowers. One of the men gives a flower to Dawoud, which he takes and keeps during part of the lesson – evidence of a profound integration with their culture – he holds it as they do.
>
> (Observation notes)

In another class:

> Dawoud showed his cultural integration by being very strict with late-comers, telling them they could not come in, but at the same time knowing when to make exceptions. He managed to make an interesting balance between theory and practice – by turning the practical language learning element of his class around the theory, as though using it as a carrier content.
>
> (Observation notes)

From my integrationist point of view, looking for signs of a skills-based, discovery-oriented, collaborative approach, I was concerned that he was being too didactic. However:

> One of Dawoud's arguments for what he was doing is that this was the way he had learnt while in English classes in his youth; and clearly he knew what was interesting and in demand for the students. I was also concerned that although he was masterful at managing learning in a very communicative way he was very worried about letting go and wanted to make every single step lecturer-controlled. He said that it would be very easy to lose the students' attention if he did not work in this way. He was also very concerned about maintaining his professorial status by presenting theory. He might be right about this. This might be where the interface between practice and theory for the local situation lies.
>
> (Observation notes)

Here Dawoud manages not only a degree of integration with the traditional aspects of the classroom culture, but also conforms to aspects of the local lecturer image implicit in the prevailing local professional-academic culture. The fact that he possesses a PhD in a theoretical subject helps to enable this; and taking on the expected lecturer image helps integration with the classroom culture as a whole. In addition, his lessons demonstrate not only how he is rationalising his classroom methodology, but also how this methodology can become culturally appropriate. Moreover, he sees that, to become culturally appropriate, the teaching methodology must be part of a wider *ethno*methodology.

There is therefore a capacity for some expatriate lecturers to move towards the traditional requirements of the local classroom culture if their rationalised approach is appropriately directed and expanded.

9.3.1   Exotic British students

All the cases of classroom conflict cited in this chapter have been of teachers and students from different national cultures. In previous chapters I have argued that it is misleading to think of problems in English language education only in terms of national cultural differences. Conflicts between people of the same national culture, but of different professional-academic cultures, have been described with reference to the Keele University integrated studies curriculum project in Chapter 7. Within the classroom, the history of secondary school teaching in Britain is rife with discipline problems which can be traced to teachers' inability to learn and understand the culture of their students. This inability may possibly but not necessarily be affected by overlays of differences in social class or generation. One of my own recent teaching experiences was particularly revealing in this respect.

I had to take three classes in applied linguistics for another department, on a diploma course for British primary school teachers. The course was already established, and the students had already formed an established culture by the time I arrived. Although they were of the same nationality, similar social class, and generally of the same generation, although we were all 'teachers' of one type or another, I felt as much an outsider to their culture as I would to the cultures of students in other-nationality classes. What was particularly interesting was that, despite sharing the same English language, without any marked differences in accent or dialect, I found their mode of communication almost as mysterious as that of the Egyptian classes already cited [3.4.1]. I could understand every word they said, but when it came to monitoring group activities, I was as much at a loss about when it was appropriate, in *their* cultural terms, to make moves to put them on task or to join in their discussion. As with the Egyptian class in which students were apparently *off*-task, but later showed that

157

they were very much in touch with the lesson [3.3], I found it difficult, with these British students, to determine whether or not they were *on-task*. There was bantering and laughter between them which represented protocols governing formality and informality which I found difficult to understand. For survival, I had to observe and learn as much as I could about their culture before proceeding.

9.4   The parameters for local teacher success

A strong implication of the argument in this chapter is that conflict between student and teacher agendas is increased where the teacher is an expatriate and thus all the more foreign to the culture of the students. The cases of the Anglo teacher and Dawoud, who go some way in succeeding to bridge the gap [9.3], are unusual.

A major advantage which local teachers have is that they have in the past been students like their own students. Dalbouni (1992) makes explicit use of this type of inside knowledge in her research on the social context of writing instruction at Damascus University; and one of Dawoud's advantages is that he was brought up as a student in a national culture cognate with that of his Egyptian students.

However, it would be dangerous to be too romantic about the innate ability of local teachers to know their students so well that conflicts are reduced. I have shown that, within the same national culture, students still have very different cultures from their teachers. Indeed, the student group in each class will have a different culture, as the culture of the classroom is different to some degree in each case. The teacher's role, whatever her or his background might be, by its nature will give the teacher a different construction on events within the classroom from those of her or his students: their agendas are essentially different; and the communication they have with each other is essentially limited. An interesting anecdote from a newly initiated teacher trainer in South Africa illustrates this point. He remembered the pleas of his British tutors, while studying in Britain, for the class to let them know how they felt about course content – to make some comment about the issues that were being raised. He now had the same difficulty with his own compatriots while carrying out training programmes in South Africa: it was very hard for him to find out how they felt about things.

Whoever the teacher is, therefore, classroom methodologies need to be developed to increase the teacher's ability to study the culture of her or his students, and to allow students the ability to express their needs to the teacher. Such a methodology will be discussed in Chapter 10.

9.5   Summary

a)   Classroom events incorporate not one lesson but a range of lessons, one for the teacher and one each for the students. These are determined by the agendas of each party.

b)   There is an inevitable conflict between the teacher's and students' lessons created by the teacher's difficulty in understanding the students' agenda. This is especially the case where the teacher has a plan or a methodology to which the students are expected to conform.

c)   The conflict is further exacerbated by the teacher being an outsider to the culture of the students.

d)   The apparent success of expatriate teachers, helped by the fact that they are native speakers of English and possess what is presumed to be a more advanced, BANA technology, may indeed be a myth if they are not behaving appropriately to their students' culture.

e)   In cases where expatriate teachers are more successful, they have built into their methodology opportunities for observing and learning about the culture of their students.

f)   The problem lies not only with teachers who belong to a different national culture from their students, however. Teachers are inevitably of a different culture from their students, no matter what their nationalities. All teachers need to develop methodologies in which they are able to learn and react to their students' cultures.

9.6   Questions for discussion

1   Is it true that conflict between teacher and students is inevitable? What are your reasons for thinking this?

2   Is the classroom really such a dangerous place?
    Think of examples of you or colleagues getting cut on the coral reef.

3   Think of examples of difficulties you have had in understanding the culture of your students.
    Think of examples from when you were a student of your teachers finding difficulty in understanding your student culture.
    What type of cultural differences were these difficulties caused by?

4   If you are or have been a student, what are the ingredients and origins of your student culture?

Part C Appropriate methodology design

10   A culture-sensitive approach

In the previous two parts of the book I have described how English language education needs to be looked at from the point of view of macro social forces within the educational environment if the micro aspects of classroom interaction are to be fully understood. I have argued that there is a problem of technology transfer between a dominant culture within the profession, which has its roots in Britain, Australasia and North America (BANA), and a very different, widely spread culture within state institutions in the rest of the world (TESEP). Again, to be fully understood, this transfer has to be seen in terms of the social *raisons d'être* of these different groups – as the product of an ethnocentric professional-academic dynamism.

In Part B, I have explored the types of conflict which emerge from this technology transfer, both in the classroom and in English language education projects. I have developed the notion that there is a deep element to what happens between people in the classroom, consisting of psycho-social, informal and micro-political factors influenced by the wider social environment, and that only by attending to these can appropriate methodologies be devised.

In Part C I intend to argue and then demonstrate how an appropriate methodology needs to be culture-sensitive if it is to address the problems raised in Part B, and that culture-sensitivity needs to be realised through ethnographic action research. This will enable both BANA and TESEP teachers, as well as curriculum developers and project managers to address these problems and to achieve a more workable, more knowledgeable, less unequal relationship with each other in this extremely important field of English language education.

160

In this chapter I shall describe the parameters for a culture-sensitive approach; in Chapter 11 I shall exemplify the process for appropriate classroom methodology development, and, in Chapter 12 I shall discuss appropriate curriculum and project design and implementation.

10.1 Learning about the classroom

The force of my argument has been that achieving an appropriate methodology depends on learning what happens between people in the classroom. I have also implied that this learning process is very much a situation-specific matter as the relationships between people will be different in different educational environments. Although it is possible to generalise about some social principles – e.g. that classroom cultures are influenced by cultures outside the classroom, or that there is likely to be conflict between teacher and student agendas – it is not possible to generalise about the precise nature of a particular classroom culture, or the other cultures which influence it, or the form which this influence takes. This means that the process of learning about these things is not a matter just for theorists and university researchers – not something that teachers can get from the literature. It is something that has to be worked through in the situation in which teaching and learning have to take place.

This has several implications. First, the process of learning what happens between people in a particular classroom should be largely in the hands of the teacher, just as the act of teaching is in the hands of the teacher. The teacher is there, in the prime position for seeing what is going on and knowing about the relevant backgrounds of the parties concerned. However, other parties, such as curriculum developers, materials or textbook writers, heads of departments etc., may also be involved in making decisions about the nature of classroom methodology. These might in some cases have more relevant knowledge than the teacher about cultures surrounding the classroom. Nevertheless, they also need to base their decisions upon what happens between people within the classroom, and should enter into a learning process in collaboration with the teacher. Another possibility is that teachers could collaborate with each other to share the learning process. (Throughout the rest of this chapter I shall refer to the teacher as the main party, although everything which I say would apply equally well to other parties collaborating with the teacher.) Secondly, to be appropriate, a methodology must be sensitive to the prevailing cultures surrounding any given classroom.

An appropriate methodology, which must by nature be culture-sensitive, therefore has two major components: a teaching methodology and a process of learning about the classroom. It is the data produced by the latter which makes the former culture-sensitive and therefore appropriate. In effect, learning about the classroom is an essential aspect of finding out how to teach. This relationship is illustrated in Figure 7.

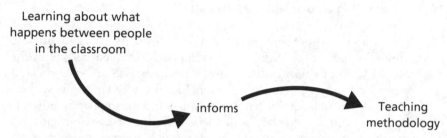

Learning about what happens between people in the classroom

informs

Teaching methodology

Figure 7 Components of a culture-sensitive methodology

Before dealing with the parameters of the teaching methodology, I shall first explain how the process of learning about the classroom involves both action research and ethnography.

10.1.1 *Ethnographic action research*

The process of learning about the classroom needs to involve research. This does not have to be the formal research one has to undertake in doing a PhD or MA thesis: it can be carried out at an informal level in such a way as to be accessible to all practitioners. The notion of teacher as informal researcher is already common in general education (see Stenhouse 1975; Ruddock and Hopkins 1985), where it has become embodied in *action research* (e.g. McNiff 1988). It is also becoming more popular in English language education (e.g. Nunan 1990; Allwright 1992) and Allwright and Bailey (1991) present the notion of 'exploratory teaching' as an even less formal means whereby teachers can carry out classroom research in such a way that it is fully integrated with their day-to-day work.

Basically, teachers do action research when they investigate aspects of their classrooms in an organised manner. The aim is usually to solve the classroom problem of how best to teach. The important thing is *action*, not research for the sake of research. The procedures which are used are the ones which fit the situation and which can most easily be applied within the course of everyday work. The purpose is for the teacher to learn what she or he needs to know about the classroom in order to develop appropriate methodologies.

However, I have demonstrated throughout that learning about the classroom necessitates looking deep at the social forces which influence student and teacher behaviour, and that this is by no means a straightforward matter. I wish to argue that to carry out this depth of social investigation successfully, action research needs to be ethnographic in approach.

Ethnography is particularly important because it is a branch of anthropology which studies the behaviour of groups of people (e.g. Spradley 1980:3; Murphy 1986:6; Hammersley and Atkinson 1983:2; Long 1983:18). As such it has developed research methodologies for investigating the teacher, student, classroom and institution cultures which make up the social context. Figure 8 shows how learning about the classroom has two essential parts – a *doing* part which is action research, and the employment of a research method which is ethnography. In general educational studies there has been a marked increase in the application of ethnography since the early 1970s, for both classroom research and wider curriculum and institutional applications (e.g. Lutz 1981:51; Spindler 1982:1–2; Delamont and Hamilton 1984:6,17; Sharp 1986:120).

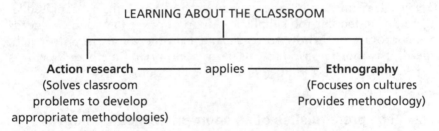

LEARNING ABOUT THE CLASSROOM

Action research ———— applies ———— **Ethnography**
(Solves classroom (Focuses on cultures
problems to develop Provides methodology)
appropriate methodologies)

Figure 8 Components of learning about the classroom

Ethnography has been applied within English language education in recent years mostly in two areas – classroom research (e.g. van Lier 1988, 1990) and the analysis of student sociolinguistic needs (e.g. Swales 1985:11; Chaudron 1988:47). However, much of the emphasis has been on what is *said* either in the classroom or a target language situation. I have already referred to Breen's suggestion that concentrating on spoken discourse alone does not address deeper cultural factors [2.1]. The research I recommend concerns a wider view of *behaviour*, which looks at what people do as well as what they say, and tries at least to scratch the surface of what Breen refers to as the coral reef of the classroom to get at the myriad life forms beneath.

I shall provide specific examples of how ethnographic action research can be carried out in Chapter 11.

10.1.2 An ongoing spiral

I do not wish to give the impression that teaching methodology is a *tabula rasa* until sufficient has been learnt about the classroom to give it form. The relationship between learning and teaching, as depicted in Figure 8, is essentially a dialogue. The teacher cannot wait until the process of learning about the classroom is finished before deciding how the teaching ought to be done. Indeed, action research by nature sets up a spiral relationship between research and action (McNiff 1988), of which the relationship in Figure 8 is only the first bend. To be realistic, this spiral has to begin with teaching; during the process of teaching the teacher learns about the classroom; this learning gives rise to an adaptation of the teaching methodology; the learning process continues to evaluate the changes to the teaching methodology, which in turn requires learning about the changed classroom situation which it brings about, and so on. The process never finishes and indeed should be a permanent, ongoing feature of the teaching methodology itself.

It is therefore important that the teaching methodology has a form to begin with – but a form which is essentially adaptable, and has a built-in propensity for learning about the classroom. The relationship between learning about the classroom and teaching as depicted in Figure 8 is in fact far too simplistic. An appropriate methodology needs to incorporate both how to teach and learning about how to teach. Indeed, it is too simplistic to call it an 'appropriate' methodology: it is in effect always a *becoming-appropriate* methodology.

10.2 The prerequisites of an appropriate methodology

To recap, therefore, it is possible to list some of the prerequisites of a becoming-appropriate English language teaching methodology as follows.

a) It should have a built-in facility for the teacher to reflect upon and learn about the social dimension of the classroom, and to continue learning.

b) It should therefore incorporate ongoing ethnographic action research.

c) It should be able to put into practice what has been learnt and should therefore be continually adaptable to whatever social situation emerges.

This list tells us what a potentially appropriate methodology must be able to do, to make it appropriate, and therefore culture-sensitive.

10.3 A communicative approach?

For several reasons I wish to place the beginning methodology within the sphere of potentials provided by the existing, communicative approach to English language education.

10.3.1 The futility of creating new myths

It is certainly true that the communicative approach has been so much interpreted, popularised and misunderstood as to have lost currency in recent years. It has retained the divisive role of being seen as a basic measure of modernity or progressiveness within the profession. Especially, but not only, members of the TESEP group often state their abilities, aspirations or resistance to new-fangledness through their attitudes to the communicative approach.

Nevertheless, I wish to argue that much of the bad press which the communicative approach has attracted is due to myths which have been built around it, especially in the TESEP side of the profession, such as 'communicative equals oral work', 'communicative equals group work' or 'communicative equals getting rid of the teacher as a major focus in the classroom' (see for example Tomlinson 1990:27). These are myths which I wish to dispose of. The forms which the communicative approach presents, rather than being restricted to group activities in which oral communication is practised, are very varied and can incorporate among other things the cognitive teaching of grammar.

The reader may think that by not only continuing to use, but also by developing the term 'communicative', I am perpetuating those myths. This is a real danger. However, creating new terms would only create new myths. Therefore, rather than suggest culture-sensitivity as a new approach with all sorts of new possibilities for myth making, I wish to argue that the communicative approach already contains potentials for culture-sensitivity which can be enhanced and developed to suit any social situation surrounding any TESEP classroom.

10.3.2 A developmental rather than a serial picture

Indeed, development is the key. Teachers, especially of the TESEP community, while trying to make sense of the battery of 'methods and approaches' that have accumulated since the 1960s, often talk of choosing a method to suit their own situation, or of being eclectic in the use of a cocktail of different methods where this is appropriate. This frame of reference is both influenced by and influences the way in which methodology is often taught as a theoretical subject in colleges of education – where methods are expressed as discrete entitities in serial.

This *serial* view is limiting in that it fails to appreciate the *developmental* nature of methodology. The serial view sees communicative language teaching as just another method to be considered amongst all the others. A developmental view, on the other hand, sees the advent of communicative language teaching as an important breakthrough in which the language learner is no longer an empty receptacle who must learn a new language by means of a new set of stimulus-response behaviour traits, but an intelligent, problem-solving person, with an existing communicative competence in a first, or perhaps second or third language. Once this breakthrough is appreciated, it is no longer possible to go back to choose an earlier method if communicative language teaching does not appeal. What is needed is a further development of the communicative approach.

For those readers who dislike communicative language teaching, who think it is essentially inappropriate to the majority of TESEP situations, I wish to argue that the communicative 'method' which they find unworkable is a limited version of what a communicative approach can be, which is supported by the very serial notion of methodology I wish to discredit.

10.3.3 *Addressing rather than avoiding ethnocentricity*

The argument I have presented throughout puts the communicative approach, at first sight, at the very centre of BANA technology. The model of classroom behaviour which the approach aims to achieve seems to be the learning group ideal [4.1] in which a skills-based, discovery-oriented, collaborative learning environment is seen as optimum. In this sense, a communicative approach looks most certainly to be central to the tenets of integrationism [5.2.2].

However, again I wish to argue that it is a particularly narrow view of communicative language teaching which fits this description. If a communicative approach is essentially adaptable, and has the capacity for a wide variety of learning modes, as well as the propensity to be truly culture-sensitive, within it the TESEP teacher should be able to grow an appropriate technology which fits her or his own situation. Of course, it cannot be denied that the communicative approach originates within the BANA camp. The very writing of this book, by a BANA practitioner, is an essentially integrationist act. My own professional-academic ethnocentricity cannot be avoided. The force of what I have to say is rather that professional-academic ethnocentricity is a fact of life, as the descriptions throughout have demonstrated, but that this ethnocentricity has to be understood and addressed so that members of both BANA and TESEP groups can see the implications of what they are doing and therefore better solve the problem of how to be appropriate. I have said that cultures naturally change and influence each other [2.6]: there is no need to be unrealistically partisan and sit only in one camp or the other.

10.4 The elements of a communicative approach

I shall begin with an analysis of the communicative approach, for the purpose of pointing out those areas which either are already or have the potential of being culture-sensitive, and of isolating and discarding the myths which limit the approach to use within BANA situations.

One of the sources of confusion is that the word 'communicative' refers to a whole range of aspects of the approach: teaching communicative competence, teaching language as communication, having students communicate with each other and with the teacher, and ensuring that the methodology communicates with the student and other concerned parties. Figure 9 attempts to map out these aspects.

10.4.1 Teaching communicative competence

The left-hand area of the figure shows the features of the approach's aim to teach communicative competence (bubble 1). In a sense this aim represents the birth of the approach – the revolutionary realisation of the nature of communication and communicative competence, which sees the language learner as somebody who already possesses certain competences, either in the mother or other tongues, or in the experience already gained of the target language, which must be capitalised and built upon (bubble 2). The student therefore brings to the classroom experience and knowledge which is of value to the learning process (bubble 4). The student can thus no longer be seen as an empty vessel which a teacher can arbitrarily fill with new knowledge or behaviour, as was the tendency in earlier grammar-translation and direct methods, and structural or audio-lingual approaches. I wish to assert that this aspect of the approach cannot be rejected. This is not to say, however, that grammar, structures and patterns of language behaviour can no longer be taught, but that they will be taught more liberally, with more respect for the individual within the communicative approach.

Although what we know about communicative competence defines how we treat the student and language in the teaching-learning process, it does not prescribe the content of the lesson. This content might concern any of the language skills and any aspect of the language system such as lexis, phonology, structure or grammar. However, I

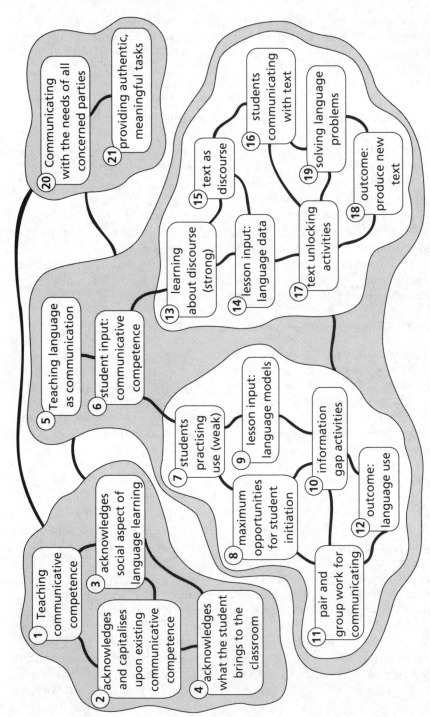

Figure 9 Being communicative

would agree with Widdowson 1992:334 that advances in linguistics make it no longer possible to view grammar as anything but a 'communicative resource'. We can no longer teach it as a purely mathematical system without pragmatic meaning. This does not mean that grammar-translation cannot be communicative. I can imagine a situation where a student is studying ancient Greek, through vocabulary learning and translation, but also communicatively, simply because the teacher has succeeded in making the content – let us say the Trojan War – so real that the language can achieve pragmatic meaning. The choice of content can depend on many things, from the needs, interests, expectations and experience of the student, to the requirements of other parties who hold stakes in what happens in the classroom (bubble 20). The latter will be discussed later [10.4.5]. I would therefore insist that there is nothing concerning the teaching of communicative competence *per se* which cannot be negotiated in accordance with the requirements of any TESEP social situation.

There are however narrow interpretations which do prescribe content. Here are the false prophets who create myths about the approach. Swan (1985) makes a very valid point when he criticises communicative courses which interpret teaching communicative competence as exhaustive instruction on how to carry out and interpret speech acts as though the students had no previous knowledge of how language works. I would suggest that such courses are *not* communicative in that they ignore the existing competence which the student brings to the classroom (bubbles 2 and 4).

10.4.2 *Teaching language as communication*

The middle area of Figure 9 depicts features of the communicative approach connected with teaching language as communication (bubble 5). There are two major areas within this area which correspond to what have become known in the literature as the *weak* and *strong* versions of the approach (e.g. Howatt 1984:279, 286–7). The descriptions of these two versions represent ideal typologies: in reality, they are intermingled and complement each other in many courses, although there is often a tendency in one direction or the other. Although they both take the communicative competence of the student as a basic input (bubble 6), the focus and lesson inputs (bubbles 9 and 14) are different. My purpose in distinguishing between them is to show that it is the weak version which contains elements which are *not* adaptable to any social situation, and which are therefore not culture-sensitive, but that, in opposition to common belief, the strong version can be almost entirely culture-sensitive.

10.4.3 Weak version

This version focuses on the practice of language use (bubble 7), with the basic lesson input as presentation of language models (bubble 9). These models can be, and often are, in the form of 'structures', albeit within a context provided by a 'function', 'notion' or 'topic', followed by a 'communicative activity' to practise the language item. This means that teachers who have been used to the lesson structure of presentation, practice and production in the earlier 'structural approach' find this version, on the surface, easier to understand and adopt than the more mysterious strong version. I have already referred to Allwright's (1982) illustration of how various aspects of the weak version can be bolted on to more traditional lesson types piecemeal [6.3].

However, although the weak version produces much of the classroom methodology in current use and has been successful in many ways, some of its elements are restricted in application to classrooms of a relatively specific type within BANA English language education. It works admirably in classes of up to fifteen students, with the right acoustics and furnishings, where the students are mainly adults who come to class with the specific purpose of learning English and are prepared to conform to the learning group ideal.

Although the focus on practising language use involves reading, writing and listening in what often amounts to very integrated learning tasks, much emphasis is, according to the common myth, placed on oral work [10.3.1]. Student oral participation is at a premium; and student talking time is an important measurement of a 'good lesson' (bubble 8). This point is illustrated in Nunan's (1987) pinpointing of the quality of student oral initiation as a crucial criterion for communicative teaching. This oral requirement is of course very difficult to manage in classes of over a certain size, especially where acoustics are very bad (cf. Holliday 1991a:367–70). Furthermore, this prescription on the type of classroom interaction is not likely to be acceptable in some social situations where the local protocols of teacher-student relations do not allow for it. The consternation among BANA teachers when Japanese students prefer not to initiate in the classroom, in the mode recommended by the learning group ideal, shows how easily this prescription on the nature of the 'communicative classroom' can be upset (Bandi and Shibata 1992).

The premium put on maximum student initiation, the principle that practising communicating will facilitate the learning of conversational strategy, and that mastery of meaning will be enhanced through negotiation (e.g. Long and Porter 1985), plus acknowledgement of the social dimension of language learning (bubble 3), sets a strong requirement for group and pair work (bubble 11). The classic device for engineering this is the 'information gap' (bubble 10), where students are given different information and need to get information from each other in order to fill the gap. Apart from the doubtfulness of the need to teach conversational strategy to people who already have this competence in their own language (Swan 1985), a common pedagogic criticism of collaborative work for the purpose of language practice, often put forward by TESEP teachers, is that during pair and group work students are very much dependent on each other for further language input, and are therefore likely to learn each other's mistakes. Although the point is often made that the weak approach makes an unfair assumption that students somehow 'already know English in some sense' (Howatt 1984:286), this criticism might not be wholly sound. However, in large classes, where teachers are not able to provide the controlled monitoring recommended in the learning group ideal, they are not able to provide the piecemeal language input needed to keep the learning process afloat. At the same time, because collaborative work is for the purpose of practice, it is essential that the students use English. To sum up, this demands a methodological régime which many teachers with large, monolingual classes find particularly hard to maintain.

10.4.4 *Strong version*

In the strong version, rather than language practice, the focus is on learning about how language works in discourse (bubble 13) as an input to new language production (bubble 18). The lesson input is language data (bubble 14) in the form of text (bubble 15) rather than language models. The student carries out tasks which are carefully designed to pose language problems (bubble 19), and which, when solved, will help the student to unlock the text (bubble 17). Here the student works out how the text is constructed and how it operates – the language rules which it incorporates – making and adjusting hypotheses very much as children do when they acquire language naturally. The task design is all-important here – to present the right kind of data and clues to help speed up this process. Central to this is the fact that the student can input the strategic aspect of her or his existing communicative competence. (See Savignon's 1983 and Canale's 1983 accounts of the components of communicative competence.) Whereas in the weak version the term 'communicative' relates more to students communicating with the teacher and with each other to practise the language forms which have been presented, in the strong version, 'communicative' relates more to the way in which the the student communicates with the text. By this, I mean that the student puts her or himself in the position of the receiver of the text, *in communication* with the producer of the text – reconstructing the language strategies used.

Here, there is less dependency on the traditional presentation, practice, production lesson format. This, and a possible liberation from an initial presentation of structures, makes this approach more within the task-based paradigm as described by Breen (1987b:161). This is perhaps a reason why the strong version is less popular than the weak version. As it is further from earlier approaches, teachers who have been brought up on structures find it more difficult to understand and digest. However, there is a wide variety of forms which the lesson can take, which allows for the adaptability referred to above [10.4.1]. The lesson input (the language data in the form of text) could be a piece of writing or a recording of speech. It is also, inevitably, whatever the teacher writes on the board, writes on student work, or says, whatever is written in textbooks or material, and whatever students say or write. It could also be grammar rules, as will be demonstrated in the example in the next chapter [11.2]. Where there is collaborative work, it is not for the purpose of students communicating with each other, but for the purpose of their helping each other to solve language problems. Therefore, students working in groups or pairs do not *have* to speak English all the time, making the approach much more manageable in monolingual large classes. They can speak in their mother tongue *about* the text. Indeed, it would be unrealistic to expect them to tackle the text analysis required by language problems in a foreign language. (For a discussion on the potentials of using the mother tongue in the classroom see Harbord 1992 and Atkinson 1987. See also my reference [6.2.4] to Phillipson's assertion that exclusive use of mother tongue in the classroom is a linguistic imperialist fallacy.) Because the aim is not to practise language forms, group and pair work does not need to be monitored closely. Indeed, much of the activity process might not be intelligible to a passing teacher.

Furthermore, the activities do not have to be carried out in groups or pairs. As long as individual students are communicating with rich text and producing useful hypotheses about the language, what they are doing is communicative. The output, the producing of new text, could certainly be the speaking or writing of something which displays the language forms taken from the first text. It could also be a report of the activity outcome. More important, it will be whatever the student thinks as a result of the activity, in the form of hypotheses. This might well be the subject of discussion with peers during the activity, but might be internalised and not produce any new external language until much later, possibly outside the classroom.

10.4.5 *Communicating with the needs of all concerned parties*

The area depicted on the right of Figure 9 is a less well-known aspect of the communicative approach (bubble 20). However, it is the core of the approach's potential for being culture-sensitive. Here, the focus of 'communicative' is communication not between students or between student and text, but between the teacher and the wider social orientation of the student. The outcome is a provision that the tasks carried out in the classroom are authentic and meaningful to the *real world* of the recipients of the methodology. Indeed, this notion of a communicative approach transcends language teaching. The term 'communicative', as in 'communicative social research', describes exploratory, interpretive procedures through which researchers attempt to get in touch with the real worlds of their subjects, sometimes through the use of ethnography (Grotjahn 1987:56–7). Research findings are seen to have communicative validity if they correspond with the viewpoints of informants (ibid.:67). Thus, the notion of communicative fits very well the notion of the teacher or curriculum developer carrying out ethnographic action research to arrive at an appropriate methodology [10.2.2].

The communicative approach should therefore already have a built-in facility for being culture-sensitive, and thus make the ideal becoming-appropriate methodology. An important function of this facility is to put the micro business of classroom teaching in touch with the macro social context with which I am concerned in this book. Hutchinson and Waters describe this aspect in the following way:

> We take the term 'communicative' to mean 'geared to the competence and expectations of those participating in the learning process'. In other words, a communicative approach is based on negotiation between all the parties concerned.
>
> (1984:108)

Candlin and Breen (1979:176) state the scope of 'all the parties concerned' as being not only the students in the classroom, but 'socio-culturally selected educational aims and ideas. Language education is to serve the individual within the context of the state and its needs'. Thus, the interests of all the relevant stake-holders in the host culture complex are considered [10.4.1]. The orientations of their *real worlds* with all their cultural behaviours and allegiances have already been considered in the design and implementation of a communicative curriculum, its texts, tasks and activities. Indeed, I would argue very strongly that any courses or materials which do not do this are essentially *not* communicative. Of course, by 'address' I mean 'try very hard to account for'; and this does not necessarily mean 'solve the problem of'. Once the intention is there, we are well on the way.

It is unfortunate, however, that Candlin and Breen neither here (1979) nor in their more seminal work (Breen and Candlin 1980) develop what they mean by this, or *how* such culture-sensitivity might be implemented; and the notion does not seem to have been developed as much as it could have been in subsequent literature. As late as 1991, Savignon notes that it is important to consider the 'broader cultural environment', including differences in learning style, national contexts and teacher perceptions, but that up to date it has been neglected. She suggests that a reason for this neglect might be the influence of the language acquisition research paradigm, 'with an emphasis on sentence-level grammatical features, [which] has served to bolster a structural focus, obscuring pragmatic and sociolinguistic issues' (1991:267). Reminiscent of my discussion of BANA professional growth [5.3.2], she suggests that:

> Researchers eager to establish SLA as a worthy field of enquiry turned their attention to more narrow, quantitative studies of the acquisition of morphosyntactic features.

> (Ibid.:271)

Now, however, she continues to argue, seemingly aware of many of the conflicts I have described in Part B, that it is becoming increasingly clear that 'specially trained ethnographers have come to replace the native speakers who were once the authorities of how language worked' (ibid.:273). There is a need for:

> teamwork of shared perspectives and insights. Researchers need to look to teachers to define researchable questions. ... Appropriate methods and materials will result only from the co-operation of all concerned.

> (Ibid.:274)

It is the *how*, which has hitherto been neglected, that I suggest ethnographic action research is able to fulfil. However, before continuing to describe the how further, there is another myth belonging to the communicative approach which I wish to discuss – the myth of learner-centredness.

10.5   The myth of learner-centredness

Communicative language teachers often claim to be 'learner-centred'. The implication, that attention which has been lacking in earlier approaches and methods is being given to the rights and integrity of the student, certainly fits the principles of the communicative revolution which acknowledges what the student brings to the classroom [10.4.1]. However, I feel that the notion of learner-centredness also carries with it a set of perhaps naive ideas which belong essentially to the BANA professional-academic culture and which inhibit technology transfer to TESEP situations. Learner-centredness has provided a banner for the moral superiority of the communicative approach and the BANA teacher group which supports it. Hutchinson and Waters suggest that learner-centredness ignores the wider social context of what happens in the classroom:

> We feel the term 'learner-centred' misleading, since it implies that the learner is the sole focus of the learning process. Education, is, by its very nature, a compromise between the individual and society. Thus, we would reject the view that a communicative approach is learner-centred: rather, it is *learning*-centred, and this implies taking into account the needs and expectations of all the parties involved.

(1984:108)

I feel that the term 'learner-centred' is especially vague, and has been largely responsible for the failures in making the communicative approach work outside the BANA classroom. The notion states an intention which is admirable, but does not say sufficient about the discipline or rigour with which it will be carried out. The purpose of teaching should be to enable learning to take place. This tells us what we have to do in the classroom, and exactly to what our technology must be directed. That the learner is the recipient of this learning goes without saying, but this does not tell us what to do.

Another side to this is that 'learner-centred' to some degree pre-supposes that we know a great deal about the learner. I would say, following my discussion so far, that we know very little about 'the learner' and the diverse cultures which she or he represents. One of the sins of the weak version of the communicative approach is that it assumes a stereotypical 'learner' who conforms to the BANA learning group ideal, and that it does not do enough to find ways of finding out about the vast array of 'learners' in real situations with whom it really has to deal. I have already made the point that the use of 'learner' is unsatisfactory as a label for members of the classroom society because it implies that the only purpose for being in the classroom is to learn [1.3]. I hope that it has become evident from my discussion throughout that this is not the case. The 'learner' is not really a person in a real social setting, but rather an almost robotic entity. One of my diploma students recently suggested that the methodologies sold in the BANA literature give the impression that the teacher is also a robot – someone who must go through all sorts of almost inhuman contortions to satisfy the régime of learner-centredness. To help methodologies relate to the realities of TESEP classrooms it is important to know not about 'learners' but about *pupils* and *students* in real classroom settings, where there may be many other influences on language learning from the society both outside and within the classroom.

Another outcome of the vagueness of learner-centredness is the lack of direction it gives to TESEP teachers who have been used to more didactic teaching modes. It seems a common perception among such teachers that what makes the communicative approach different is that students are set free, both in that they can follow their own agendas in group work, and in that they can produce their own language. This notion immediately threatens the order of many established classroom cultures by implying that the status of the teacher, often involving her or his ability to control language input and output, is threatened by allowing a language output which is controlled by the students. The teacher is not given anything to replace this loss of status, especially if she or he feels less than competent to field the uncontrolled language output. Mastery of various techniques in group work organisation, error correction, student monitoring etc. which come with the communicative package is not sufficient to provide a consolidated teacher status. Just what is the teacher master of under these circumstances? What carries many BANA teachers through, often regardless of their professional competence, is that they are native speakers, and therefore have a natural, unassailable status (see Pociecha 1992; Harbord 1992).

TESEP teachers derive much of their often considerable status, and indeed power, from their position in their education system and their society. They also have power from their considerable experience and knowledge of their teaching situation. It has been feared that learner-centredness erodes this power. A South African teacher reported, in a seminar I recently attended, that 'learner-centredness has been quite misinterpreted. ... We felt guilty to stand up in front of the class'.

10.5.1 *A disciplined learning-centredness*

A learn*ing*-centred approach, on the other hand, which acknowledges the social context of education (Hutchinson and Waters 1984) gives power back to the TESEP teacher. It puts such worries about the communicative approach as group work clearly in their place. The aim is to enable students to learn. Group work and free language production are possible means to this end, amongst a potential of many more. The stronger version of the communicative approach described in [10.4.4] makes this variety possible and can be informed entirely by communicative, ethnographic action research, which will decide whether or not such procedures as group work are appropriate to a specific classroom setting. The essence of masterful classroom practice is thus the engineering of appropriate classroom activity for the purpose of bringing learning about. This requires considerable masterfulness on the part of the teacher, which will give rise to considerable status.

The implication of the weak version of the communicative approach has been that students have to be able to work in groups with a prescribed degree of teacher monitoring. Although 'learner-centred', high teacher presence is an essential within the BANA régime – almost as though the students cannot be trusted to be free by themselves. In a learning-centred approach, teacher monitoring is one factor that has to be decided about in the light of what strategy will bring learning about. If the class is large – 300, never mind over fifteen – close student monitoring will not be possible. On the other hand, perhaps the students do not need this monitoring; or perhaps tasks can be designed in such a way that self-monitoring is built in.

10.6   Becoming-appropriate classroom methodology

I have argued in the second part of this chapter that the existing communicative approach, with changes in focus to enhance its more culture-sensitive features, and reduce its less culture-sensitive features, is sufficient for the role of the initial becoming-appropriate methodology in the ethnographic action research cycle. However, I wish to stress again that this becoming-methodology is only a beginning, and that whatever further development the methodology takes in its ongoing route to greater appropriacy, this form will always be ephemeral. The course of the action research spiral will continue: not only will the methodology continue to develop, the nature of the culture of the classroom will also develop as the other influence in the dialogue. In the last analysis, it is what the teacher does as action researcher and implementer that will make the act of learning more or less successful. What the student is asked to do will depend on the outcome of the action research spiral. Figure 10 shows this spiral. It is expressed as a cycle; but each new turn of the cycle will be at a higher level of understanding and development.

10.6.1 The text of the classroom

In much the same way as the student in the strong communicative classroom investigates discourse as text, unlocks it to find how it works, and then produces her or his own text on the basis of what has been

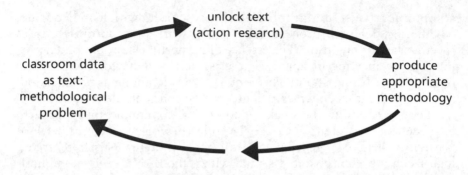

Figure 10 *Action research cycle*

found out [10.4.4], the teacher investigates the text of the classroom, which presents a methodological problem. This text consists of all the elements of the culture of the classroom so far described – the realities of student groups, and the constructions imposed upon these realities by the teacher's own presence as representative of teacher groups, and the realities of the host institution, the wider educational environment and the society beyond. All these, plus what is known to be important in how people learn languages, and in the language itself, present the enormous complexity of the text of the classroom.

The teacher must attempt to unlock the text of the classroom, to discover its rules, to enable the formulation of hypotheses for action. As language students tap their natural resources of communicative competence, the teacher taps her or his natural social ability to learn new cultures. As argued in Chapter 9, the position of the teacher is seen as that of an outsider newcomer to the culture of the classroom, who has to learn how best to deal with this culture. This learning is rather like that which a newcomer to any social situation needs to embark upon. In many ways in modern complex society we are all outsiders to some cultural group we wish to join, for example as colleagues in a new job or the members of a new club, or with which we need to deal, such as car mechanics or people who sell computers. In Parsons' words, we are all 'objects of one another' (1951:93).

The process by which the teacher unlocks the text is the action research, and the focus and methodology are essentially ethnographic [10.1.1].

10.7 Summary

a) A culture-sensitive approach to English language education is needed if the question of appropriate methodologies is to be fully addressed. The type of learning about the classroom which this requires can be best carried out by ethnographic action research.

b) A reflective approach to English language education can contribute to culture-sensitivity; but it needs to be driven by what is to be reflected upon. It needs to address the macro social influences on classroom behaviour described in previous chapters.

c) The action research spiral needs to begin with a becoming-appropriate methodology which can be developed in dialogue with the findings of the research.

d) The communicative approach to English language teaching already contains the basic elements of an initial methodology with which to begin the action research spiral. In its stronger version it contains the necessary adaptability. Furthermore, being communicative should also involve intepretive research into the needs of the wider social environment.

e) The weak version of the communicative approach, which prescribes the nature of classroom activities, is unable to be appropriate to TESEP needs. Its learner-centredness prescribes forms of democratic student collaboration which might not be appropriate to all classroom, professional-academic and student cultures.

f) In the same way as students unlock language texts to formulate hypotheses about language, the teacher needs to unlock the text of the classroom to formulate hypotheses about appropriate methodologies.

10.8 Questions for discussion

1   How far can ethnographic action research be a natural part of teaching?
    How far is ethnographic action research just common sense?
    Think of instances when you solved classroom problems by watching, learning about what was going on, and then changing direction slightly as a result of this learning.

2   Think of examples, from your own teaching style, which are non-communicative according to the weak version, but communicative according to the strong version.

3   Is it possible to be teacher-centred and communicative at the same time?

4   In what ways can learner-centredness be 'bogus co-authorship'?

11   Solving classroom problems

In this chapter I shall look at some examples of how ethnographic action research can be used by the teacher to solve classroom problems, and come closer to an appropriate methodology. It is not my intention to define specific steps or rules for procedure. There has been too much dogma and prescription in the past; and to be truly culture-sensitive is to develop steps and procedures for each situation according to its needs. What I am looking for is a variety of possibilities, all of which follow a broad culture-sensitive approach as described briefly in Chapter 10. The examples provided in this chapter, and in the next one on curriculum and project design, are ones from my own work or with which I am familiar, which follow this broad approach. Each one highlights different aspects of the approach, which I shall discuss in some depth.

11.1   A methodological attitude

Several examples of classroom problems have already been cited in Chapter 9. The first was the conflict between a British teacher and Iranian students. The researcher was a third party who observed the class over a period of time and then arbitrated a solution which enabled the overall aims of the course to be realised in a methodology which suited the cultural needs of the students [9.1.2]. The second was the expatriate Mr Scout, who had unusually succeeded in teaching in a way which seemed to blend with the culture of local Eskimo children. He had taken care to observe the culture of his pupils and had thus learnt how to teach appropriately [9.3]. The third example was the expatriate Dawoud, who had succeeded, again unusually, in blending his highly rationalised, BANA methodology with the more traditional, TESEP expectations of his students. Significant in his approach, too, was the creation of opportunities to observe his students at work [9.3].

It is important to note that only in the first of these examples was ethnographic action research carried out explicitly. Indeed, in the first case, although I was carrying out explicit research, I was not conscious of the term 'action research'. The adoption of terminologies is often only the naming of things that have been going on all the time. Although Mr Scout and Dawoud were clearly actively solving the problem of how to communicate with their students' real worlds, they were not consciously following defined action research steps. What they did, which I think is essential to a culture-sensitive approach, was to subjugate their methodology to what they observed – to their interpretation of the text of the classroom. It is not just the steps, nor the research instruments that might be used (cf. Nunan 1990), that make action research work, but the interpretive attitude of the teacher.

11.1.1 *Being interpretive*

At the end of Chapter 1 I suggest that an important attribute of research into the cultures surrounding what happens in the classroom is that it should be able to *interpret* events in and around the classroom. This involves being as non-prescriptive as possible, so as to allow meaning to emerge from the situation being studied. This interpretive approach is inherent in modern ethnography. Ethnographers try hard to interpret what they find, not to impose preconceptions and models from outside the situation.

The difference between an interpretive and a more traditional *normative* approach, which tends to begin with theories about how reality ought to be, and with a definite plan as to which research instruments are going to be used, might in effect be very slight. It is perhaps more a difference of attitude, as expressed in Table 5. Ironically, anthropology, the parent discipline to ethnography, has not always used an interpretive approach. It had a strong functionalist tradition until the 1960s, and was seen by some to be instrumental in maintaining a colonialist status quo until that time (Asad 1973:9–19; M. Kennedy 1987:1–3). Hempel (1968:190–2) argues that the functionalist approaches of Malinowski and Radcliffe-Brown involve the imposition of *a priori* 'laws' about the structuring of societies. It was thus normative in its approach in that it started with the assumption that Western society was complex and that non-Western societies were simple and in need of modernisation [2.6, 3.5.3]. Further discussion of the differences between normative and interpretive approaches, with specific reference to English language education, can be found in van Lier (1988:xiv, 55), Breen (1986:151), Sevigny (1981:75), Chaudron (1988:47), Long (1983:16,18).

Table 5: Research attitudes

Normative	Interpretive
Conviction about what it is important to look for.	Conviction that what it is important to look for will emerge.
Confidence in research instruments.	Confidence in an ability to devise research procedures to fit the situation as it is revealed.
Reality is not so problematic if the research instruments are adequate.	Reality contains mysteries to which the researcher must submit and can do no more than interpret.
Steps:	**Steps:**
1 Decide what to look for.	1 Decide the subject is interesting.
2 Devise instruments for description (e.g. categories, definitions, checklists).	2 Explore the subject.
	3 Decide what to focus on.
3 Approach the subject.	4 Devise instruments for description.

Spradley illustrates this difference when he explains how:

> In most forms of social science research, the questions asked by the researcher tend to come from *outside* the cultural scene. ... Ethnography begins with a different assumption ... as far as possible, *both questions and answers must be discovered in the social situation being studied.*
>
> (1980:32)

Thus, Spradley asserts that the research does not begin until *after* entering the social situation. At this point, a research cycle commences: a) a generalised asking of ethnographic questions, moving on in stages to b) the collection of data, which progresses gradually from broad, to focused, to selective observation, c) the making of an ethnographic record and d) analysis of the data (ibid.:29). Thus 'the development of the research problem is rarely completed before fieldwork begins' (Hammersley and Atkinson 1983:40). This methodological procedure, despite conflicts between various schools within ethnography, is commonly followed by other ethnographers (Hammersley and Atkinson 1983; Strauss *et al.* 1969; Gearing and Epstein 1982; Wilcox 1982).

Collier (1979), McCarty (1975), de Brigard (1975:23) and Temaner and Quinn (1975:54) discuss the same basic procedure in ethnographic filming. McCarty describes his progress through 'culture shock and language familiarity', 'tripod methodology' and finally 'close portraiture of everyday life'. Temaner and Quinn describe how in *cinéma vérité*, domumentary filming is 'organized by a "found structure" ... and not by the imposed structure of an artificial story or a ... theory'.

In the case of pure ethnography, the ethnography is then *written* after the research is complete, but may often initiate a continuance of the research cycle (Spradley 1980:29). However, for practising teachers who use ethnography for action research, this writing up is not necessary unless they wish to publish their findings.

A word of caution is necessary in this respect. It is important to distinguish between *applied* and *pure* ethnography. In the latter ethnographers describe human groups for the purpose of scientific advancement. The English language educator is not embarking on 'pure' research. In Figure 7, action research applies ethnography for its own purposes of solving classroom problems [10.1, 10.1.1]. The specific steps of the research cycle recommended by Spradley are for use by pure ethnographers who are carrying out full-scale ethnographic research. This is sometimes possible in ethnographic action research, but not always.

In my own research regarding the British teacher and Iranian students [9.1.2], I was able to begin observing classes with a wide focus and then gradually narrow the focus as I began to see what the crucial issues were. This was possible because it was a longitudinal study of one class; and the same would be possible for a teacher carrying out action research with her or his own class. However, Mr Scout and Dawoud [9.3] might not have been so conscious of these steps: their research would be determined by the life of their involvement with a particular class, and not by a series of steps. Furthermore, many teachers will already have experience of certain types of student culture and will not be entering virgin territory.

As an aside, I wish to make a link between an interpretive approach to looking at the classroom and what has become known as a *reflective* approach to teacher education (Wallace 1991), where trainees reflect upon their classroom experience to help them find what are in effect appropriate methodologies. Perhaps what I am arguing for is a reflective approach to teaching as a whole, a central message being that learning about the classroom is not just something that trainees have to do, but that certain expatriate teachers have to learn about classrooms with 'foreign' cultural orientations, and that local teachers also have to continue to learn about classrooms to which in a sense they never cease to be outsiders. A reflective approach should not therefore be confined to teacher education, but should be seen as applicable to all aspects of education, especially where appropriate methodologies are the focus of attention. Similarly, the rejection of an 'applied science model' of teacher education where theorists inform trainees of state of the art practice (ibid.:9) should extend to the rejection of an applied science model of education generally. The hegemony of a so-called superior BANA technology, which I am arguing against, is in effect such an applied science model.

11.2   Teaching grammar in a large class

The interpretive nature of ethnographic action research can be seen in the way in which Azer, an Egyptian lecturer, approached the problem of teaching grammar to undergraduate trainee teachers at Tanta University in Egypt, with classes of more than 350. He began with a dissatisfaction with current classroom practice:

> I wish to maintain that straight lecturing on grammar, which seems to be the norm, cannot be hoped to achieve any course objectives with students whose English is already poor and who hardly ever engage in any sort of communication. ... How will they communicate with their pupils when they themselves have communication problems?

> (1990:33)

In this case, the first step was to consult literature on communicative language teaching. This included a recommendation for a methodology to teach reading in large classes in which students would work in groups on texts accompanied by worksheets in a 'distance learning' mode (Zikri 1990; Holliday 1993). This was compared with his experience of his students and the classroom culture to which they belonged. Thus far, his procedure was similar to that of Shamim (in process) who also began with a dissatsifaction with current methods and looked to literature on communicative teaching for help [6.4.1]. However, Azer seems to have found this literature more useful than Shamim. His decision to adopt a communicative approach was influenced by the culture-sensitive strong version referred to in [10.3.3]:

> A communicative curriculum is what I recommend for the teaching of grammar to large classes. I believe that [Candlin and Breen's (1979)] ... three questions are still valid. These are: what is to be learned, how is the learning to be undertaken and achieved; and to what extent is the former appropriate and the latter effective? In other words, a CC determines some specified purposes and the methodology adopted will see to it that those purposes are achieved.

> (Azer 1990:36)

An example of the tasks which he produced is as follows:

Topic: The Passive

I wrote the following sentences on the blackboard:
a. The landlord was robbed (by his butler).
b. The rioters were persuaded to leave (by the police).
c. I was given this watch as a birthday present (by my parents).
d. He was considered a genius (by his teachers).
e. The painting has already been sold (by ?).
f. The boy got hurt on his way back from school.

Instructions:

1 Study the sentences on the blackboard. They are all of the type you know as 'passive'.
2 Think of the actives of which these passives are transforms.
3 Write down in points how the passive sentences are constructed from their active counterparts.
4 Check your findings against the reference grammar book you have with you.
(Ibid.:45)

His report on the methodology as follows shows how the task was carried out in a manner which he felt appropriate to the classroom conditions and the expectations of his students:

> In handling the tasks ... I used the blackboard for setting the task, giving short statements, or questions, about what to look for. After setting the task for the students I never interfered in their negotiations as I believe that such interference can easily undermine their sense of independence while allowing other groups to expect similar help.

> (Ibid.:41)

An interpretive approach to solving the problem is evident in the way in which Azer bases the action he takes on observation of the culture of the classroom. He sees the text of the classroom unfolding before him as he watches the way in which his students behave in reaction to his new approach, step by step. It is significant that the rationale he presents in his paper consists largely of descriptions of student behaviour at different stages.

Handouts were not practical with such large numbers, as was the normal, received, BANA method for organising and monitoring group work. Anyway, the students did not expect such attention. As I have already mentioned, Egyptian students in large classes were used to looking after themselves, co-operating with each other and taking responsibility for their learning [4.3.1–2].

185

Azer expected some resistance, as his students were unused to an inductive, discovery-oriented approach [4.3.3]:

> It must not be ignored that Egyptian students of grammar are used to 'rules' and these are often given to them first, sometimes supplemented by examples with no effort whatsoever on their part to infer these rules or at least try to. It therefore took the students some time to get used to doing this themselves in grammar. First of all, they did not know what to look for, even with clearly set tasks and instructions they were apprehensive of their ability to 'perform a task' rather than do an exercise.

(Ibid.)

Eventually they got used to the idea, despite having to trade quantity for participation:

> From what I have observed, the motivation it provided the students, the novelty of their being asked to observe and infer rules rather than getting them first, the enthusiasm with which they negotiated tasks, tolerated differences and deliberated the selection of a speaker [to report back] were all indicative of a favourable reception. ... It is true that in terms of quantity, large classes following a communicative methodology are bound to cover fewer topics than in traditional lecturing, but there is the added bonus that 'all' students participated in the process and many of them had the chance to 'talk' and 'discuss', some for perhaps the first time, grammatical rules which they have been trained to regard as unquestionable.

(Ibid.:48)

Azer was himself surprised at how far his students would conform to certain aspects of the tasks:

> I asked the students to bring with them to class their reference grammars for immediate reference after the completion of the task. ... I had been reluctant ... fearing that some may straight away refer to the book rather than perform the task first and consult the reference later. I must admit that my fears were ungrounded as the students were so much involved in their task, which they seemed to like because of the challenge it represented to their ability, that they had no time to refer to their reference grammars.

(Ibid.:44)

Although he is not part of the student culture, and stands very much on the margin, watching, his special insider knowledge, as an Egyptian lecturer, is revealed in one of the ways in which he expects the task to be maintained. 'I also counted on serious students' reporting of any cases of students not doing what they were told to do in the instructions' (ibid.:44).

This might be where his approach was more successful than that of Shamim (in process). Whereas she seems to have seen a certain type of democratic student collaboration as part and parcel of her new communicative methodology, and its 'failure' as a failure in the methodology, Azer, in his stronger, more culture-sensitive communicative approach, was prepared to adapt the mode of student collaboration according to what he observed as consonant with their culture. (Shamim acknowledges that her attempt at a new methodology was weakened by the fact that she imported it [6.4.1].) What he asked his students to do in groups was carefully structured and still ruled by the teacher authority to which they were used, even though he was unable to monitor their work carefully. Interestingly, Shamim found the more 'distant' she was to her students, the more inclined they were to do what she wanted [6.4.1].

This balance between collaboration and teacher authority, to suit the culture of the students, is seen in the way Dawoud maintained his 'professorial status' while creating a relatively decentralised classroom [9.3], and also in Szulc-Kurpaska's approach [9.2.1]. It was essential as well to blend collaboration with firm insurances of security:

> Despite initial resistance, the following strategy has proved effective in introducing the inductive approach in the teaching of grammar to undergraduate students with large classes of 150 students: 1) Assure the students that arriving at the rule is guaranteed, that if they cannot arrive at the rule by themselves, the lecturer will provide the rule at the end of the lesson. State that the lesson aim is to arrive at the rule. 2) Assure the students that they are not totally alone. If there are diversions, the lecturer is there to rescue the lesson and set the right course. 3) Design activities so carefully that the students are almost left with no choice but to arrive at the rule.
>
> This strategy has instilled so much confidence in a significant number of students that they have also taken well to collaborative learning.
>
> (Barjesteh and Holliday 1990:91)

Point 3 was included to reassure very worried students faced with a very new, alien classroom methodology. Students always need time to get used (acculturate) to new things, after which the adventure might begin.

11.2.1 Activities as formative evaluation

The classroom activities which Azer set his students thus doubled as formative evaluation. As in the classes of Mr Scout and Dawoud [9.3], the group activities enabled Azer to observe his students and thus gauge their reaction to the methodology and aspects of their progress. Indeed, being unable to take an interactive monitoring role in group work, because of the size of the class, enforced a situation in which the teacher interferes less and can be more conscious of the effect of her or his lesson agenda. It was not only the number of students that prevented interactive monitoring in most of the classes seen in Egyptian faculties of education, but the fact that the furniture and general overcrowding did not enable teachers to move between the students, and, in some cases, there was not even access to the sides of the classroom (Holliday 1991a: 225–6). The diagrams of classroom composition [3.4.5] represent literally wall-to-wall students. Azer reports:

> Nothing is easier or more satisfying to the lecturer than an active class in which learner participation is a true parameter whereby to evaluate their performance. ... The teacher may observe how much involved the students are in their task by the noise level in the room, the ease with which groups are formed and the tone of conversation among the students. ... The students too can see for themselves how they are doing, and this in itself can give them tangible incentive to carry on and improve their performance.

> (1990:46)

This might only be a rough guide to student assessment; but it is more effective than what can be done in a lecture situation with a class of many hundreds where assessment depends on the marking of minimal pieces of written work (see Dalbouni 1992). Indeed:

> The evidence ... is essentially qualitative. Quantitative data would be very difficult to collect given the size of the classes ... and the lack of control over attendance. When the recommended methodology has been tried for some time, the students can be given a questionnaire to gauge their reaction to it.

> (Azer 1990:34)

This evaluation of student behaviour is an essential aspect of the teacher unlocking the text of the classroom; and in a culture-sensitive methodology, classroom activities should have a dual role, both transactional (using Widdowson's terminology here [4.5.1]) and evaluative. This can be seen in Figure 11. Within the evaluative role, two different types of things can be observed, both the nature of the interaction – the student and hence the classroom culture – and the quality of the transaction – the degree to which learning is taking place.

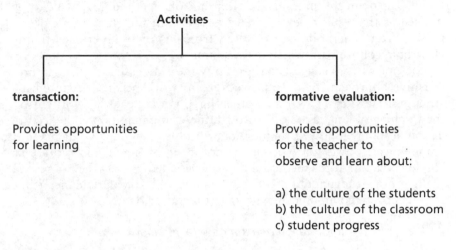

Figure 11 *Roles of classroom activities*

Classroom activities should thus be designed with the formative evaluation role in mind. This was the case in the 'distance learning' methodology designed by Zikri and myself (Zikri 1990; Holliday 1993) [11.2]. The students were given written instructions which asked them to do certain things with a reading text. This required them to cross-refer between the instructions and the text. They were asked to solve a problem in the text, take notes on what they found out and prepare to report to the whole class. The whole thing was to be carried out in groups. From the beginning, the lecturer would not interfere, and would certainly not help the students by reading out or explaining the instructions.

The lecturer's job was to observe before doing anything else. If the students quickly got on task, if no significant numbers were seen to be looking into space or confused, if they began to point at parts of the reading text, to start taking notes, and then, eventually, when asked, to be able to stand up and, pointing to the bit of the text to which they were referring, report to the whole class, this would mean that they had been able to 1) read the instructions, 2) cross-refer, 3) read the text sufficiently well to find what they needed to find (skimming, scanning or whatever), 4) organise their findings, 5) plan an oral explanation, and (at least one of them) make an oral explanation. If the lecturer observed that a significant number of students appeared to be having difficulty, she or he would then intervene.

This is, of course, only one possible way to proceed. I by no means wish to present this 'distance learning' approach as a method to be used by all. The point I wish to make is that it is one methodology which was devised as the result of extensive observation of the classroom culture, just as Azer's methodology resulted from his own experience of the classroom culture with which he was familiar.

I do not wish to suggest that group work is an essential of a culture-sensitive approach. Azer employed group work because it suited his situation. Hawkey (1986) and other Egyptian colleagues, working on the teaching of language skills through literature, maintained the lecture as initial input, followed by individual problem solving. What made it communicative was not whether or not group work or pair work was employed, but that the methodology was designed to meet the interactive reality of the student culture – to find a culturally appropriate means for the students to communicate with target language data.

11.2.2 A local interpretation of expatriate technology

A further point I wish to make about Azer's methodology is that it constituted a local interpretation, from a TESEP point of view, of a piece of BANA technology. Azer's paper is written at the end of over ten years of expatriate project involvement in Egyptian faculties of education in the Ain Shams University project to which I referred in Chapter 7. A mountain of materials, reports and curriculum recommendations had accumulated over this period with relatively modest sustainable effect (see Zikri 1992). Azer was able to consult this material, but instead of trying to adopt any of the courses and methodologies which it contained, he set it alongside the other literature he consulted and his own experience of his own classroom situation. This total experience he converted into his own approach. For example, there were reports on classroom conditions and locally oriented recommendations. These, although written by expatriates and perhaps lacking true local knowledge, might, on the one hand, have made Azer feel less isolated, and, on the other hand, given him something against which to set and focus his local experience. Outsider views thus become useful as commodities to be looked at and reacted to. However, similar data from local sources is also needed. Azer's own paper is one such source.

11.3 Unfinished, thick descriptions

In Chapter 1 I suggest that research for the purpose of finding appropriate classroom methodologies need not be 'finished' [1.5]. Findings need to be sufficient to take the teacher, curriculum developer or project manager on to the next stage, where the effect of ensuing action will be the test. I have already made the point that action research is never 'finished' [10.1.4]. Ethnography is also always 'unfinished' in the sense that the mysteries of what is being studied can never be fully unravelled (cf. Delamont and Hamilton 1984:19). Azer's description of student behaviour [11.2] only scratches the surface, but he finds out sufficient to get him on to the next stage. There is an important holism implicit in this view of reality:

> Education is a complex practical activity. Any effort to reduce that complexity to singularistic perspectives tends to distort the reality, and may mislead those who seek to understand the reality. ... It is this belief that is behind a holistic approach.

> (MacDonald 1971:167)

This aspect of ethnography is characterised by 'thick description', which relies on the breadth of holistic description for validation, rather than on the replication of individual phenomena in experimental conditions (Lutz 1981:57). (For discussion of the holistic nature of ethnography see Long 1983:22; van Lier 1988:56; Lim 1987; Delamont and Hamilton 1984:18–19; MacDonald 1971:167.) This breadth of description is very important because it allows teachers freedom to develop their own common-sense perceptions of the social world, unrestricted by the confines of specialist knowledge:

> 'Thick description' ensures that whilst ... [we] are *informed* by specialist pre-occupations [i.e. applied linguistics and pedagogy], the pedagogical shaping of those activities is not necessarily *determined* by specialist pre-occupations.

> (Swales 1985:13–14)

Stenhouse suggests that ethnography is similar to history in that they both use the language of the subjects under study, whereas social scientists are interested in more generalised social and political behaviour (1985a:13). Like history, 'the virtue of ethnography is verisimilitude as opposed to abstracted analysis' (1985c:53). This, he argues, is in contrast to more quantitative research, which 'is concerned to establish by calculation the relationship between a sample studied and a target population', and where 'abstraction starves judgement' (ibid.). An example of this difference is as follows:

> The contrast is between the breakdown of questionnaire responses
> of 472 married women respondents who have had affairs with men
> other than their husbands and the novel, *Madame Bovary*. The
> novel relies heavily on that appeal to judgement which is appraisal
> of credibility in the light of the reader's experience. You cannot
> base much appeal to judgement on the statistics of survey.

(Stenhouse 1985b:31)

Stenhouse presents a critique of the over-application of what he terms
the 'psychostatistical' research paradigm to educational issues in which
he says that:

> Predictions of statistical levels of confidence are applicable only
> when the same treatment must be given throughout the entire
> population. This condition does not apply in education. It is the
> teacher's task to differentiate treatments. It is in part the recognition
> of this problem that accounts for the spread of interest in
> naturalistic or ethnographic styles of educational research.

(1985a:12)

He describes how the psycho-statistical paradigm is derived from
agriculture which presents easily quantifiable values. In education on
the other hand, 'the criterion of yield is difficult to establish'
(ibid.:20–1); and 'meaningful action is not quantifiable' (ibid.:22).

11.4 The question of expertise

Although I have treated ethnographic action research in the classroom
as a very open-ended affair, which might change its form substantially
in different classroom situations, there *is* need for a highly professional
approach. Lutz (1981:51) warns against ethnography being
'bastardized' by educators who are not ethnographers and who 'twist
the tool to fit their data'. Similar worry is expressed by Spindler
(1982:1–2) and Atkinson and Delamont (1986:240–1) over the
'obscurity of purpose' often found in school ethnography.

Lutz insists that as a minimum, educational ethnographers should be
trained in basic ethnographic research methods, have a grounding in the
principles of anthropology, and have actually done some ethnographic
work (1981:57). This clearly has implications for in- and pre-service
teacher training, full discussion of which is beyond the scope of this
book. However, it might be that current movements towards classroom
problem solving, with an emphasis on using classroom experience,
through observation and teaching practice, as data (Richards and

Nunan 1990; Wallace 1991) might be the beginning of what is required. One area that needs more attention is the development of teachers' faculties of observation, with perhaps less attention to the mastery of prescribed methodology.

However, the current movements I am thinking of here are firmly within BANA territory. In TESEP faculties of education the pressure for prescription and theory, to support the established professional-academic cultures of language, linguistics and literature, might be too strong to allow integrative social science into the syllabus in a formal way. Changes of attitude, which are partially hindered by influence of prescribed methods from the BANA sector, need to be grown from within. Szulc-Kurpaska (1992) reports how in her methodology classes in Poland she asks her students to keep diaries of their personal observations while on teaching practice. This type of interpretive work, with a little more rigour, is in fact virtually ethnographic action research.

11.5 Summary

The following principles of ethnographic action research and a culture-sensitive approach can be derived from the examples cited:

a) It is important to interpret the real world of the students from the inside, rather than to impose categories of investigation from outside.

b) Gradual focusing, from an initial open-ended approach to the subject, is recommended. However, this might not be possible in some classroom situations; and often teachers will already have experience of their students' culture.

c) Classroom activities should be developed in dialogue with observation of student behaviour.

d) Group work is useful in that it allows the teacher opportunities to observe how the students are taking to it. However, group work is not an essential of a culture-sensitive approach, or of a strong communicative approach; and where group work is employed it can be blended with strong teacher authority.

e) 'Communicativeness' is therefore based on creating culturally appropriate means for students to communicate with language data, rather than with each other, in oral practice.

f) Formative evaluation should be built into classroom activities. As well as providing opportunities for learning, activities should also provide opportunities for the teacher to observe student progress and reaction to the activity design.

g)   Ethnographic action research is never 'finished' and can achieve no
more than 'thick description'. Findings need only be sufficient to
formulate hypotheses which can inform the next stage of action.

h)   As much training as possible in interpretive observation must be
built into existing training courses.

11.6   Questions for discussion

1   What have you observed about your students during teaching
which has enabled you to improve your methodology?
How far do you think this observation did or could have
constituted ethnography?

2   Are there any principles in what Azer did with his university class
of 450 intermediate students which could be applied to either a
primary or secondary school class of 50 students?

3   What forms of formative evaluation do you carry out naturally
during the course of your teaching?
What sort of activities could you develop to enable you to do more
formative evaluation?

4   Think of examples of appropriate methodologies having been
developed independently of BANA influence.
How were they developed?

12　Curriculum and project design

In Chapter 11 I provided some examples of how a culture-sensitive approach to English language education, using ethnographic action research, could help teachers to solve their classroom problems and move closer to appropriate methodologies. However, throughout this book I have demonstrated that the whole range of activities in English language education, from syllabus design to project management, needs to be led by a deeper understanding of the social forces acting on the classroom, which a culture-sensitive approach hopes to provide. In this chapter I shall look at this wider canvas.

As in Chapters 7 and 8 I shall focus once again on English language projects because they encapsulate many of the problems encountered. However, I use the term project loosely to be anything from a small-scale, staged process of curriculum development within one course, department or institution, to large-scale national projects.

12.1　The project and the curriculum

As shown in Figure 5 [7.1], the purpose of an English language project is to introduce curriculum change within a host institution or set of institutions. I am taking 'curriculum' in a wide sense to encompass a range of possible project aims from improving language teaching curricula to teacher education, teacher trainer education and staff development curricula. It also involves various types of curricular element such as syllabuses, materials and textbooks. Figure 12 shows how the project introduces a new or changed curriculum within the host institution. If it is going to work, and to avoid *tissue rejection* [8.3], the changed curriculum must belong to the host institution and connect absolutely with the *real world* of all the parties within it – with the social deep action that pervades all its relationships. As I have argued in Chapter 8, it is this avoidance of tissue rejection which presents projects with the greatest difficulty.

The figure shows that there are two methodologies involved here.

There is the methodology inherent in the curriculum and that of the project itself. The methodology of the curriculum involves the way in which the whole educational process is perceived and implemented – from the design and arrangement of subjects, syllabuses and materials, to the classroom teaching methodology. The methodology of the project, on the other hand, involves its strategies for action and the strategies for managing this action. Elsewhere (Holliday 1992b:412) I refer to Bowers' (1986) discussion of the ways in which these two methodologies, which he calls *M-1* and *M-2*, are similar in that they both need to be appropriate to the host institution, and indeed, to the wider educational environment.

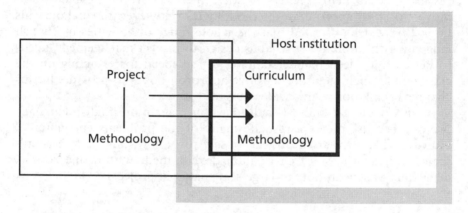

Figure 12 *The relationship between projects, curricula and host institutions*

However, there also needs to be a process of learning about the host institution which provides information as to how the methodologies of both the project and the curriculum can be appropriate. This process of learning about the host institution requires a third methodology – *M-3*. The relationship between these three methodologies is expressed in Figure 13. Just as M-1 and M-2 both have to be appropriate to the host institution, so does M-3: the research methodology, for learning about the host institution, has to be appropriate to what it is investigating. This process of learning about the host institution for the project manager or curriculum developer is very similar to the process of learning about the classroom carried out by the teacher [10.1]. The difference is one of focus. Much of the data will be the same, as what happens between people in both the classroom and the host institution is interconnected, and learning about both spheres requires an understanding of the wider host educational environment [2.7].

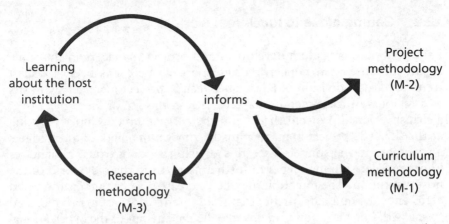

Figure 13 *Three methodologies*

As with learning about the classroom, learning about the host institution is concerned with the interaction of cultures – with different teacher groups within the profession, influenced by their different professional-academic cultures. Hence, Figure 14 sees ethnographic action research as central to learning about the host institution, just as it is central for the teacher to learn about the classroom [10.1.2]. As with learning about the classroom, the interpretive nature of the ethnography will help its research methodology to achieve its own appropriacy by building itself on the exigencies of the situation [11.1.1].

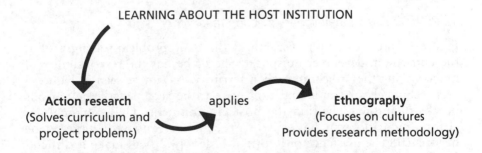

Figure 14 *Components of learning about the host institution*

12.2   Getting close to local 'real worlds'

I speak about curriculum developers and project managers in the same breath because their concerns often merge. There has been a recent trend towards a division of labour between a 'project manager' who sits in a regional office sometimes far away from the site of the project (e.g. a British Council project officer) and the curriculum developer working at the site. The project manager thus becomes a manager of aid budgets and expatriate personnel. I see this division as dangerous, as it takes important decision making even further away from the real world of the host institution. The intention may be to create greater organisation and efficiency by making project management more centralised and specialised. In reality, however, this may be the attempt of the hyperrational funding agency to avoid confrontation with the problematic real world of the host institution with which it cannot cope [8.4.2] – a device for calculated procrastination. This hyperrational 'organisation' and 'efficiency' merely fabricate a higher institution in which to house more sophisticated looking 'busy work' [cf. 8.1.1].

A project manager therefore needs to be a curriculum developer just as a teacher needs to be a classroom manager. She or he needs to develop the methodology of both the project and the target curriculum simultaneously, in reaction to the same set of cultural parameters discovered within the host institution and educational environment. The project only works if the curriculum change it creates works: the same set of criteria affects both. I shall use 'curriculum developer' in this chapter to refer also to 'project manager'.

12.2.1 *Curriculum developer as action researcher*

Figure 14 presents action research as the basic problem-solving tool at the curriculum developer's disposal. She or he has the responsibility of manoeuvring the project into alien territory. As can be seen in Figure 5 [7.1], channels of communication have to be set up with the various blocks of influence within the host environment. These channels of communication will have little precedence, and will have to be negotiated. The existence of informal orders [8.2] will make it difficult for the curriculum developer to collect the information she or he needs to establish these relationships easily. This process will therefore have to be negotiatory, will require as much investigation as any other part of project work, and may go on for much of the project's life. This will be one focus for ongoing action research. The project will move forward step by step, forming hypotheses about how to act which will be in a constant state of repair. I am thinking primarily here of the curriculum developer as an outsider foreigner, with BANA ideals. However, similar problems and courses of action would have to be taken even by an insider taking on the role of curriculum developer, as has been seen in the case of the Keele project [7.2]. Just as all teachers are in many ways outsiders to the cultures of their classrooms, so are curriculum developers, no matter how 'local' they are, outsiders to the real worlds of the students and teachers who act out the curriculum. I have been working recently with South African secondary school teachers who are gradually achieving the role of innovators within their own system. This role itself makes them different; and the new interests which it involves will distance them in some ways from the real worlds of other teachers.

12.2.2 The means analysis

I have referred elsewhere to this process of learning as a means analysis [8.2.1]:

> an ongoing survey of the cultural, sociopolitical, logistical,
> administrative, psycho-pedagogic and methodological features of
> the host educational environment as it changes in time before and
> during the process of innovation.

(Holliday 1992b:411)

Most of the features which the means analysis surveys are those defined by Munby (1978:217) as the factors which remain as 'constraints' on syllabus specifications produced by his needs analysis. The significant difference is that in the means analysis these are addressed from the outset. I have already discussed how these so-called 'constraints' are thus turned to advantage and treated as *conditions* for design [6.4.2]. In Munby's model the needs analysis puts off attention to 'constraints' until after the syllabus has been specified; within the means analysis, the needs analysis becomes a lower order investigation device which the means analysis uses and controls according to the needs of the situation (Holliday 1992b:415, 1990). This can be seen in Figure 15. The constant evaluation leading to syllabus adjustment on the right of the figure is in effect an ongoing process of formative evaluation similar to that advocated in classroom teaching [11.2.1].

Curriculum and project design

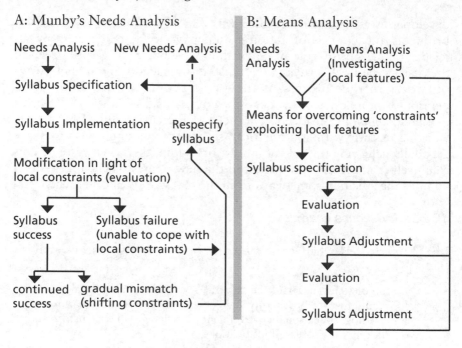

Figure 15 *The means analysis model*
(taken from Holliday and Cooke 1982:135)

12.2.3 *Simultaneous methodologies of management and curriculum*

The setting up and maintenance of communication will in effect be a major part of the methodology of the project, and will be a basis for the means analysis necessary for the purpose of evolving appropriate curriculum change. This is because, as can be seen in the Keele project [7.2], any curriculum has to be meaningful to *people* before it can be put into practice. In the part of the Ain Shams project with which I was involved – to develop the language curriculum in Egyptian faculties of education – curriculum development was, over a period of five years, parallel to a development in project management policy. At the beginning of the project the management policy was to develop materials in collaboration with local lecturers through committees. On discovering that these committees were not producing real change in the classroom [7.3.4], the management policy was changed to one in which action research at the classroom level was put into the hands of an interested core of local lecturers. Azer's (1990) work [11.2] was one such piece of individualised action research. This gradual change in project policy towards decentralisation is catalogued in Holliday (1991b).

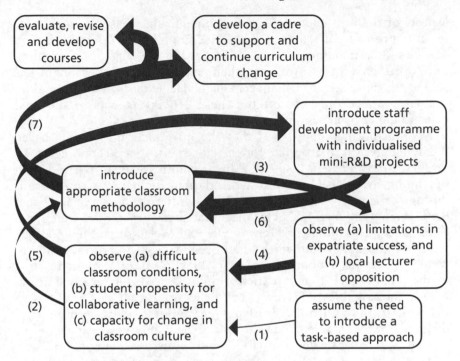

Figure 16 *Spiral process*
(developed from Holliday 1991:411)

The process of the means analysis through which the classroom methodology of the curriculum was developed, intertwined with the process of the project methodology already described, can be seen in Figure 16. The spiral nature of the process [10.1.4], which McNiff (1988:26–41,43) refers to as 'generative action research' can also be seen in the figure.

12.2.4 Spiral process

As with classroom action research [10.1.4], essential to this spiral is the systematic formulation, testing and reformulation of hypotheses in the light of ongoing investigation. The aim is to professionalise what might currently exist as 'folk knowledge' among curriculum developers (cf. Kelley 1980:78). Indeed, I am not suggesting that the means analysis is looking at areas which experienced curriculum developers have not always looked at: it is rather the formalisation of the process which is important. To provide a basis for accountability and effective reporting to funding agencies is an important aim here. I have already argued that what is reported about project work often fails to represent crucial aspects of the host educational environment. One reason is that these aspects are too soft to satisfy the needs of hyperrational funding agencies [8.2.1]; but another reason is that English language curriculum developers have only formalised their expertise in applied linguistics [1.3] and, more recently, management [1.1], neither of which enables them to report and account for these crucial aspects of the host educational environment in acceptably formalised ways.

My starting hypothesis was that the introduction of a task-based methodology was appropriate for the classroom – step (1) in Figure 16 and Holliday (1991a:183–5). This assumption was treated as a beginning hypothesis, to be tested, adapted, or perhaps thrown out during the course of investigation. It is significant, however, in that it derived from my own BANA professional-academic culture, which was essentially integrationist. This was after all a classroom methodology which I knew about and which I had been brought up professionally to believe in. It was supported by suggestions in my pre-project briefing material that 'more student participation' was needed in largely 'lecture-based' local classes. However, the need for the means analysis to investigate the appropriacy of project inputs, such as this initial diagnosis of the 'problem' and this initial view of how well it should be 'solved', as well as the local situation, will be discussed later [12.6.2].

The findings of the means analysis, some of which are referred to in previous chapters, are a good example of the thick description characteristic of classroom action research [11.3]. The observations revealed a large number of phenomena which, if taken in isolation, did not seem to relate. However, when taken within a holistic view of a total social scenario, they became the pieces of a huge jigsaw puzzle, which, when put together, took on meaning. The hypotheses which they motivated could be no more than working assumptions on the part of the outsider curriculum developer. The test of their validity would be in how far they stood up to subsequent action.

My initial observations – step (2) in Figure 16 – of student gregariousness, responsibility for learning and group problem-solving abilities in difficult circumstances have already been discussed [4.3.1–2]. This was sufficient evidence for taking the first action in the change process: introducing some trial lessons involving collaborative learning – step (3) in Figure 16.

The next step in the spiral was to observe the effects on the classroom culture that this change brought about – step (4). The methodology's incompatibility with the local professional-academic culture, despite the ability of the students to handle the new methodology when taught by expatriate lecturers, has been discussed earlier [5.4].

I will not go into detail about what happened in the rest of the process: my aim here is rather to exemplify the dialogue between observation and action. Like classroom action research [11.3], the spiral process of the means analysis is never finished. The process went on for several more years while I was involved. There is no before, during and after, but only a constant state of evaluation and action. The change which this constant process directs and monitors is not a new once-and-for-all package but an ongoing dynamism which, if effective, should become a permanent feature of the host educational environment.

12.3 Curriculum developer as ethnographer

As with the action research carried out in the classroom, the action research necessary for curriculum development should be ethnographic in nature. Ethnography provides the means by which the curriculum developer *finds out* what she or he needs to know during the process of negotiating both the project and curriculum methodology. The informal orders which prevent a straightforward view of the host environment are accompanied by tacit psycho-cultural and micro political aspects of local behaviour [8.2] which can only be understood through an ethnographic learning process.

12.3.1 Curriculum developer as marginal

Whereas the role of ethnographer in the classroom might be problematic for teachers [11.4], I would like to argue that it might be a more natural role for the curriculum developer. Much of the discipline of ethnography is a rationalisation of the natural learning process anyone goes through when approaching a new culture. All of us, at different points in our lives, need to learn new cultures – of new work places, of new neighbourhoods, of new schools, of mechanics, of pubs, and so on. Schutz (1964:104) argues that there is a distinct methodology in this learning of culture. In daily life, this methodology is tacit. However, curriculum developers, who are used to working in very foreign environments, acquire a more conscious experience of learning new cultures. They possess a professional marginality. Shipman *et al.* see this marginality as representing the tenuousness of the curriculum developer role (1974:113–14); however, I see it as a potential.

Stenhouse's comparison between history and ethnography [11.3] is once again interesting here. Whereas history is carried out by insiders, and assumes a shared understanding of human behaviour, deals in the foreground of action and can thus rely on documents and 'the discussion and interpretation of evidence accessible to scholars', ethnography is essentially the work of outsiders who need to 'call into question the commonplace' (1985c:53). Stenhouse cites Levi-Strauss as saying that whereas history deals with the 'conscious', ethnography deals with the 'unconscious' (ibid.) – a distinction which I see as roughly corresponding to my surface and deep action.

Referring back to my discussion of deep and surface action [8.3.1], I wish to suggest that curriculum developers who are mainly preoccupied by surface action phenomena are like the historians in Stenhouse's analysis. Their failure to see imminent tissue rejection is largely due to their reliance on what they can see in the foreground of the host educational environment, as though they were insiders. It is central to my argument that they should call this foreground information into question, and behave more as the outsiders which in reality they are. A marginal viewpoint is thus essential.

Stonequist links marginality to 'cultural transitions and cultural conflicts' (1937:3). On a grander note, although in fact relevant to the cultural turmoil sometimes found in projects [7.3], marginal people can be:

> creative agents not only [to] adjust themselves but also [to]
> contribute to the solution of the conflict of races and cultures. ...
> [Thus] marginal [woman or] man is the key personality in the
> contacts of cultures. ... The practical efforts of the marginal person
> to solve [her or] his own problem lead [her or] him consciously or
> unconsciously to change the situation itself.

(Ibid.: 220–1)

Hammersley and Atkinson stress that this *marginal* position of ethnographers must be maintained and capitalised upon no matter how familiar they become with the situation under study:

> The researcher generates 'creative insight' out of this marginal
> position of simultaneous insider-outsider. The ethnographer must
> be intellectually poised between 'familiarity' and 'strangeness',
> while socially he or she is poised between 'stranger' and 'friend'...
> – a 'marginal native'.

(Ibid.:100, citing Lofland, Powdermaker and Freilich)

This intermediate position is very much the situation of the teacher, who knows her or his students, and yet is an outsider to their culture [9.4]. It is also the position of practitioners such as Shamim (in process) [6.4.1] who practise curriculum development from inside their own institution. It would be naive to distinguish here between expatriates and local actors, especially in the type of developing industrial societies in which English language projects are often located, which tend to be cosmopolitan, and where expatriates can be an established part of the local scene. In the Ain Shams project means analysis expatriate lecturers were subjects of the investigation along with local lecturers.

This methodology, although not appreciated, can be seen at work in the Keele project [7.2]. The identity crisis which was an inevitable consequence of marginality was instrumental in working out a methodology for making sense of, and finding out about, what was going on – in developing a means analysis with a heavy emphasis on participant observation. Some of the 'mistakes' made by the Keele project, which this identity crisis brought about, might have been avoided or reduced if both the inevitability and the advantages of marginality had been understood and mobilised from the beginning.

Just as we ask language learners to mobilise and rationalise their communicative competence to solve language problems, so teachers and curriculum developers, like any social researcher, need to do the same with their ability to learn new cultures if appropriate methodologies are to be achieved.

12.3.2 Wide-ranging classroom observation

The application of ethnography to the means analysis is also demonstrated in the Ain Shams project. As in classroom action research [11.2], the investigation of the host educational environment took the form of ethnographic observation. Over three years I visited 17 faculties of education, 20 lecturers and 28 groups of students. Although I was interested in all aspects of the host educational environment, most observations were of classes. This was partly because, as I have argued throughout, classroom interaction seemed to represent many of the social forces of the wider environment, and partly because the classroom was a convenient focus to which I had automatic access as a curriculum developer (Holliday 1991a:196–8). Some observations were of other events such as seminars and presentations. Figure 16 [12.2.2.] shows that the observations went through several stages, in dialogue with actions that were taken in the curriculum change process.

The need for wide-ranging observations has already been discussed [8.2.1]. In Holliday (1992b:410) I refer to similar wide-ranging observation carried out to inform project work by Andrews (1984) and Coleman (1992). Similar observations were also carried out at Damascus University, where they were catalogued as:

> a) Observing classes in the widest possible sense (including observation of how students came in and left, sat and waited outside, not only of classes attended by the investigator, but also of classes going on throughout the university);

b) Observing lecturer behaviour in and out of the class, in seminars, in meetings and on social occasions (a large number of lecturers, both English language and other subjects, visit the ... [Language] Centre for a friendly chat, advice etc.);

c) Observation of student behaviour, particularly how they behave towards and are treated by lecturers (it was possible to witness a lot of lecturer-student interaction outside the classes, in lecturers' offices and in corridors, and a lot of students come to the ... Centre, curious to find out what is going on or asking directions);

d) Observation of how the university operates, how ... administrators, clerks and janitors get on with their work, the problems they have with the bureaucracy and so on (particularly easy because a lot of ... Centre business requires personal appearance by one or both of the ... [curriculum developers], and a lot of other business and general coming and going is carried on while the ... business is being dealt with - or not);

e) Experience of people's attitudes to the project, ... ideas about new courses etc. (not only from the Rector and Vice-rector in meetings, or from lecturers in seminars and meetings, but from the lecturers and students generally when conversation often leads on to these topics).

(Cooke and Holliday 1982:16–17)

12.3.3 Gaining access

A common problem with ethnographic means analysis is gaining access to situations for the purpose of observation. On the one hand, the curriculum developer has an advantage over the ethnographer in that her or his work provides a ready-made licence for access. Whereas ethnographers have to fabricate 'normal' roles to enable them to carry out their research – e.g. getting a job in a restaurant, being a customer in a shop, being blood donors, for the purpose of observing behaviour (Spradley 1980:51–2), curriculum developers start out with a normal role within the environment to be studied. The pre-existing social routines and realities of their job allow for wide movement and the type of behaviour normally characteristic of the ethnographer. Curriculum developers working in language projects are often expected to observe classes, interview a large variety of host personnel, visit offices, departments and staffrooms, travel on institutional transport, attend social gatherings in and out of the work setting, carry out questionnaire surveys, and generally collect information. This would be the case in classroom observation especially, which the curriculum developer would often be expected to do for professional-evaluative reasons.

On the other hand, many aspects of project work, from negotiating lines of communication with host bodies [12.2.2] to gaining access to lessons for observation, require informal networking with which ethnographic field practice can help. At Ain Shams I had no formal licence to enter other people's classes; my ability to do this was due to the informal professional relations which I was able to set up, but which took a long time. It is common, in my experience, for curriculum developers to spend a considerable amount of time, on first arriving in a new host situation, working through false leads. Finding accurate informants who will provide access to the real world of local personnel is equally problematic for ethnographers and curriculum developers, but formalised only by the former. Ethnographers refer to key local personalities as *gatekeepers*. They can grant or withhold access to a situation, regardless of permission granted by formal authorities. They hold an unofficial power at a local level and 'may attempt to exercise some degree of surveillance or control, either by blocking off certain lines of enquiry, or by shepherding the fieldworker in one direction or another' (Hammersley and Atkinson 1983:65). It would benefit English language curriculum developers to add a formalised approach to gaining access to their currently acknowledged expertise in applied linguistics and curriculum design.

12.3.4 Field relations

Literature on ethnography stresses the importance of the *field relations* which underlie gaining access. Much of this might seem common sense to the curriculum developer, and the tendency to place them in low priority against applied linguistics is, I suggest, contributory to the 'calculated procrastination' [Chapter 8] which keeps them from really addressing the real worlds of their local colleagues.

Hammersley and Atkinson stress the need for the researcher to mobilise natural social skills in repartee, empathy, sensitivity (ibid.:58), and 'the normal requirements of tact, courtesy, and "interaction ritual"' (ibid.:83, citing Goffman) when dealing with local people – in 'penetrating informants' "fronts"' (ibid.:62, citing Hoffman). They warn against the expectations that local people can develop of the researcher, seeing her or him as 'the expert', 'the evaluator' with special powers to 'sort out' local problems (ibid.:75). This sort of thing was seen as an inhibition to curriculum development work by Cooke and myself at Damascus University:

> Local attitudes to, and expectations of ... foreign aid advisors can
> be a potent source of friction and misunderstanding. ... Probably
> the most widespread misconception is that [the advisors] ... 'have
> the answers' before coming to Syria; their qualifications and

> expertise have equipped them with a battery of ready-made
> solutions to every English language teaching problem. Hence there
> is very little appreciation of the need for, and value of, research,
> planning, piloting, feedback, gradual change etc.

(Cooke and Holliday 1982:32)

False expectations may prove barriers to access. Furthermore:

> Ethnographers are sometimes conspicuous for an apparent lack of
> activity as well. This too can militate against their being treated
> seriously by their hosts. ... Rumours about ... [one researcher]
> included beliefs that he was a communist spy, a CIA agent, a
> protestant missionary, or a government tax agent.

(Hammersley and Atkinson 1983:76, citing the experience of Barrett)

Thus local people may be 'more concerned with what kind of person
the researcher is than with the research itself' – hence the need for the
researcher to become expert in *'impression management'*, including
'personal appearance' (ibid.:78, 81). Both as curriculum developer and
researcher I found myself particularly sensitive to this issue, as some of
my notes show: 'I never wear a suit and tie when teaching postgraduate
groups "in-house", but feel it is expected on consultancy visits'
(Observation notes). Another factor, recognised as commonplace by
ethnographers, but often missed by curriculum developers in English
language projects, is that what the investigator wishes to see, and what
local people are prepared to show, do not always correspond.
Hammersley and Atkinson point out that:

> It is often the most sensitive things that are of most *prima facie*
> interest. Periods of change and transition, for example, may be
> perceived as troublesome by the participants themselves, and they
> may wish, therefore, to steer observers away from them: the conflict
> of interest arises from the fact that such disruptions can be
> particularly fruitful research opportunities for the fieldworker.

(1983:66)

They go on to suggest that often researchers in education '"with limited
time and money available to them"' never see anything but established
classroom routines where teachers can be at their best (ibid.:67, citing
Ball). I have already referred to this difficulty in collecting the right
information [8.2].

Shamim (1993) in her account of research she carried out in Pakistani
secondary schools, not as a curriculum developer, but, interestingly, in a
setting in which curriculum developers often find themselves, describes
how she was received and how her role was perceived by local teachers

and heads. Although she is Pakistani too, she was in effect an outsider and had to manage her image very carefully indeed, and found that gaining access to classes depended on this as well as on formal agreements. Indeed, although she does not say this, her detailed account of local reactions becomes valuable data regarding the nature of the host educational environment in its own right. Attention to the way in which the local scene responds to the researcher not only helps the researcher to gain access, but also provides valuable data.

Using the experience of doing research in the local situation as data about the local situation is an important feature of the *reflexivity* of ethnographic research (Hammersley and Atkinson 1983:14; Holliday 1991a:145–52). Reflexivity overcomes the problem of the 'observer paradox' (Labov 1972:181), where the observer fears that her or his presence will upset the local scene to the extent that what is observed is no longer real. Hammersley and Atkinson suggest that 'rather than engaging in futile attempts to eliminate the effects of the researcher, we should set about understanding them' (1983:17). The way in which the local situation responds to the presence of the observer, rather than ruining the research, reveals important aspects of that situation. This principle was evident in my own research [3.4.3] when, on entering classrooms, I was requested to sit at the front next to the teacher. Rather than ruining my attempt to be inconspicuous, this revealed the hospitality and formality of the classroom culture.

12.4 Curriculum developer as opportunist

Although curriculum developers have the advantage of having a range of ready-made research settings at their disposal, these settings are rarely ideal and might not facilitate the standard ethnographic research cycle where the researcher enters a situation and gradually focuses [11.1.2]. The curriculum developer needs to be much more *opportunistic*, making the best of what is available (see Hammersley and Atkinson 1983:40). Indeed, this opportunism is part and parcel of the process of developing the research methodology in dialogue with the local situation. The way in which opportunistic research grew out of the exigencies of the local situation in the Ain Shams project is summarised in Table 6. The left-hand column of the table lists the relevant features of the local situation, which necessitated the approach to data collection summarised in the middle column of the table. Although the procedures in the middle column are eccentric in 'normal' ethnographic terms, and may appear to be making the best of the difficult situation depicted in the first column, they did in some cases give rise to insightful outcomes

Table 6: Summary of means analysis procedures
[From Holliday 1992a:428]

Local situation exigencies	*Opportunistic procedures*	*Outcomes*
A Integration with normal curriculum development work	**1** Observation of large number of different classes	
B Difficult geographical locations		
C Time allowed for beginning innovation is short	**2** Observation before and during innovation simultaneously	**i** Insight into whole innovation process
D Difficulty in collecting information about where and when	**3** Observation of eccentric classroom situations	**ii** Examination of factors in isolation
E Difficulty of access to sufficient 'normal' classroom situations	**4** Observation of own guest lectures and of expatriate lecturers	**iii** Insight into feasibility of innovation for students and classroom conditions
	5 Use of local lecturers as co-observers	**iv** Valuable form of comparison
F Viewpoints of observer and observed differed too widely	**6** Record of discussion with lecturer after observation	**v** No final reconciliation of conflicting viewpoints
	7 Many findings kept covert	**vi** Innovation remains a subversive activity

which might not otherwise have been possible. The third column summarises these outcomes – (i)–(iv).

The left-hand column refers to constraints of geography, time, protocols and differences in perception regarding the nature of research and education. The project involved faculties of education spread all over a large country – (A). The need for me, as a curriculum developer, to see what was going on in the whole range of institutions, the time required to travel between them, and the difficulty in setting up visits due to problems with telephonic and postal communication within the state education sector, meant that textbook longitudinal observation of particular classrooms, developing from the wide to the more focused, was not possible. Furthermore, the project did not allow the time for long-term research prior to innovation – (C). I therefore defined the location for the investigation as a large number of similar classroom contexts and related non-classroom events – (1) in the middle column. Although the investigation ranged over five years, the shape of the emergent jigsaw puzzle was broad rather than long, and, as has been described earlier, was simultaneous and in dialogue with the process of innovation – (2) in the middle column. The difficulty I had in collecting information about timetables and locations of classes, due to the opacity of the informal order [8.2], coupled with difficulty in gaining access – (D) and (E) in the left-hand column – meant that I had to observe classes wherever and whenever I could, whether or not they seemed eccentric to the norm. I had to make maximum use of classes which I taught myself – (3) and (2) in the middle column. Partly to compensate for this, and because it was good practice anyway, I triangulated where possible with the views of local co-observers and post-observation discussion – (5) and (6) in the middle column. The procedures in the middle column were thus essentially culture-sensitive in the way that they responded to the local situation and were not imported. The workability of the procedures in the middle column is demonstrated in the right-hand column.

12.5   Learning from project experience

It is possible to learn from the procedures generated by the project and to evolve principles which might be transferable to other projects. The need to integrate the means analysis with normal curriculum development work – (A) in the left-hand column – would be the case in all projects, unless there was funding for a specialist ethnographer. The shortage of time allowed for beginning innovation (C) is likely to be the case in all projects, where the hyperrational funding agency is looking for a short project lifetime, of up to five years, and rapid, quantitative output [8.4.2]. As I shall explain [12.6], the differing viewpoints of observer and observed (F) are unavoidable. Even where curriculum development is initiated from within a host institution, it will take on a culture which is different from, and in conflict with the indigenous cultures of the institution. (cf. the Keele Humanities Project, where the curriculum developers were ex-local teachers [7.2]).

It is now possible to see which of the procedures listed in the middle column of Table 6 follow (A), (C) and (F) from the first column in being transferable to other projects. Observation before and during innovation simultaneously (2), observation of eccentric classroom situations (3), the use of local lecturers as co-observers (5), and keeping a record of discussion with lecturers after observation (6), would all be necessary in any local situation, barring very unusual circumstances. Procedure (7), the keeping covert of many findings, clearly relates to (F), and is therefore also transferable.

The procedures from one project can thus be carried as hypotheses to other projects, to be tested and confirmed, adapted or rejected by the means analysis in other projects. A bank of formalised experience of how to carry out the means analysis can thus be built up.

12.6 Moral issues

A significant, less desirable outcome of the means analysis procedures catalogued in Table 6 is the covert nature of the findings (middle column) caused by the inevitably differing viewpoints between observer and observed (left-hand column). The implication here is that curriculum development seemed to be an irreconcilably subversive activity in the terms of the host institution (right-hand column v–vi).

12.6.1 The inevitability of researcher-subject conflict

I wish not to justify but to explain this inevitability that the means analysis should be covert. There is an unavoidable lack of a 'community of interest' or of a consensus of norms between the researcher and those he or she studies, and there is therefore a necessary conflict between them (Becker 1969:265). A good piece of research will inevitably make someone angry (ibid.:268), and for this reason social scientists often need to repress 'conflict-provoking findings' (ibid.:270).

The dilemma arising out of this fact of life is central to the discussion in Hammersley (1986) on the appropriacy of 'democratic' research, which seeks to protect the interests of the research subjects. (I discuss this debate in some detail along with the whole ethics of participant observation in Holliday 1991a:158–65.) It is sufficient to say here that those who support democratic research insist that it should always represent the wants of the people being studied. The other side of the debate says that this would create a censorship effect which would inhibit true research, and that anyway, any 'democracy' which the researcher might claim could be no more than the type of 'bogus co-authorship' to which I have already referred in connection with the relationship between curriculum developer and target local personnel [8.1.2]: because of the irreconcilable difference of interest between researcher and researched, there can in reality be no such thing.

The conflict to which Becker refers does not always need to come to the surface. Shamim (1993), in her survey of Pakistani secondary school classrooms, notes that it was when she tried to 'come clean' and explain to those she was observing exactly what the aims of her research were, and that she would make her findings of use to them, that a potential conflict came to the surface. Heads and teachers seemed relatively happy with her role as 'a researcher', but did not seem to want to know very much about the findings or to get too involved in the process. These things were her business and not theirs. In my view, they seemed to have no romantic illusions about how their world and the world of the researcher could be integrated. Had this integration been forced, Shamim felt that conflict would have surfaced and ruined the relationship with them that she had formed [12.3.4]. It may well have been that the introduction of research findings into the ecology of the school might have disrupted existing protocols and tacit understandings.

In the case of the Ain Shams project, I felt that the 'coming clean' about the ethnographic nature of the means analysis and its findings would have been counterproductive for the following reasons. First, the means analysis was instigated by the project, which was being shown, in its integrationist form, to be culturally very different from the collectionist host institution. I have already described the communication problems this difference created [7.3]. If conflicting perceptions regarding pedagogy were common, there would undoubtedly be conflicting perceptions with regard to the more complex issue of ethnographic research. This would have been exacerbated by the fact that qualitative research was not traditionally an acceptable form of research in the humanities in the local university system. The communication problem is therefore quadrupled. There is the conceptual gap between what researchers and researched, and curriculum developers and teachers do and think, in all curriculum projects (demonstrated in the Keele project [7.2]), and in the case of English language projects, between BANA and TESEP, and between 'foreigners' and local personnel.

213

Because of the inevitable inability of curriculum developers to understand fully the real worlds of local personnel, not just because of being 'foreign' where they are expatriates in other people's institutions, but because of the ethnocentricity of the culture of change underlying BANA curriculum development, I feared that I would not have the necessary perceptions to know *how* to report my means analysis findings to local personnel effectively.

It therefore seems that a degree of covertness in the means analysis is unavoidable. In effect, the means analysis is part of the 'thinking in private' of the curriculum developer. Elsewhere, I suggest that this is what makes it different from formal formative evaluation, which, although similar in many respects, serves the needs of an interested party or parties who need to be involved in its design and execution (Holliday 1992b:416).

This discussion brings home an extremely important factor in the use of ethnography in curriculum development. Ethnography can put curriculum developers in better touch with the real worlds of the people with whom they are working. This is necessary if appropriate methodologies are to be achieved. However, ethnography will not *solve* the problems which these real worlds present. It will rather expose all their sensitivities and dangers. The 'coral gardens' of cultural reality, although fascinating, will all too easily cut the intruder, who can in turn easily destroy their ecology. All I am arguing for in this book is that curriculum developers should proceed with their eyes open, so that they can *see* the effects of their work. The inevitability of conflicting viewpoints between curriculum developer and local personnel reminds one that the area at which the means analysis looks is culturally sensitive and opaque. Ethnography may help to remove some of the opacity; and indeed, the overall aim is to prevent rather than create conflict; but the sensitivity remains. Ethnography is itself a dangerous tool if not handled carefully. The whole ethics of technology transfer is thus again brought into question.

12.6.2 *Addressing conflicting viewpoints*

Although the initial ethnocentricity on the part of the curriculum developer is unavoidable – seen in the initial decision to introduce a task-based approach in the Ain Shams project [2.2.4] – what is important is that the curriculum developer should acknowledge and account for this ethnocentricity. The means analysis must investigate the implications of this bias for the host environment. The means analysis must therefore address not only the 'foreign' cultures of the host educational environment, but also the culture of the project or curriculum developer as it interacts with them. The job of the means analysis is to investigate the cultural interface of the change process.

12.7 Achieving an 'appropriate methodology'

Whether or not a really appropriate methodology is ever achieved is something that only history can judge; and 'appropriate' is inevitably a very relative term. Swales (1989:88) describes the approach characterised by the means analysis as alchemy. The outcome is a reconstituting of elements which are indigenous to the cultures of the host educational environment – to produce something which is changed, but which also has its roots within the traditional.

The working of this alchemy at the classroom level can be seen in Azer's approach to teaching grammar in large classes, where he changes the classroom methodology from didactic to collaborative problem solving, while building on basic cultural elements [11.2]. On the wider scale of the Ain Shams project, it can be seen in the eventual decentralisation of action research into the hands of local lecturers [12.2.3]. The means analysis had revealed the following factors surrounding the situation of local lecturers:

1   the local lecturers' status, independence, professional influence and local knowledge
2   the need they saw for change, and their understanding that the teaching of theoretical linguistics was not succeeding in giving their students the language skills they needed
3   their need to publish research for the purpose of promotion
4   their desire for contact with the international English language teaching community
5   the propensity of the local classroom culture to accept change – seen in its resilience and hospitality under the pressure of outsider interference [3.4.3–4]
6   the students' propensity for collaboration, independent study and group problem solving [12.2.4].

All of these points were still hypotheses on the part of the curriculum developer, to be maintained or thrown out in the light of further action. (1–4) are consistent with the local lecturer viewpoint expressed in the rudimentary soft system analysis referred to earlier [7.3.4]. (3) is particularly interesting in that it was very much a feature of the prevailing collectionist professional-academic culture, which demanded evidence of subject knowledge. Indeed, it represented the centre of what could be interpreted as a compromise with the integrationist culture of the project, which was interested in the development of classroom management skills. Hence, the publications which grew out of the action research were designed both to satisfy the collectionist need and to motivate the integrationist need. How far this compromise is either desirable or workable in the long term remains to be seen.

Another important factor is the motivation of the particular local lecturers who joined the scheme to wish to step even partly out of the collectionism which might have made many of their colleagues less so inclined. It is always people who are dissatisfied with some aspect of their own organisation who desire change of any form – and there will be many complex professional and personal reasons for this, as already seen [5.5.1].

12.7.1 A basis for meaningful exchange

Furthermore, it needs to be remembered that these professional-academic cultures, as I have been describing them, are only heuristic descriptions of groups of people, which are not sealed hermetically. There will always be movement and exchange between these cultures. The sort of innovation which I hope this staff development scheme achieved can be likened to a trade – where one group provides a commodity which another group can import according to its needs. In a sense, the means analysis plays the role of ongoing market research, finding out what form this commodity should take to ensure fair and meaningful exchange (Holliday 1992b:416). (There is no reason, in these terms, to pretend that the aid donor is not getting anything in return. 'Making friends and influencing people' seems to me perfectly respectable as long as the trade is clear and meaningful.) The concern with cultural or linguistic imperialism is surely reduced in the event of fair and meaningful trading; and, as I have already argued it is in the very nature of cultural groups to influence and be influenced by each other [2.7].

As in the case of classroom methodology [11.2.3], the appropriate methodology in curriculum design or project management terms is therefore not so much a means for doing as a means for allowing the relevant parties to take part in a process of meaningful exchange.

12.8 Summary

a) Project work and curriculum development are inextricably bound together. Both have methodologies which need to be appropriate to the same set of cultures within the host educational environment.

b) Project work and curriculum development both need to incorporate a process of learning about the host educational environment. As in classroom work, this process needs to be action research supported by ethnography, termed means analysis.

c) Curriculum developers have a natural marginality which can be mobilised in the ethnography of the means analysis.

d) Curriculum developers can learn much from the ethnographer, who has professional means for gaining access and field relations with local parties.

e) The means analysis might have to be a covert procedure because of the inevitability of cultural differences between the curriculum developer and local personnel.

f) The means analysis needs to address these differences, and to appraise the appropriateness of project ethnocentricity; but, although it uncovers real worlds, it cannot ultimately solve the problems which they present.

g) Achieving appropriate methodologies, rather than removing the differences between the parties concerned, can make the technology transfer between them meaningful.

12.9 Questions for discussion

1 How much of the work you do as a curriculum developer involves informal ethnography, and how might your effectiveness be improved if this were formalised and developed professionally?

2 Think of examples of important deep action phenomena which have been left out of reports because they were not considered sufficiently serious, technical or quantifiable.

3 An area which has not been discussed in this chapter is that of understanding and communicating effectively with the 'hyperrational' funding agency. Is the funding agency simply another culture block within the host educational environment? Could a curriculum developer use ethnographic action research to learn how to communicate with the funding agency?

4 Think of cases where the design of a needs analysis has depended on social factors discovered in the host institution.

5 From your experience, is the means analysis only necessary when the curriculum developer is a foreigner?
Have you ever felt like a foreigner as a curriculum developer in an institution in your own country? Why was this?

6 Think of examples of successful 'means analysis' procedures you have used in one project which i) have been useful or ii) have not worked in another project.

7 What would be the justifications for either covert or overt action research in different institutions with which you are familiar?

Conclusion

In this final chapter I have brought together several strands of my argument and shown how ethnographic action research can be used not only by the teacher, to collect the information necessary for developing an appropriate classroom methodology, but also, in the form of a means analysis, by the curriculum developer, to help develop an appropriate curriculum project methodology. In this way, the three types of methodology are brought together – the methodology for teaching or implementing curricula, for designing and managing classroom activities or projects, and for collecting the necessary information through ethnographic action research.

The three methodologies all follow the same principle – that of gradual interaction with the relevant features of the host educational environment. The different social contexts encountered in different educational environments thus become more than simply backdrops for the practice of English language education: they become a significant input to the process.

Through case studies, I have illustrated how these methodologies might work. I have indicated some of the areas which need to be addressed. However, the specifics of what to do can only be realised in specific environments, in response to what investigations reveal. It is now for the reader to look at her or his own social context, to attempt ethnographic action research, and to begin to discover appropriate methodology.

References

Adams, A., B. Heaton and P. Howarth (Eds.) 1991. *Socio-Cultural Issues in English for Academic Purposes*. Review of English Language Teaching, vol.2. London: Modern English Publications.

Adams-Smith, D.E. 1984. Planning a university language centre in Oman: Problems and Proposals. In J. Swales and H. Mustafa (Eds.) *ESP in The Arab World*, 197–210. Birmingham: Language Services Unit, University of Aston.

Allwright, R.L. 1982. Communicative curricula in language teaching. Paper presented at the international conference on language science and the teaching of languages and literatures. Bari, Italy.

Allwright, R.L. 1988. *Observation in the Language Classroom*. London: Longman.

Allwright, R.L. 1992. Integrating 'Research' and 'Pedagogy': Appropriate Criteria and Practical Possibilities. *Working Paper* 13. Lancaster: Centre for Research in Language Education.

Allwright, R.L. (in process). Social and pedagogic pressures in the language classroom: The role of socialization. In H. Coleman (Ed.) *Society and the Classroom: Social Explanation for Behaviour in the Language Class*.

Allwright, R.L. and K.M. Bailey. 1991. *Focus on the Language Classroom*. Cambridge. Cambridge University Press.

Andrews, S. 1984. The effect of Arabicization on the role of Service English. In J. Swales and H. Mustafa (Eds.) *ESP in The Arab World*, 172–84. Birmingham: Language Services Unit, University of Aston.

Asad, T. (Ed.) 1973. *Anthropology and the Colonial Encounter*. London: Ithaca Press.

Atkinson, D. 1987. The mother tongue in the classroom: a neglected resource? *English Language Teaching Journal*, 41(4).

Atkinson, P. and S. Delamont. 1984. Mock-ups and cock-ups: The stage-management of guided discovery instruction. In A. Hargreaves and P. Woods (Eds.) *Classrooms and Staffrooms: The Sociology of Teachers and Teaching*, 36–47. Milton Keynes: Open University Press. Reprinted from P. Woods and M. Hammersley (Eds.) 1977. *School Experience*, 87–108. London: Croom Helm.

References

Atkinson, P. and S. Delamont. 1986. Bread and dreams or bread and circuses? A critique of 'Case Study' research in education. In M. Hammersley, 238–54. Reprinted from M. Shipman (Ed.) 1985, *Educational Research: Principles, Policies and Practices*. Lewes: Falmer Press.

Azer, H. 1990. Can a communicative approach to university grammar cope with large classes? *Occasional Papers in The Development of English Language Education* 12. Cairo: Centre for Developing English Language Teaching, Ain Shams University.

Ballard, B. (in process). Through language to learning: Preparing overseas students for study in western universities. In H. Coleman (Ed.) *Society and The Classroom: Social Explanation for Behaviour in The Language Class*.

Bandi, G. and M. Shibata. 1992. *Japanese Students in The English Classroom: Is There a Problem?* Unpublished project, Department of Language Studies, Canterbury Christ Church College, Canterbury.

Barjesteh, D. and A.R. Holliday. 1990. How to introduce inductive learning in the teaching of grammar. In M. Aboussena (Ed.) 1989. *Proceedings of The National Symposium on Teaching English in Egypt: Linguistics, Literature and Culture*, 89–94. Cairo: Centre for Developing English Language Teaching, Ain Shams University.

Barmada, W. 1983. *Ten English Language Centres in the Arab World: An Investigation into their 'Macro ESP Problems'*. Unpublished MSc Dissertation. Birmingham: University of Aston.

Barrow, R. 1990. Culture, values and the classroom. In B. Harrison, 3–10.

Bartlett, L. 1990. Teacher development through reflective teaching. In J.C. Richards and D. Nunan, 202–14.

Becker, H.S. 1969. Problems in the publication of field studies. In G.J. McCall and J.L. Simmons (Eds.) *Issues in Participant Observation*, 260–75. Reading, Massachusetts: Addison Wesley. Reprinted from Problems in the publication of field studies. In A.J. Vidich, J. Bensman and M.R. Stein (Eds.) 1964, *Reflections on Community Studies*, 267–84. New York: Wiley.

Berger, P.L., B. Berger and H. Kellner. 1974. *The Homeless Mind*. Harmondsworth: Penguin.

Bernstein, B. 1971. On the classification and framing of educational knowledge. In M.F.D. Young (Ed.) *Knowledge and Control*, 47–69. London: Collier Macmillan.

Bloor, M. and T. Bloor. 1991. Cultural expectations and socio-pragmatic failure in academic writing. In A. Adams, B. Heaton and P. Howarth, 1–12.

220

Bourdieu, P. 1971. Systems of education and systems of thought. In M.F.D. Young (Ed.) *Knowledge and Control*, 198–207. London: Collier Macmillan.

Bowers, R. 1980a. The background of students from the Indian subcontinent. In The British Council, 104–13.

Bowers, R. 1980b. War stories and romances: Exchanging experiences in ELT. In *Projects in Materials Design*, ELT Documents Special, 99–118. London: The British Council.

Bowers, R. 1983. Project Planning and Performance. In *ELT Documents 116, Language Teaching Projects in The Third World*, 99–118. Oxford: Pergamon Press.

Bowers, R. 1986. Appropriate methodology. Unpublished paper presented at Dunford House in dialogue with H.G. Widdowson.

Bowers, R. 1987. Language teacher education: An integrated approach. In R. Bowers (Ed.) *ELT Documents 125, Language Teacher Education: An Integrated Programme for ELT Teacher Training*, 3–9. London: Modern English Publications.

Bowers, R. 1991. ELT development: projects and power. In *Dunford Seminar Report 1991: The Social and Economic Impact of ELT in Development*, 29–35. London: The British Council.

Bowers, R. and H.G. Widdowson. 1986. Debate on appropriate methodology. In R. Webber and T. Deves, (Eds.) *1986 Dunford House Seminar Report: Appropriate Methodology*, 6–10. London: The British Council.

Breen, M.P. 1986. The social context of language learning – a neglected situation. *Studies in Second Language Acquisition*, 7, 135–58.

Breen, M.P. 1987a. Contemporary paradigms in syllabus design. Part I. *Language Teaching* 20(2), 81–92.

Breen, M.P. 1987b. Contemporary paradigms in syllabus design. Part II. *Language Teaching* 20(3), 157–74.

Breen, M.P. and C.N. Candlin. 1980. The essentials of a communicative curriculum in language teaching. *Applied Linguistics*, 1(2), 89–11.

de Brigard, E. 1975. The history of ethnographic film. In P. Hockings (Ed.) *Principles of Visual Anthropology*, 13–44. The Hague: Mouton.

The British Council. 1980. *ELT Documents 109, Study Modes and Academic Development of Overseas Students*. London: The British Council.

Britten, D. and F. Sow. 1981. Designing a micro-teaching programme in the third world. In *ELT Documents 110: Focus on The Language Teacher*, 22–33. London: The British Council.

Brown, G. 1989. Sitting on a rocket: An interview with Professor Gillian Brown. *English Language Teaching Journal*, 43(3), 167–72.

References

Brumfit, C. 1980. Education, ideology and materials design: A Tanzanian experience. In *Projects in Materials Design*, ELT Documents Special, 164–71. London: The British Council.

Canale, M. 1983. From communicative competence to communicative language pedagogy. In J. Richards and R.W. Schmidt (Eds.) *Language and Communication*. London: Longman.

Candlin, C.N. and M.P. Breen. 1979. Evaluating and designing language teaching materials. *Practical Papers in English Language Education* 2, 172–216. Lancaster: Lancaster University.

Chamberlain, R.G.D. and M.K.S. Flanagan. 1978. Developing a flexible ESP programme design. In R. Hawkey (Ed.) *ELT Documents 101, English For Special Purposes*, 46–55. London: The British Council.

Chaudron, C. 1988. *Second Language Classrooms: Research on Teaching and Learning*. Cambridge: Cambridge University Press.

Chick, J.K. (in process). Safe-talk: Collusion in Apartheid education. In H. Coleman (Ed.) *Society and The Classroom: Social Explanation for Behaviour in The Language Class*.

Coleman, H. 1987. Teaching spectacles and learning festivals. *English Language Teaching Journal*, 41(2), 97–103.

Coleman, H. 1988. Analysing language needs in large organizations. *English for Specific Purposes*, 7, 155–69.

Coleman, H. 1991. The testing of 'appropriate behaviour' in an academic context. In A. Adams, B. Heaton and P. Howarth.

Coleman, H. 1992a. Moving the goalposts: Project evaluation in practice. In J.C. Alderson and A. Beretta (Eds.) *Evaluating Second Language Education*, 222–49. Cambridge: Cambridge University Press.

Coleman, H. 1992b. BATQI: British Association of TESOL Qualifying Institutions. *ELT Management* 8, 8–9.

Coleman, H. (in process). Interpreting classroom behaviour in its cultural context. In H. Coleman (Ed.) *Society and The Classroom: Social Explanations for Behaviour in The Language Class*.

Collier, M. 1979. *A Film Study in Classrooms in Western Alaska*. Fairbanks: Center for Cross-Cultural Studies, University of Alaska.

Cooke, T.M. and A.R. Holliday. 1982. *Damascus University ESP Project, Research Findings, 1980–2*. Unpublished report.

Cortazzi, M. 1990. Cultural and educational expectations in the language classroom. In B. Harrison, 54–65.

Cortis, G. 1977. *The Social Context of Teaching*. London: Open Books.

Daft, R.L. and S.W. Becker. 1978. *Innovations in Organizations*. New York: Elsevir North-Holland.

Dalbouni, H. 1992. An investigation into the relations between the educational context and the written projects of university EFL students, with implications for the teaching of writing. Unpublished PhD thesis. Department of Linguistics, University of Leeds.

Delamont, S. and D. Hamilton. 1984. Revisiting classroom research: A continuing cautionary tale. In S. Delamont (Ed.) *Readings on Interaction in The Classroom*, 3–37. London: Methuen.

Dudley-Evans, T. and J. Swales. 1980. Study modes of students from the Middle East. In The British Council, 91–101.

Eggleston, J. 1980. Action and reaction in science teaching. In M.J. Galton (Ed.) *Curriculum Change: The Lessons of a Decade*, 81–94. Leicester: Leicester University Press.

Elley, W.B. 1989. Tailoring the evaluation to fit the context. In R.K. Johnson (Ed.) *The Second Language Curriculum*, 270–85. Cambridge: Cambridge University Press.

Esland, G.M. 1971. Teaching and learning as the organization of knowledge. In M.F.D. Young (Ed.) *Knowledge and Control*, 70–116. London: Collier Macmillan.

Fullan, M. 1982. *The Meaning of Educational Change*. Ontario: The Ontario Institute for Studies in Education Press.

Gabriel, A.C. 1991. Classrooms and chessboards: An ethnographic enquiry into classroom culture. Unpublished MA dissertation. Canterbury Christ Church College, Canterbury.

Gearing, F. and P. Epstein. 1982. Learning to wait: An ethnographic probe into the operations of an item of hidden curriculum. In G. Spindler, 240–67.

Gellner, E. 1964. *Thought and Change*. London: Weidenfeld and Nicolson.

Goodson, I. 1988. Beyond the subject monolith: subject traditions and sub-cultures. In A. Westoby (Ed.) *Culture and Power in Educational Organizations*, 181–97. Oxford: Open University Press.

Grotjahn, R. 1987. On the methodological basis of introspective methods. In C. Faerch and G. Kaspar (Eds.) *Introspection in Second Language Studies*. Clevedon: Multilingual Matters.

Hammersley, M. (Ed.) 1986. *Controversies in Classroom Research*. Milton Keynes: Open University Press.

Hammersley, M. and P. Atkinson. 1983. *Ethnography*. London: Tavistock.

Handy, C.B. 1985. *Understanding Organizations*. Harmondsworth: Penguin.

Harbord, J. 1992. The use of the mother tongue in the classsroom. *English Language Teaching Journal*, 46(4), 350–5.

References

Hargreaves, A. 1984. The significance of classroom strategies. In A. Hargreaves and P. Woods (Eds.) *Classrooms and Staffrooms: The Sociology of Teachers and Teaching*, 64–85. Milton Keynes: Open University Press. Reprinted from L. Barton and R. Meighan (Eds.) 1978. *Sociological Interpretations of Schooling and Classrooms: A Reappraisal*, 73–96. Driffield: Nafferton Books.

Hargreaves, A. 1986. The micro–macro problem in the sociology of education. In M. Hammersley 154–75. Reprinted from R.G. Burgess (Ed.) 1985, *Issues in Educational Research: Qualitative Methods*. Lewes: Falmer Press.

Harrison, B. (Ed.) 1990. *ELT Documents 132: Culture and The Language Classroom*. London: Modern English Publications and The British Council.

Hawkey, M. 1986. The literature component of the BA in Education with English. Unpublished report. Centre for Developing English Language Education, Ain Shams University, Cairo.

Hawkey, R. and C. Nakornchai. 1980. Thai students studying. In The British Council, 70–8.

Hempel, C.G. 1968. The logic of functional analysis. In M. Broadbeck (Ed.) *Readings in The Philosophy of The Social Sciences*, 179–210. New York: Macmillan.

Herrera, L. 1992. *Scenes of Schooling Inside a Girls' School in Cairo. Cairo Papers in Social Science* 15(1). Cairo: American University in Cairo Press.

Holliday, A.R. 1984. Research into classroom culture as necessary input to syllabus design. In J. Swales and H. Mustafa (Eds.) *ESP in The Arab World*, 29–51. Birmingham: Language Services Unit, University of Aston.

Holliday, A.R. 1986a. *Interim Report for 1985–6 for The Phonetics and Grammar Components of The BA in Education with English*. Unpublished report. Cairo: Centre for Developing English Language Teaching, Ain Shams University.

Holliday, A.R. 1986b. *Interim Report for 1985–6 for The Essay and Comprehension Components of The BA in Education with English*. Unpublished report. Cairo: Centre for Developing English Language Teaching, Ain Shams University.

Holliday, A.R. 1988. Project work as an evaluation device. *System* 61(1), 77–86.

Holliday, A.R. 1990. A role for soft systems methodology in ELT projects. *System* 18(1), 77–84.

Holliday, A.R. 1991a. *Dealing with Tissue Rejection in EFL Projects: The Role of an Ethnographic Means Analysis*. Unpublished PhD Thesis. University of Lancaster.

Holliday, A.R. 1991b. From materials development to staff development: An informed change in direction in an EFL project. *System* 19(3), 301–8.

Holliday, A.R. 1992a. Intercompetence: Sources of conflict between local and expatriate ELT personnel. *System* 20(2).

Holliday, A.R. 1992b. Tissue rejection and informal orders in ELT projects: Collecting the right information. *Applied Linguistics* 13(4), 404–24.

Holliday, A.R. 1993. *Large University Classes in Egypt: The Application of a 'Distance Learning' Methodology*. Working paper 17, International Network for Class Size Studies.

Holliday, A.R. (in process). Large and small class cultures in Egyptian university classrooms: A cultural justification for curriculum change. In H. Coleman (Ed.) *Society and The Classroom: Social Explanations for Behaviour in The Language Class*.

Holliday, A.R. and T.M. Cooke. 1982. An ecological approach to ESP. In A. Waters (Ed.) *Issues in ESP, Lancaster Practical Papers in English Language Education* 5, 124–44. Oxford: Pergamon Press.

Holly, D. 1990. The unspoken curriculum – or how language teaching carries cultural and ideological messages. In B. Harrison, 11–19.

Howatt, A. 1984. *A History of English Language Teaching*. Oxford: Oxford University Press.

Hoyle, E. 1970. Planning organizational change in education. *Research in Education*, May, 1–22.

Hoyle, E. 1988. Micropolitics of educational organizations. In A. Westoby (Ed.) *Culture and Power in Educational Organizations*, 255–69. Oxford: Open University Press.

Hutchinson, T. 1989. Learning how to manage. In M. Abousenna (Ed.) *Professional Development: Education and Training, Proceedings of The 8th National Symposium on English Language Teaching in Egypt, March 1988*, 23–34. Cairo: Centre for Developing English Language Teaching, Ain Shams University.

Hutchinson, T. and A. Waters. 1984. How communicative is ESP? *English Language Teaching Journal*, 38(2), 108–13.

Hyde, M. 1992. *The Moroccan Association of Teachers of English XIIth Conference*. Unpublished report. Canterbury: Canterbury Christ Church College.

Jackson, P.W. 1968. *Life in Classrooms*. New York: Holt, Rinehart and Winston.

Jenkins, D. 1986. An adversary's account of SAFARI's ethics of case study. In M. Hammersley (Ed.) *Controversies in Classroom Research*, 220–7. Milton Keynes: Open University Press. Reprinted from C. Richards (Ed.) *Power and The Curriculum: Issues in Curriculum Studies*. Driffield: Nafferton Books.

References

al Jubbouri, A.J.R. 1984. The role of repetition in Arabic argumentative discourse. In J. Swales and H. Mustafa (Eds.) *ESP in the Arab World*, 99–117. Birmingham Language Services Unit, University of Aston.

Kelley, P.J. 1980. From innovation to adaptability: The changing perspectives of curriculum development. In M.J. Galton (Ed.) *Curriculum Change: The Lessons of a Decade*, 65–80. Leicester: Leicester University Press.

Kennedy, C. 1987. Innovation for a change: Teacher development and innovation. *English Language Teaching Journal*, 41(4), 164–70.

Kennedy, M.C. 1987. Differential dimensions of the crisis of relevance in Middle Eastern Social Sciences. Unpublished paper. Department of Anthropology, American University in Cairo.

Kharma, N.N. and A.H.S. Hajjaj. 1985. Tradition and innovation in ELT: An Arab perspective. In W. Littlewood (Ed.) *Tradition and Innovation in English Language Teaching*, 54–70. London: Longman.

Kirwan, D. and A. Swales. 1981. Group-work – an attempt to change teacher attitudes. In *ELT Documents 110: Focus on The Teacher*, 64–70. London: The British Council.

Kowitz, J. 1986. The methodology component of the BA in Education with English. Unpublished report. Center for Developing English Language Teaching, Ain Shams University, Egypt.

Krasnick, H. (in process). Cultural 'Faux Amis'. In H. Coleman (Ed.) *Society and The Classroom: Social Explanation for Behaviour in The Language Class*.

Kuhn, T.S. 1970. *The Structure of Scientific Revolutions*. Reprinted and enlarged. Chicago: University of Chicago Press.

Labov, W. 1972. The study of language in its social context. In J.B. Pride and J. Holmes (Eds.) *Sociolinguistics*, 180–202. Harmondsworth: Penguin. Reprinted from *Studium Generale* 23, 1970, 30–87.

Layton, D. 1973. Science as general education. *Trends in Education*. January.

van Lier, L. 1988. *The Classroom and The Language Learner*. London: Longman.

van Lier, L. 1990. Ethnography: Bandaid, bandwagon, or contraband. In C. Brumfit and R. Mitchell (Eds.) *ELT Documents 133: Research in the language classroom*, 33–55. London: Modern English Publications, The British Council.

Lilley, A.D. 1984. The establishment of an independent inter-faculty ESP centre. In J. Swales and H. Mustafa (Eds.) *ESP in The Arab World*, 184–96. Birmingham: Language Services Unit, University of Aston.

Lim, S. 1987. Peer group versus teacher–pupil interaction. In B.K. Das (Ed.) *Patterns of Classroom Interaction in Southeast Asia*, 103–28. Singapore: SEAMEO Regional Language Centre.

LoCastro, V. 1989. *Large Size Classes: The Situation in Japan*. Lancaster-Leeds Language Learning in Large Classes Research Project, Report No.5.

LoCastro, V. (in process). English language education in Japan. In H. Coleman (Ed.) *Society and The Classroom: Social Explanation for Behaviour in The Language Class*.

Long, M.H. 1983. Inside the 'Black Box': Methodological issues in classroom research on language learning. In H.W. Seliger and M.H. Long (Eds.) *Classroom Oriented Research in Second Language Acquisition*, 3–35. Massachusetts: Newbury House. Reprinted from *Language Learning* 30(1), 1–42.

Long, M. and P. Porter. 1985. Group work, interlanguage talk and second language acquisition. *TESOL Quarterly* 19(2).

Lutz, F.W. 1981. Ethnography – the holistic approach to understanding schooling. In J.D. Green and C. Wallet (Eds). *Ethnography and Language in Educational Settings*, 51–63. New Jersey: ABLEX.

MacDonald, B. 1971. The evaluation of the humanities curriculum project: A holistic approach. *Theory and Practice* 10, 163–7.

McCarty, M. 1975. McCarty's Law and how to break it. In P. Hockings (Ed.) *Principles of Visual Anthropology*, 45–51. The Hague: Mouton.

McNiff, J. 1988. *Action Research: Principles and Practice*. London: Macmillan.

Maley, A. 1980. Making sense: Reconciling ideas and constraints in materials production. In *Projects in Materials Design*, ELT Documents Special. 47–60. London: The British Council.

Maley, A. 1986. Xanadu – 'A miracle of rare device': The teaching of English in China. In J. M. Valdes, 102–11.

Martindale, D. 1960. *The Nature and Types of Sociological Theory*. London: Routledge and Kegan Paul.

Miller, T. and L. Emel. 1988. Modern methodology or cultural imperialism. Paper presented at TESOL, Chicago.

Mills, C.W. 1970. *The Sociological Imagination*. Harmondsworth: Penguin. First published in 1959 by Oxford University Press.

Morain, G.G. 1986. Kinesics and cross-cultural understanding. In J.M. Valdes, 64–76.

Morris, T. 1991. *The Despairing Developer: Diary of an Aid Worker in The Middle East*. London: Tauris.

Munby, J. 1978. *Communicative Syllabus Design*. Cambridge: Cambridge University Press.

Murphy, R.E. 1986. *Culture and Social Anthropology: An Overture*. Englewood Cliffs, N.J.: Prentice Hall.

Nolasco, R. and L. Arthur. 1986. Try doing it with a class of forty. *English Language Teaching Journal* 40(2), 100–6.

Nunan, D. 1987. Communicative language teaching: Making it work. *English Language Teaching Journal*, 41(2), 136–45.

Nunan, D. 1990. Action research in the language classroom. In J.C. Richards and D. Nunan, 43–61.

Osterloh, K. 1986. Intercultural differences and communicative approaches to foreign language teaching in the Third World. In J.M. Valdes, 77–84.

Parker, O.D. and Educational Services Staff AMIDEAST. 1986. Cultural clues to the Middle-Eastern student. In J.M. Valdes, 94–101.

Parsons, T. 1951. *The Social System*. London: Routledge and Kegan Paul.

Pett, J. 1987. Course development in restricted circumstances: Reading and writing. In R. Bowers, 43–66.

Phillipson, R. 1991. Linguistic imperialism. In *Dunford Seminar Report 1991: The social and economic impact of ELT in development*, 27–8. London: The British Council.

Phillipson, R. 1992. *Linguistic Imperialism*. Oxford: Oxford University Press.

Pociecha, S.H. 1992. Open letter to the Peace Corps, the US Embassy English Teaching Office, NKJO Directors and whom it may concern. *IATEFL Newsletter* 17, 12–13.

Rea, P.M. 1984. Evaluation of educational projects, with special reference to English language education. In *ELT Documents 116, Language Teaching Projects in The Third World*, 85–98. Oxford: Pergamon Press.

Reynolds, J. and M. Skilbeck. 1976. *Culture and the Classroom*. London: Open Books.

Richards, J.C. and D. Nunan (Eds.) 1990. *Second Language Teacher Education*. Cambridge: Cambridge University Press.

Robinson, P. 1988. The management of language training. *Language Teaching*, 21(3), 146–57.

Roe, P. 1980. The English Language Centre, Jeddah. In *Projects in Materials Design*, 172–89. ELT Documents Special. London: The British Council.

Ruddock, J. and D. Hopkins (Eds.) 1985. *Research as a Basis For Teaching: Readings from the Work of Lawrence Stenhouse*. Oxford: Heinemann.

Rugh, A. 1985. *Family in Contemporary Egypt*. Cairo: American University in Cairo Press.

Sa'adeddin, M.A.A.D. 1991. Writing across language communities: The structure of Arabic text. In A. Adams, B. Heaton and P. Howarth, 53–73.

Safty, M., M. Palmer and M. Kennedy. 1985. *An Analytic Index of Survey Research in Egypt*, Cairo Papers in The Social Sciences 8, Monographs 1 and 2. Cairo: American University in Cairo Press.

Said, E. 1993. The Idea of Empire. *Arena*: February 12th. London: BBC.

Saunders, J.J. 1971. *The History of the Mongol Conquest*. London: Routledge and Kegan Paul.

Savignon, S.J. 1983. *Communicative Competence: Theory and Classroom Practice*. Reading, Massachusetts: Addison-Wesley.

Savignon, S.J. 1991. Communicative language teaching: State of the art. *TESOL Quarterly* 25(2).

Schutz, A. 1964. The stranger. *Collected Papers*, vol. 2, 91–105. The Hague: Martinus Nijhoff.

Sevigny, M.J. 1981. Triangulated enquiry – a methodology for the analysis of classroom interaction. In J. Green and C. Wallet (Eds.) *Ethnography and Language in Educational Settings*, 65–86. New Jersey: ABLEX.

Seymour, A. and M. Bahloul. 1992. Project sustainability: A case study of the Tunisian ESP project. *ELT Management*, no.8, 2–6.

Shamim, F. 1993. *Teacher-Learner Behaviour and Classroom Processes in Large ESL Classes in Pakistan*. Unpublished PhD Thesis. International Education, School of Education, University of Leeds.

Shamim, F. (in process). Towards an understanding of learner resistance to innovation in classroom methodology. In H. Coleman (Ed.) *Society and The Classroom: Social Explanation for Behaviour in The Language Class*.

Sharp, R. 1986. Self-contained ethnography or a science of phenomenal forms and inner relationships. In M. Hammersley, 120–34. Reprinted from *Boston University Journal of Education* 164(1), 48–63 (1982).

Shipman, M.D., D. Bolam and D.R. Jenkins. 1974. *Inside a Curriculum Project*. London: Methuen.

Slavin, R., S. Sharan, S. Kagan, R. Hertz-Lazarowitz, C. Webb, and R. Schmuck (Eds.) 1985. *Learning to Cooperate, Cooperation to Learn*. New York: Plenum.

Smith, H.N.J. 1989. *ELT as AID: Projects, Processes and Professionals*. Paper presented at the IATEFL conference, Warwick, revised version.

Spindler, G. (Ed.) 1982. *Doing The Ethnography of Schooling*. New York: Holt, Rinehart and Winston.

Spradley, J.P. 1980. *Participant Observation*. New York: Holt, Rinehart and Winston.

References

Stenhouse, L. 1975. *An Introduction to Curriculum Research and Development*. London: Heinemann.
Stenhouse, L. 1985a. What counts as research. In J. Ruddock and D. Hopkins, 8–19. Reprinted from What counts as research, *British Journal of Educational Studies*, 29(2), June 1981.
Stenhouse, L. 1985b. The illuminative research tradition. In J. Ruddock and D. Hopkins, 31–2. Reprinted from The problem of standards in illuminative research. *Scottish Educational Review* 11(1), 1979.
Stenhouse, L. 1985c. The case-study tradition and how case studies apply to practice. In J. Ruddock and D. Hopkins, 52–5. Reprinted from A note on case study and educational practice. In R.G. Burgess (Ed.) *Field Methods in The Study of Education*, Lewes: Falmer Press.
Stonequist, E.V. 1937. *The Marginal Man, A Study in Personality and Culture Conflict*. New York: Russell and Russell.
Straker Cook, R.H. 1986. Effecting ELT curriculum change in developing education systems. Paper presented at TESOL 20th Annual Convention, Annaheim, California.
Strauss, A., L. Schatzman, R. Bucher, D. Ehrlich, and M. Sabshin. 1969. In G. McCall and J.L. Simmons (Eds.) *Issues in Participant Observation*, 24–8. Reading, Massachusetts: Addison-Wesley. Reprinted from A. Strauss, L. Schatzman, R. Bucher, D. Ehrlich and M. Sabshin. 1964. *Psychiatric Ideologies and Institutions*, 19–21. New York: Free Press.
Sussex, E. 1975. *The Rise and Fall of The British Documentary*. California: University of California Press.
Swales, J. 1980. The educational environment and its relevance to ESP programme design. In *Projects in Materials Design*, 61–70. ELT Documents Special. London: The British Council.
Swales, J. 1985. ESP – the heart of the matter or the end of the affair. In *English in The World*. London: The British Council.
Swales, J. 1989. Service English programme design and opportunity cost. In R.K. Johnson (Ed.) *The Second Language Curriculum*. Cambridge: Cambridge University Press.
Swan, M.A. 1985. A critical look at the communicative approach (1). *English Language Teaching Journal* 39(1), 2–12.
Szulc-Kurpaska, M. 1992. *Evaluation in Legnica Foreign Language Teacher Training College*. Unpublished Report. Foreign Language Teacher Training College, Legnica, Poland.
Temaner, G, and G. Quinn. 1975. Cinematic social enquiry. In P. Hockings (Ed.) *Principles of Visual Anthropology*, 53–64. The Hague: Mouton.

Thomas, A. 1985. *CDELT Curriculum Recommendation No 1: Third and Fourth Year Grammar and Phonetics for English Specialists in Faculties of Education*. Unpublished report. Cairo: Centre for Developing English Language Teaching, Ain Shams University.

Tomley, D. 1980. The selection of curriculum content: Issues and problems. In M.J. Galton (Ed.) *Curriculum Change: The Lessons of a Decade*, 33–50. Leicester: Leicester University Press.

Tomlinson, B. 1990. Managing change in Indonesian high schools. *English Language Teaching Journal* 44(1), 25–37.

Valdes, J.M. (Ed.) 1986. *Culture Bound*. Cambridge: Cambridge University Press.

Wadel, S. 1979. The hidden work of everyday life. In S. Wallman (Ed.) *Social Anthropology of Work*, 366–84. London: Academic Press.

Wallace, M.J. 1991. *Training Foreign Language Teachers*. Cambridge: Cambridge University Press.

Watson, O.M. and T.D. Graves. 1973. Quantitative research in proxemic behaviour. In M. Argyle (Ed.) *Social Encounters: Readings in Social Interaction*, 34–46. Harmondsworth: Penguin. Reprinted from *American Anthropologist*, 68, 971–85 (1966).

White, R.V. 1987. Managing innovation. *English Language Teaching Journal*, 41, 211–18.

White, R.V. 1988. *The ELT Curriculum*. Oxford: Blackwell.

White, R.V. 1989a. Curriculum studies and ELT. *System* 17(1), 83–93.

White, R.V. 1989b. Professional management and the management of change. In M. Abousenna (Ed.) *Professional Development: Education and Training, Proceedings of The 8th National Symposium on English Language Teaching in Egypt, March 1988*, 204–12. Cairo: Centre for Developing English Language Teaching, Ain Shams University.

Whitty, G. 1985. *Sociology and School Knowledge: Curriculum Theory, Research and Politics*. London: Methuen.

Widdowson, H.G. 1984. *Explorations in Applied Linguistics 2*. Oxford: Oxford University Press.

Widdowson, H.G. 1987. The roles of teacher and learner. *English Language Teaching Journal* 41(2), 83–8.

Widdowson, H.G. 1992. English language teaching and ELT teachers: matters arising. *English Language Teaching Journal* 46(4), 333–9.

Wilcox, K. 1982. Ethnography as a methodology and its applications to the study of schooling: A review. In G. Spindler, 456–87.

Wolcott, H.F. 1982. Mirrors, models and monitors: Educator adaptations of the ethnographic innovation. In G. Spindler, 68–95.

References

Woods, P. 1984. Teaching for survival. In A. Hargreaves and P. Woods, (Eds.) *Classrooms and Staffrooms: The Sociology of Teachers and Teaching*, 48–63. Milton Keynes: Open University Press. Reprinted from P. Woods. and M. Hammersley (Eds.), 1977. *School Experience*, 271–93. London, Croom Helm.

Wright, T. 1987. *Roles of Teachers and Learners*. Oxford: Oxford University Press.

Young, M.F.D. 1971. An approach to the study of curricula as socially organised knowledge. In M.F.D. Young (Ed.) *Knowledge and Control*, 19–46. London: Collier Macmillan.

Zikri, M.S. 1979. *A Comparative Study of Lexical Relations in English and Egyptian Arabic*. Unpublished PhD Thesis. Department of General Linguistics, University of Manchester.

Zikri, M. 1990. The linguistic and situational validity of an undergraduate course in reading and essay. *Occasional Papers in The Development of English Language Education*. Cairo: Centre for Developing English Language Teaching, Ain Shams University.

Zikri, M. 1992. *A case study of two approaches to upgrade English language proficiency at Egyptian universities through the Centre for Developing English Language Teaching, Ain Shams University*. Unpublished paper. Cairo: Centre for Developing English Language Teaching, Ain Shams University, Cairo.

Index